Enhancing Entrepreneurial Education and Training With AI

Monia Ben Ltaifa
King Faisal University, Saudi Arabia

IGI Global
Scientific Publishing
Publishing Tomorrow's Research Today

Published in the United States of America by
IGI Global Scientific Publishing
701 East Chocolate Avenue
Hershey, PA, 17033, USA
Tel: 717-533-8845 | Fax: 717-533-7115
Website: https://www.igi-global.com E-mail: cust@igi-global.com

Library of Congress Cataloging-in-Publication Data

LCCN: 2026017410 (CIP Data Pending)
ISBN13: 979-8-2600-0487-6
Isbn13Softcover: 979-8-2600-0488-3
EISBN13: 979-8-2600-0489-0
British Cataloguing in Publication Data
A Cataloguing in Publication record for this book is available from the British Library.

Table of Contents

Detailed Table of Contents

Entrepreneurial education has undergone a significant transformation in response to globalization, digitalization, and the rapid evolution of technological ecosystems. Among emerging technologies, Artificial Intelligence (AI) stands out as a disruptive force capable of redefining how entrepreneurial knowledge is created, delivered, and applied. This chapter explores the integration of AI in entrepreneurial education and training, highlighting its role in personalized learning, simulation-based training, predictive analytics, and innovation ecosystems. It examines how AI-driven tools can foster entrepreneurial competencies such as creativity, critical thinking, decision-making, and opportunity recognition. The chapter also discusses practical applications, benefits, challenges, ethical considerations, and future directions for AI-enhanced entrepreneurship education. By presenting conceptual insights and real-world examples, this chapter provides a comprehensive framework for educators, policymakers, and institutions seeking to leverage AI for developing future-ready entrepreneurs.

This study examines the impact of artificial intelligence (AI) on entrepreneurship education and training in Saudi Arabia within the framework of Vision 2030. It proposes that the integration of AI enhances entrepreneurial skills and fosters adaptive teaching approaches. A mixed-methods approach is employed, combining semi-structured interviews (n=40) and a quantitative survey of students (n=300). The data are analyzed using thematic analysis and structural equation modeling. The results show that the use of AI significantly strengthens learners' creativity, decision-making, and engagement, while also revealing limitations related to inequalities in access and teacher skills. The originality of this research lies in its empirical approach integrated within an emerging context. It contributes to the literature on the digital transformation of entrepreneurship education.

The integration of Artificial Intelligence (AI) into entrepreneurial training is reshaping how future innovators acquire skills, make decisions, and build trust in digital ecosystems. This study examines the ethical dimensions, trust-building mechanisms, and transformative potential of AI through qualitative perspectives drawn from diverse educational and entrepreneurial contexts. Using interviews, focus groups, and narrative analysis, the research uncovers how learners and educators perceive AI's role in fostering responsible entrepreneurship. Key findings highlight tensions between efficiency and ethics, the importance of transparency in AI-driven pedagogy, and the need for trust as a foundational element in entrepreneurial learning. The study also reveals how AI can act as a catalyst for transformation empowering learners with adaptive tools while simultaneously raising questions about accountability, inclusivity, and cultural sensitivity. By synthesizing these qualitative insights.

Artificial Intelligence (AI) is rapidly transforming entrepreneurship education, offering new pedagogical tools, experiential learning models, and innovation pathways. Yet, its narratives and applications vary significantly across cultural and economic contexts. This study explores cross-cultural narratives of AI in entrepreneurship education, with a particular focus on lessons emerging from developing and transitional economies. Drawing on comparative case studies, policy reviews, and institutional practices, the research highlights how cultural values, resource constraints, and local innovation ecosystems shape the integration of AI into entrepreneurial learning.

Preface

INTRODUCTION

As editor of this volume, I am pleased to introduce *Enhancing Entrepreneurial Education and Training With AI*, a work that brings together diverse perspectives at a moment of profound transformation. Across the globe, educational systems and entrepreneurial ecosystems are being reshaped by the rapid advancement of artificial intelligence. This book seeks to capture, analyze, and critically examine that transformation through an interdisciplinary lens.

The chapters assembled here explore the integration of AI into entrepreneurial training, the rise of EdTech startups and AI-driven ventures, and the shifting landscape of entrepreneurial skills in what may be described as the algorithmic age. At the same time, contributors engage with the ethical, regulatory, and societal questions that inevitably accompany technological disruption, ensuring that innovation is considered not only in terms of efficiency and growth, but also responsibility and impact.

This volume builds upon established foundations in technological entrepreneurship, applied artificial intelligence, and the evolving concept of the entrepreneurial university. However, it moves beyond these traditions by proposing an integrated conceptual framework linking AI, skills development, innovation, value creation, and societal impact. In doing so, it aims to help structure an emerging field situated at the intersection of entrepreneurship, education, and intelligent technologies.

A key ambition of this book is to advance hybrid theoretical models—particularly those that combine effectuation principles with AI-driven innovation dynamics—while grounding these ideas in international empirical research. Several contributions also propose indicators and evaluation tools to better assess the role and impact of AI in entrepreneurial education, an area that remains underdeveloped yet increasingly critical.

This work is designed to serve multiple audiences and purposes. It can function as a reference for MBA programs, engineering schools, technological innovation curricula, and faculties of education. Beyond academia, it speaks to broader societal goals: strengthening startup ecosystems, enhancing the employability of graduates, promoting digital inclusion, and supporting the development of national AI strategies.

The intended readership reflects this diversity. Researchers in entrepreneurship and innovation, educational technology specialists, doctoral and postdoctoral scholars, policymakers, and university incubator managers will all find relevant insights within these pages. The breadth of perspectives represented is a direct result of our collaborative approach—drawing on contributions from colleagues, research networks, conferences, and interdisciplinary groups worldwide.

As editor, I view this volume not as a definitive conclusion, but as an invitation: to rethink how we educate future entrepreneurs, to question how intelligent systems reshape human capability, and to collaboratively define pathways toward inclusive and sustainable innovation.

I extend my sincere gratitude to all contributors for their intellectual rigor and commitment, and to the broader community whose ongoing work continues to shape this evolving field.

ORGANIZATION OF THE BOOK

From the vantage point of the editor, each chapter in this volume contributes a distinct yet interconnected perspective on how artificial intelligence is reshaping entrepreneurial education across contexts, methodologies, and levels of analysis.

Chapter 1 by Ilham Firmansyah sets the conceptual foundation by examining the transformative role of AI in entrepreneurship education within emerging digital economies. The chapter articulates how adaptive systems, generative AI, and data analytics enable more personalized and innovation-driven learning environments, while also confronting structural constraints such as digital inequality and infrastructural limitations. Particularly noteworthy is the proposed integrative framework linking AI, entrepreneurial skills, innovation, and value creation—an anchor that resonates throughout the volume.

Chapter 2, authored by Aarthi Selvakumar, Ravikumar Natarajan, Karimov Rashid Salayevich, and Sadirdin Khudoykulov, advances the discussion into experiential learning through the introduction of "Synthetic Startup Labs." This innovative pedagogical model leverages generative AI to simulate entrepreneurial ecosystems, allowing learners to experiment with venture creation in immersive, risk-free environments. The chapter compellingly demonstrates how simulation, adaptive feedback, and virtual stakeholder interaction can significantly enhance entrepreneurial thinking and accessibility to startup education.

Chapter 3 by Abdelraouf Ishtaiwi introduces a highly specialized yet increasingly critical domain: cybersecurity entrepreneurship. Through a synthesis of learning analytics, intelligent tutoring systems, and domain-specific knowledge structures, the chapter proposes a pedagogical architecture for cultivating AI-augmented risk assessment capabilities. Its emphasis on artifact-based learning, legal awareness, and trust productization reflects the complex realities faced by technology startups operating under conditions of uncertainty.

Chapter 4, contributed by Ravikumar Natarajan, Aarthi Selvakumar, Umid Otajanov, and Makhmudov Asliddin, explores AI-driven recommender systems as a mechanism for personalizing entrepreneurial learning. By integrating collaborative filtering, content-based methods, and deep learning, the chapter illustrates how tailored learning pathways can enhance engagement, skill acquisition, and startup readiness. Importantly, it also engages with pressing concerns ב ב privacy, algorithmic bias, and the ethical scalability of such systems.

Chapter 5 by Amrik Singh offers a comprehensive synthesis of AI's role in entrepreneurial education and training. The chapter bridges theory and practice by examining applications such as simulation-based learning, predictive analytics, and innovation ecosystems, while also outlining the competencies required for future-ready entrepreneurs. Its balanced treatment of opportunities, challenges, and ethical considerations positions it as a central reference point within the book.

Chapter 6, authored by Walid Chouari, provides valuable empirical insight through a mixed-methods study situated in Saudi Arabia's Vision 2030 context. By combining qualitative and quantitative data, the chapter demonstrates how AI integration enhances creativity, engagement, and decision-making among learners, while also revealing persistent gaps related to access and educator readiness. This contribution underscores the importance of context-sensitive implementation in national innovation strategies.

Chapter 7 by P. Yadav shifts the focus toward qualitative inquiry, examining ethics, trust, and transformation in AI-enabled entrepreneurial training. Drawing on interviews and narrative analysis, the chapter reveals the nuanced perceptions of learners and educators, highlighting tensions between efficiency and ethical responsibility. It foregrounds trust as a foundational element in digital learning ecosystems and calls for greater attention to inclusivity, transparency, and cultural sensitivity.

In Chapter 8, P. B. Narendra Kiran adopts a comparative lens to explore cross-cultural narratives of AI in entrepreneurship education. Through case studies and policy analysis, the chapter illustrates how local contexts—shaped by cultural values, resource constraints, and institutional dynamics—profoundly influence the adoption and adaptation of AI-driven pedagogies. This contribution enriches the volume by situating technological transformation within diverse global realities.

Taken together, these chapters reflect the richness and complexity of an emerging field. They collectively demonstrate that the integration of AI into entrepreneurial education is not merely a technological shift, but a profound reconfiguration of how knowledge is created, shared, and applied in pursuit of innovation and societal impact.

CONCLUSION

In bringing this volume to completion, it becomes evident that the integration of artificial intelligence into entrepreneurial education is not a passing trend, but a structural transformation with far-reaching implications. The contributions collected in this book collectively affirm that we are witnessing the emergence of a new educational paradigm—one in which intelligent systems, human creativity, and entrepreneurial action are increasingly intertwined.

From conceptual frameworks to empirical studies, from immersive simulations to ethical reflections, each chapter has illuminated a different dimension of this evolving landscape. Together, they underscore a central insight: artificial intelligence is not merely enhancing existing pedagogies, but redefining how entrepreneurial knowledge is constructed, experienced, and applied. Learning is becoming more personalized, more data-informed, and more experiential—yet also more complex, raising new questions about equity, governance, and responsibility.

As editor, I am particularly struck by the balance this volume achieves between optimism and critical inquiry. While many chapters highlight the transformative potential of AI in fostering innovation, creativity, and opportunity recognition, they also remind us of the persistent challenges—digital divides, algorithmic bias, infrastructural gaps, and ethical dilemmas—that must be addressed if these technologies are to serve inclusive and sustainable development.

This book also reinforces the importance of context. Whether in emerging digital economies, national strategic frameworks, or cross-cultural environments, the adoption and impact of AI in entrepreneurial education are deeply shaped by local conditions. As such, there can be no single, universal model. Instead, what emerges is a mosaic of approaches, each contributing valuable insights into how AI can be meaningfully integrated into diverse educational and entrepreneurial ecosystems.

Looking ahead, the task before educators, researchers, policymakers, and practitioners is both ambitious and urgent. It requires not only the development of new tools and models, but also the cultivation of ethical awareness, interdisciplinary collaboration, and institutional adaptability. The future of entrepreneurial education will depend on our ability to align technological advancement with human values, ensuring that innovation remains both purposeful and inclusive.

It is my hope that this volume serves not only as a reference, but as a catalyst—for further research, for pedagogical experimentation, and for informed policy dialogue. More importantly, I hope it inspires a new generation of learners and educators to engage critically and creatively with artificial intelligence as they shape the entrepreneurial landscapes of tomorrow.

In closing, I extend my deepest appreciation to all contributors whose work has made this volume possible. Their scholarship reflects a shared commitment to advancing knowledge at the intersection of education, entrepreneurship, and intelligent technologies—an intersection that will undoubtedly continue to define the future of innovation.

Funding: This work was supported by the Deanship of Scientific Research, Vice Presidency for Graduate Studies and Scientific Research, King Faisal University, Saudi Arabia [Grant No. KFU261570]

Chapter 1
Artificial Intelligence in Entrepreneurship Education in Emerging Digital Economies:
AI for Entrepreneurial Skills and Innovation

Ilham Firmansyah
http://orcid.org/0009-0007-6104-9966
Universitas Esa Unggul, Indonesia

ABSTRACT

Artificial intelligence is transforming entrepreneurship education, especially in emerging digital economies. This chapter examines how AI enhances learning, skill development, and innovation in entrepreneurial contexts. AI tools such as adaptive systems, generative AI, and data analytics enable personalized and data-driven learning experiences. The chapter also highlights challenges including digital inequality, limited infrastructure, and skill gaps. A conceptual framework is proposed linking AI, entrepreneurial skills, innovation, and value creation. The study provides insights for educators, institutions, and policymakers to support effective and inclusive AI-driven entrepreneurship education.

DOI: 10.4018/979-8-2600-0487-6.ch001

1. INTRODUCTION

Artificial intelligence (AI) has rapidly evolved into a transformative technology that reshapes economic activities, educational systems, and entrepreneurial practices worldwide. Its integration into various sectors has enabled new forms of innovation, automation, and data-driven decision making. Within this transformation, the intersection between AI and entrepreneurship education has become increasingly important, particularly in the context of emerging digital economies (Wei et al., 2026).

Entrepreneurship education plays a crucial role in fostering innovation, economic growth, and job creation. It equips individuals with essential competencies such as opportunity recognition, business development, and strategic decision making. However, the rapid advancement of digital technologies has altered the nature of entrepreneurship, requiring new skills related to digital innovation, data utilization, and technological adaptability. This shift highlights the need to redesign entrepreneurship education to align with the demands of the digital economy (Guo, 2026).

Artificial intelligence provides significant opportunities to enhance entrepreneurship education through innovative learning approaches. AI-driven tools, including intelligent tutoring systems, generative AI platforms, and simulation-based learning environments, enable more personalized and interactive learning experiences. These technologies support students in developing entrepreneurial skills, testing business ideas, and making data-driven decisions, thereby improving their readiness for real-world entrepreneurial challenges (Ogunsola et al., 2026).

The relevance of AI becomes even more critical in emerging digital economies, where rapid technological adoption coexists with structural challenges such as limited access to quality education and gaps in entrepreneurial skills. In these contexts, AI has the potential to democratize access to knowledge, improve learning efficiency, and support the development of entrepreneurial ecosystems. However, the integration of AI also raises challenges related to digital inequality, data privacy, and ethical concerns, which must be carefully addressed to ensure inclusive and responsible implementation (Gal & Rachevski, 2026).

In addition, the evolving landscape of entrepreneurship requires individuals to develop new competencies, including AI literacy, digital skills, and innovation capabilities. Educational institutions, particularly universities, play a strategic role in preparing future entrepreneurs by integrating AI into their curricula and training programs. This transformation supports the development of innovation-driven economies and strengthens the role of higher education in entrepreneurial ecosystem building (Adetunji & Ade-Ibijola, 2026).

Despite the growing importance of AI in entrepreneurship education, there remains a limited understanding of how these domains intersect, especially within emerging digital economies. Existing studies often examine AI in education or entrepreneurship separately, leaving a gap in integrated perspectives. Addressing this gap is essential for developing effective educational models and strategies that respond to contemporary economic and technological challenges (Lai, 2026).

This chapter aims to explore the role of artificial intelligence in transforming entrepreneurship education and to propose a conceptual perspective linking AI, entrepreneurial skills, and innovation in emerging digital economies. By providing this integrated view, the chapter contributes to a deeper understanding of how AI can enhance entrepreneurial learning and support sustainable economic development.

2. ARTIFICIAL INTELLIGENCE IN HIGHER EDUCATION

The integration of artificial intelligence (AI) into higher education has significantly transformed teaching, learning, and institutional management practices. As universities increasingly adopt digital technologies, AI has emerged as a key enabler of innovation in educational environments. From personalized learning systems to data-driven decision making, AI is reshaping how knowledge is delivered, accessed, and applied in higher education institutions (Zhou, 2026).

One of the most prominent applications of AI in higher education is the development of intelligent tutoring systems and adaptive learning platforms. These systems utilize machine learning algorithms to analyze student performance, identify learning patterns, and provide personalized feedback. By tailoring content and learning pathways to individual needs, AI enhances student engagement and improves learning outcomes. This shift from standardized instruction to personalized education represents a fundamental transformation in pedagogical approaches (Yang & Li, 2026).

In addition to adaptive learning, generative artificial intelligence has introduced new possibilities for knowledge creation and academic support. Tools such as large language models enable students and educators to generate content, explore ideas, and receive real-time assistance in problem solving. These technologies support critical thinking, creativity, and independent learning, while also raising questions about academic integrity, originality, and the role of human cognition in the learning process (Khotimah et al., 2026).

AI is also increasingly used in administrative and institutional contexts within higher education. Universities leverage AI for student enrollment management, academic advising, performance prediction, and resource allocation. Predictive analytics, for example, can identify students at risk of academic failure and enable early interventions. Such applications improve institutional efficiency and contribute to better student retention and success rates (Yoshida et al., 2026).

Despite these advantages, the integration of AI in higher education presents several challenges. One major concern is the issue of digital inequality, where unequal access to technological resources may create disparities in learning opportunities. Students in developing regions or under-resourced institutions may face barriers in accessing AI-driven educational tools, potentially widening existing educational gaps (Jiang, 2026).

Another critical issue is data privacy and ethical governance. AI systems rely heavily on large volumes of student data, including academic performance, behavioral patterns, and personal information. The collection and processing of such data raise concerns regarding consent, transparency, and data protection. Ensuring that AI applications comply with ethical standards and regulatory frameworks is essential to maintain trust in educational institutions (Mah et al., 2026).

Furthermore, the increasing reliance on AI in education raises questions about the role of educators. While AI can enhance teaching efficiency and provide valuable support, it cannot fully replace the human elements of education, such as mentorship, emotional intelligence, and contextual understanding. Therefore, the integration of AI should be viewed as a complement to, rather than a substitute for, human educators (Deng & Sun, 2026).

The adoption of AI in higher education also contributes to the development of digital competencies among students. As learners interact with AI-driven tools, they acquire skills related to data interpretation, technological literacy, and digital problem solving. These competencies are essential in preparing students for participation in digital economies and innovation-driven environments (Festiyed et al., 2026).

In the context of entrepreneurship education, the role of AI in higher education becomes even more significant. AI technologies provide students with tools to simulate business environments, analyze market trends, and develop data-driven business strategies. This enhances experiential learning and supports the development of entrepreneurial skills, bridging the gap between theoretical knowledge and practical application (Maleki, 2026).

Overall, artificial intelligence is reshaping higher education by introducing new models of teaching, learning, and institutional management. While it offers significant opportunities for enhancing educational quality and accessibility, its implementation must be carefully managed to address ethical, social, and technological challenges. Understanding the role of AI in higher education provides a critical foundation for exploring its application in entrepreneurship education, which is discussed in the following section.

3. ARTIFICIAL INTELLIGENCE AND ENTREPRENEURSHIP EDUCATION

The integration of artificial intelligence (AI) into entrepreneurship education represents a significant shift in how entrepreneurial competencies are developed, delivered, and applied in modern learning environments. As digital technologies continue to reshape economic systems, entrepreneurship education must evolve to prepare individuals not only for traditional business creation but also for innovation within digitally driven and data-intensive contexts (Pöcher et al., 2026). In this regard, AI serves as both a pedagogical tool and a transformative force that redefines entrepreneurial learning processes.

Entrepreneurship education traditionally emphasizes experiential learning, where students engage in activities such as business simulations, case studies, and project-based learning. These approaches aim to develop critical competencies including opportunity recognition, creativity, risk management, and decision making. However, the emergence of AI introduces new dimensions to these learning processes by enabling real-time data analysis, intelligent feedback, and predictive insights. For instance, AI-driven simulation tools allow students to test business models under dynamic market conditions, enhancing their ability to make strategic decisions (Sun, 2026).

One of the key contributions of AI in entrepreneurship education lies in its ability to enhance opportunity recognition. Identifying viable business opportunities is a fundamental entrepreneurial skill, yet it often depends on access to information and analytical capabilities. AI tools can analyze large datasets, detect emerging market trends, and provide insights into consumer behavior, thereby supporting students in identifying potential business opportunities more effectively (Essel et al., 2026). This data-driven approach shifts entrepreneurship education from intuition-based learning to evidence-based decision making.

Moreover, generative AI technologies have introduced new possibilities for idea generation and innovation. Students can leverage AI-powered platforms to brainstorm business concepts, develop value propositions, and refine their entrepreneurial ideas. These tools can act as cognitive partners, supporting creativity while also providing structured guidance in the ideation process. However, this also raises important questions regarding originality, authorship, and the role of human creativity in AI-assisted innovation (Brezovec et al., 2026).

Another important aspect of AI integration is its role in supporting entrepreneurial decision making. In traditional entrepreneurship education, decision making is often based on limited data and hypothetical scenarios. AI enables students to access real-time data, perform predictive analysis, and evaluate multiple scenarios simultaneously. For example, machine learning models can be used to forecast market demand, optimize pricing strategies, and assess business risks. Such capabilities enhance students' analytical skills and prepare them for data-driven entrepreneurial environments (Pingmuang et al., 2026).

AI also contributes to the personalization of entrepreneurial learning. Different learners possess varying levels of experience, knowledge, and learning preferences. AI-driven adaptive learning systems can tailor educational content to individual needs, providing customized feedback and learning pathways. This personalized approach enhances student engagement and allows learners to progress at their own pace, improving the overall effectiveness of entrepreneurship education (Guo, 2026).

Despite these advantages, the integration of AI into entrepreneurship education presents several challenges. One major concern is the risk of over-reliance on AI tools, which may reduce students' ability to think critically and independently. While AI can provide valuable insights, entrepreneurial success still requires human judgment, creativity, and the ability to navigate uncertainty. Therefore, it is essential to strike a balance between leveraging AI capabilities and maintaining human-centered learning approaches (Gal & Rachevski, 2026).

In addition, ethical considerations play a crucial role in the adoption of AI in entrepreneurship education. Issues such as data privacy, algorithmic bias, and transparency must be addressed to ensure responsible use of AI technologies. For example, biased datasets may lead to misleading insights, potentially affecting students' understanding of markets and opportunities. Ensuring ethical AI usage is therefore essential to maintain the integrity of entrepreneurial education (Lai, 2026).

The integration of AI also has implications for educators and institutions. Educators are required to adapt their teaching methods and develop new competencies related to AI technologies. Rather than acting solely as knowledge providers, educators increasingly take on the role of facilitators, guiding students in using AI tools effectively and critically. Institutions, on the other hand, must invest in technological infrastructure and develop policies that support the responsible integration of AI into educational systems.

Furthermore, AI enables the development of more immersive and experiential learning environments. Technologies such as virtual simulations, AI-driven business games, and digital incubators allow students to engage in realistic entrepreneurial scenarios. These environments provide opportunities for experimentation, failure, and learning without real-world risks, thereby enhancing students' entrepreneurial readiness (Yang & Li, 2026).

In the context of emerging digital economies, the role of AI in entrepreneurship education becomes even more significant. Many developing regions face limitations in access to quality education and entrepreneurial resources. AI-driven platforms can help overcome these barriers by providing scalable and accessible learning solutions. However, challenges related to infrastructure, digital literacy, and resource availability must be addressed to ensure that the benefits of AI are distributed equitably.

Overall, artificial intelligence is redefining entrepreneurship education by transforming how entrepreneurial skills are developed, how learning experiences are designed, and how innovation is fostered. By integrating AI into educational practices, institutions can better prepare students for the complexities of modern entrepreneurial environments. At the same time, it is essential to address the associated challenges to ensure that AI-driven entrepreneurship education remains ethical, inclusive, and effective.

4. ENTREPRENEURSHIP EDUCATION IN EMERGING DIGITAL ECONOMIES

The rapid expansion of digital technologies has significantly transformed economic structures across the globe, particularly in emerging digital economies. These economies are characterized by accelerating digital adoption, expanding internet penetration, and increasing engagement with innovation-driven activities. Within this context, entrepreneurship education plays a critical role in fostering economic development, promoting innovation, and enhancing employability among young populations (Yoshida et al., 2026). However, the effectiveness of entrepreneurship education in emerging economies is often shaped by structural, technological, and institutional challenges.

Artificial intelligence (AI) introduces new opportunities to address these challenges while simultaneously redefining how entrepreneurial knowledge and skills are developed. Understanding the dynamics of entrepreneurship education in emerging digital economies is therefore essential for designing effective AI-driven educational strategies.

4.1 Characteristics of Emerging Digital Economies

Emerging digital economies are typically characterized by rapid technological adoption combined with uneven development in infrastructure, education, and institutional capacity. Countries in regions such as Southeast Asia, Africa, and parts of Latin America are experiencing significant growth in digital platforms, e-commerce, and startup ecosystems. This transformation is driven by increased access to mobile technologies, digital payment systems, and online services (Mah et al., 2026).

However, despite these advancements, emerging economies often face disparities in access to digital resources and educational opportunities. While urban areas may benefit from advanced technological infrastructure, rural and underserved regions frequently lack reliable internet access and digital tools. This digital divide creates unequal opportunities for participation in entrepreneurship education and innovation ecosystems (Festiyed et al., 2026).

In addition, emerging digital economies are often characterized by a growing youth population with high entrepreneurial potential. Many young individuals are motivated to pursue entrepreneurship as a pathway to economic mobility and job creation. This demographic advantage presents a unique opportunity for leveraging AI-driven educational tools to support large-scale entrepreneurial skill development.

4.2 Challenges in Entrepreneurship Education

Entrepreneurship education in emerging digital economies faces several critical challenges that limit its effectiveness. One of the primary challenges is the lack of access to high-quality educational resources. Many institutions struggle with outdated curricula, limited teaching materials, and insufficient exposure to real-world entrepreneurial practices (Pöcher et al., 2026).

Another significant challenge is the gap between theoretical knowledge and practical application. Traditional entrepreneurship education often focuses on conceptual frameworks without providing students with opportunities to engage in hands-on learning experiences. As a result, students may lack the practical skills required to develop and manage businesses in dynamic market environments.

Furthermore, there is a notable deficiency in digital and technological competencies among students. As entrepreneurship increasingly relies on digital tools, data analytics, and online platforms, the absence of digital literacy becomes a major barrier. Without adequate training in these areas, students may struggle to adapt to modern entrepreneurial ecosystems (Essel et al., 2026).

Institutional limitations also play a crucial role. Many universities and educational institutions lack the infrastructure, funding, and strategic direction needed to integrate advanced technologies such as AI into their programs. Additionally, educators may not have sufficient training or experience in utilizing digital tools effectively in teaching entrepreneurship.

4.3 Opportunities for AI Integration

Artificial intelligence presents significant opportunities to overcome the challenges associated with entrepreneurship education in emerging digital economies. One of the most important contributions of AI is its ability to provide scalable and accessible learning solutions. AI-driven platforms can deliver educational content to a large number of learners, regardless of geographical location, thereby reducing barriers to access (Pingmuang et al., 2026).

AI also enables personalized learning experiences, which are particularly valuable in diverse educational contexts. Students with different backgrounds, skill levels, and learning preferences can benefit from adaptive learning systems that tailor content to their individual needs.

This enhances learning efficiency and supports more effective skill development (Wei et al., 2026).

In addition, AI can facilitate experiential learning through simulation-based environments. Students can engage in virtual business scenarios, test entrepreneurial ideas, and receive real-time feedback. These interactive learning experiences bridge the gap between theory and practice, allowing students to develop practical entrepreneurial skills in a risk-free environment.

Another key opportunity lies in data-driven decision making. AI tools can analyze market trends, consumer behavior, and competitive landscapes, enabling students to develop more informed business strategies. This exposure to data analytics prepares students for the realities of modern entrepreneurship, where data plays a central role in decision making.

4.4 AI and Entrepreneurial Ecosystem Development

Beyond individual learning, AI plays a crucial role in strengthening entrepreneurial ecosystems in emerging digital economies. Entrepreneurial ecosystems consist of interconnected actors, including universities, startups, investors, government institutions, and support organizations. The effectiveness of these ecosystems depends on knowledge exchange, innovation capacity, and access to resources (Guo, 2026).

AI can enhance these ecosystems by facilitating collaboration and knowledge sharing. Digital platforms powered by AI can connect entrepreneurs with mentors, investors, and industry experts, creating more dynamic and inclusive innovation networks. This is particularly important in emerging economies, where access to such networks may be limited (Yoshida et al., 2026).

Furthermore, AI-driven analytics can support policymakers in designing more effective entrepreneurship development programs. By analyzing data on startup performance, employment trends, and innovation activities, governments can develop targeted policies that foster entrepreneurial growth and economic development.

Universities also play a central role in ecosystem development by acting as hubs of innovation and entrepreneurship. The integration of AI into university programs can enhance research capabilities, support startup incubation, and strengthen collaboration between academia and industry.

4.5 Ethical and Societal Considerations

While AI offers numerous benefits, its integration into entrepreneurship education and ecosystems raises important ethical and societal considerations. One of the primary concerns is digital inequality, where unequal access to AI technologies may exacerbate existing disparities. Ensuring equitable access to AI-driven educational tools is essential for promoting inclusive development (Ogunsola et al., 2026).

Data privacy is another critical issue, as AI systems rely on large volumes of data for analysis and decision making. Educational institutions must ensure that student data is collected, stored, and used in a responsible and transparent manner. Failure to address these concerns may undermine trust in AI-driven educational systems.

Algorithmic bias also presents a significant challenge. AI systems trained on biased data may produce inaccurate or discriminatory outcomes, which can negatively impact learning experiences and entrepreneurial decision making. Addressing bias requires careful design, continuous monitoring, and ethical governance of AI systems (Adetunji & Ade-Ibijola, 2026).

In addition, there is a need to balance technological innovation with human-centered values. While AI can enhance learning efficiency, it should not replace critical human elements such as creativity, ethical reasoning, and social interaction. Entrepreneurship education must therefore maintain a balance between technological integration and human development.

4.6 Toward Sustainable AI-Driven Entrepreneurship Education

The successful integration of AI into entrepreneurship education in emerging digital economies requires a strategic and sustainable approach. This includes investing in digital infrastructure, developing AI literacy among students and educators, and fostering collaboration between educational institutions, industry, and government (Zhou, 2026).

Capacity building is essential to ensure that both students and educators can effectively utilize AI technologies. Training programs, workshops, and continuous professional development initiatives can help build the necessary skills and competencies. At the same time, institutions must develop policies and frameworks that support ethical and responsible AI usage.

Moreover, there is a need to align entrepreneurship education with broader national and regional development strategies. By integrating AI into education, countries can strengthen their innovation capacity, support startup ecosystems, and enhance global competitiveness. This alignment ensures that entrepreneurship education contributes to long-term economic and social development.

4.7 Summary

Entrepreneurship education in emerging digital economies is undergoing a significant transformation driven by digital technologies and artificial intelligence. While these economies face structural and institutional challenges, AI provides powerful tools to enhance learning, improve accessibility, and strengthen entrepreneurial ecosystems. However, the successful implementation of AI-driven education requires careful consideration of ethical, social, and technological factors.

Understanding these dynamics provides a critical foundation for developing a comprehensive framework that links artificial intelligence, entrepreneurial skills, innovation, and value creation. The following chapter builds on this foundation by proposing a conceptual framework for AI-enhanced entrepreneurship education.

5 . PROPOSED CONCEPTUAL FRAMEWORK FOR AI-ENHANCED ENTREPRENEURSHIP EDUCATION

The rapid integration of artificial intelligence (AI) into educational and entrepreneurial contexts calls for a structured conceptual understanding of how AI contributes to entrepreneurial development (Mah et al., 2026). While previous sections have explored the role of AI in higher education and entrepreneurship education, there remains a need for a comprehensive framework that connects AI capabilities with entrepreneurial outcomes in emerging digital economies.

This chapter proposes a conceptual framework that illustrates how artificial intelligence enhances entrepreneurship education by influencing the development of entrepreneurial skills, fostering innovation processes, and ultimately contributing to value creation and broader societal impact. The framework provides a holistic perspective that links technological capabilities with educational and economic outcomes.

5.1 Conceptual Foundation of the Framework

The proposed framework is grounded in the idea that artificial intelligence functions as an enabling layer that enhances learning processes and entrepreneurial activities. Rather than replacing traditional educational approaches, AI augments them by providing intelligent support, data-driven insights, and adaptive learning environments.

At its core, the framework establishes a sequential and interrelated relationship between five key components:

- Artificial Intelligence
- Entrepreneurial Skills
- Innovation
- Value Creation
- Societal and Economic Impact

These components are interconnected and form a continuous cycle, where improvements in one dimension influence and reinforce the others.

5.2 Artificial Intelligence as an Enabler

Artificial intelligence serves as the foundational element of the framework. It enables new forms of learning, decision making, and innovation by leveraging technologies such as machine learning, natural language processing, and predictive analytics.

In the context of entrepreneurship education, AI supports:

- Personalized learning experiences
- Intelligent feedback and mentoring
- Data-driven business analysis
- Simulation-based entrepreneurial training

Through these capabilities, AI enhances both the accessibility and effectiveness of entrepreneurship education, particularly in environments with limited resources.

Importantly, AI acts not as a substitute for human learning but as an augmentation tool that enhances cognitive processes and decision-making capabilities.

5.3 Development of Entrepreneurial Skills

The second component of the framework focuses on the development of entrepreneurial skills. AI contributes to the enhancement of both traditional and emerging competencies required in modern entrepreneurial environments.

These skills include:

- Opportunity recognition
- Critical and strategic thinking
- Innovation and creativity
- Data literacy and analytical skills
- Digital and technological adaptability

AI enables students to engage with real-world data, test business ideas, and receive immediate feedback, thereby accelerating the learning process. For example, AI-driven tools can help students analyze market trends or simulate startup scenarios, improving their ability to make informed decisions.

As a result, entrepreneurship education shifts from theoretical knowledge acquisition to practical, data-driven skill development.

5.4 AI-Driven Innovation Processes

The development of entrepreneurial skills leads to the next stage of the framework: innovation. AI plays a crucial role in facilitating innovation by providing tools that support idea generation, experimentation, and problem solving.

AI enhances innovation in several ways:

- Supporting ideation through generative AI tools
- Enabling rapid prototyping and testing of business concepts
- Providing predictive insights for market validation
- Facilitating iterative learning and improvement

This stage emphasizes that innovation is no longer solely driven by intuition but increasingly supported by data and intelligent systems. AI reduces uncertainty in the innovation process and allows entrepreneurs to explore multiple possibilities more efficiently.

5.5 Value Creation in Digital Economies

Innovation, when effectively applied, leads to value creation. In the context of entrepreneurship, value creation refers to the development of products, services, or solutions that address market needs and generate economic benefits.

AI contributes to value creation by:

- Improving efficiency and productivity
- Enabling scalable digital business models
- Enhancing customer experience through personalization
- Supporting data-driven strategic decision making

In emerging digital economies, value creation is particularly important as it contributes to economic growth, job creation, and increased competitiveness. AI-driven entrepreneurship enables new forms of value that were previously difficult to achieve, especially in resource-constrained environments.

5.6 Societal and Economic Impact

The final component of the framework focuses on the broader impact of AI-enhanced entrepreneurship education. Beyond individual learning outcomes and business success, the integration of AI contributes to wider societal and economic transformation.

These impacts include:

- Increased employability among graduates
- Strengthening of startup ecosystems
- Promotion of digital inclusion
- Support for innovation-driven economic development

In emerging digital economies, these outcomes are particularly significant, as they contribute to reducing inequality, fostering economic resilience, and supporting national development strategies.

5.7 Integrated Framework Dynamics

The proposed framework is not linear but dynamic and iterative. Each component influences and reinforces the others:

- AI enhances skill development
- Skills drive innovation
- Innovation leads to value creation
- Value creation generates societal impact
- Societal needs further drive the adoption of AI

This cyclical relationship highlights the continuous nature of learning, innovation, and economic development in AI-driven environments.

5.8 Implications of the Framework

The framework has several important implications:

- **For Educators**

Educators need to integrate AI tools into teaching practices while ensuring that students develop both technical and critical thinking skills.

- **For Institutions**

Universities must invest in digital infrastructure and create supportive environments for AI-driven entrepreneurship education.

- **For Policymakers**

Governments should develop policies that promote AI adoption in education while ensuring ethical and inclusive implementation.

- **For Students and Entrepreneurs**

Learners must develop a combination of entrepreneurial, digital, and analytical skills to succeed in AI-driven economies.

5.9 Summary

This chapter proposes a conceptual framework that links artificial intelligence with entrepreneurial skills, innovation, value creation, and societal impact. The framework provides a structured perspective on how

AI can transform entrepreneurship education, particularly in emerging digital economies.

By understanding these relationships, stakeholders can design more effective educational strategies, foster innovation, and support sustainable economic development. The next chapter builds on this framework by discussing practical implications and recommendations for implementation.

6. IMPLICATIONS AND DISCUSSION

The integration of artificial intelligence (AI) into entrepreneurship education presents significant implications for various stakeholders, including educators, institutions, policymakers, and learners. Building upon the conceptual framework proposed in the previous chapter, this section discusses how AI-driven entrepreneurship education can be effectively implemented and the broader implications it holds for educational systems and economic development.

6.1 Educational Implications

The adoption of AI in entrepreneurship education requires a fundamental transformation in teaching and learning practices. Traditional lecture-based approaches are no longer sufficient to equip students with the skills needed in dynamic and technology-driven entrepreneurial environments. Instead, education must shift toward more interactive, adaptive, and experiential learning models.

AI enables educators to design personalized learning experiences that accommodate diverse student needs. Adaptive learning systems allow students to progress at different paces while receiving targeted feedback. This not only improves learning outcomes but also enhances student engagement and motivation. However, educators must ensure that the use of AI does not diminish critical thinking and independent problem-solving abilities.

Furthermore, the role of educators is evolving. Rather than serving solely as knowledge providers, educators increasingly act as facilitators and mentors who guide students in utilizing AI tools effectively. This requires educators to develop new competencies, including digital literacy, data interpretation skills, and an understanding of AI technologies.

6.2 Institutional Implications

Higher education institutions play a central role in implementing AI-driven entrepreneurship education. To fully leverage the benefits of AI, institutions must invest in digital infrastructure, technological resources, and faculty development.

One key implication is the need for curriculum redesign. Entrepreneurship programs should integrate AI-related topics such as data analytics, digital innovation, and AI literacy. This integration ensures that students are equipped with the competencies required in modern entrepreneurial ecosystems.

In addition, universities must foster interdisciplinary collaboration. The intersection of AI and entrepreneurship requires knowledge from multiple disciplines, including business, computer science, and social sciences. Encouraging collaboration across these fields can enhance innovation and improve the quality of entrepreneurship education.

Institutions also need to establish clear policies and guidelines for the ethical use of AI in education. Issues such as data privacy, academic integrity, and responsible AI usage must be addressed to maintain trust and accountability within educational environments.

6.3 Implications for Policymakers

Policymakers have a critical role in supporting the integration of AI into entrepreneurship education, particularly in emerging digital economies. Governments must create enabling environments that facilitate the adoption of AI technologies in educational institutions.

One important area is investment in digital infrastructure. Access to reliable internet connectivity and technological tools is essential for implementing AI-driven learning systems. Without adequate infrastructure, the benefits of AI in education cannot be fully realized.

Policymakers should also develop national strategies that align education with digital transformation goals. This includes promoting AI literacy, supporting innovation-driven education, and fostering collaboration between academia, industry, and government.

Additionally, regulatory frameworks are needed to ensure the ethical and responsible use of AI. Policies related to data protection, algorithmic transparency, and digital inclusion are essential to prevent misuse and ensure equitable access to AI technologies.

6.4 Implications for Students and Future Entrepreneurs

For students and aspiring entrepreneurs, the integration of AI into education presents both opportunities and challenges. AI provides access to powerful tools that can enhance learning, support innovation, and improve decision-making capabilities.

Students can leverage AI to analyze market trends, develop business strategies, and test entrepreneurial ideas. This exposure to data-driven approaches prepares them for real-world entrepreneurial environments where technology plays a central role.

However, there is also a need for students to develop critical awareness of AI technologies. Over-reliance on AI tools may reduce creativity and independent thinking. Therefore, students must learn to use AI as a support tool rather than a replacement for human judgment.

In addition, developing digital and AI-related competencies is essential. Skills such as data literacy, technological adaptability, and critical thinking are increasingly important for success in digital economies.

6.5 Societal and Economic Implications

The integration of AI into entrepreneurship education extends beyond individual learning outcomes and has broader societal and economic implications. AI-driven education can contribute to the development of innovation-driven economies by fostering entrepreneurial skills and supporting startup ecosystems.

In emerging digital economies, AI has the potential to enhance employability and reduce unemployment by equipping individuals with relevant skills. It also supports the growth of digital entrepreneurship, which plays a crucial role in economic diversification and competitiveness.

Moreover, AI-driven entrepreneurship education can promote social inclusion by providing access to learning opportunities for individuals in remote or underserved areas. However, this potential can only be realized if issues related to digital inequality and access to technology are effectively addressed.

6.6 Challenges and Limitations

Despite its potential, the implementation of AI in entrepreneurship education faces several challenges. One major limitation is the digital divide, which may prevent certain groups from accessing AI-driven learning tools. Addressing this issue requires coordinated efforts from governments, institutions, and technology providers.

Another challenge is the ethical use of AI. Concerns related to data privacy, algorithmic bias, and transparency must be carefully managed to ensure responsible implementation. Failure to address these issues may undermine trust in AI-based educational systems.

There are also institutional challenges, including resistance to change and limited readiness among educators and institutions. Adopting AI-driven approaches requires significant investment in training, infrastructure, and curriculum development.

6.7 Discussion

The findings of this chapter highlight the transformative potential of AI in entrepreneurship education, particularly within emerging digital economies. The proposed framework demonstrates how AI can enhance skill development, drive innovation, and contribute to value creation.

However, the successful implementation of this framework depends on a balanced approach that integrates technological capabilities with human-centered values. AI should be used to enhance, rather than replace, human creativity, critical thinking, and ethical reasoning.

The discussion also emphasizes the importance of collaboration among stakeholders. Educators, institutions, policymakers, and industry actors must work together to create an ecosystem that supports AI-driven entrepreneurship education. This collaborative approach is essential for maximizing the benefits of AI while minimizing its risks.

6.8 Summary

This chapter has examined the implications of integrating artificial intelligence into entrepreneurship education across multiple dimensions. It highlights the need for educational transformation, institutional readiness, supportive policies, and the development of new competencies among students.

By addressing both opportunities and challenges, this chapter provides a comprehensive understanding of how AI-driven entrepreneurship education can be effectively implemented. The final chapter concludes this study by summarizing key insights and outlining future directions for research and practice.

7. FUTURE DIRECTIONS OF AI IN ENTREPRENEURSHIP EDUCATION

The rapid advancement of artificial intelligence (AI) continues to reshape the landscape of education and entrepreneurship, creating new opportunities while simultaneously introducing complex challenges (Festiyed et al., 2026). As digital transformation accelerates across emerging economies, the future of entrepreneurship education will be increasingly influenced by the evolution of AI technologies. Understanding these future directions is essential for ensuring that educational systems remain relevant, adaptive, and capable of preparing individuals for rapidly changing economic environments.

7.1 The Evolution of AI Technologies in Education

Artificial intelligence is expected to become more sophisticated and integrated into educational systems. Emerging technologies such as advanced machine learning models, generative AI, and multimodal learning systems are likely to further enhance the capabilities of educational platforms.

Future AI systems will not only provide personalized learning experiences but also offer predictive insights into student performance, learning behaviors, and career trajectories. These developments will enable more proactive and data-driven approaches to education, allowing institutions to better support students throughout their learning journeys.

In entrepreneurship education, these advancements will facilitate more realistic simulations, intelligent mentoring systems, and enhanced decision-support tools, enabling learners to engage in complex entrepreneurial activities with greater confidence and accuracy.

7.2 The Rise of AI-Driven Entrepreneurial Learning Ecosystems

The future of entrepreneurship education will extend beyond traditional classroom settings toward more integrated and dynamic learning ecosystems. AI will play a central role in connecting various components of these ecosystems, including universities, startups, investors, mentors, and industry partners.

Digital platforms powered by AI will enable seamless collaboration and knowledge sharing among stakeholders. For example, students may interact with AI-driven mentors, participate in global startup networks, and access real-time market data through integrated platforms. These ecosystems will provide continuous learning opportunities and support entrepreneurial development beyond formal education.

Such developments are particularly important in emerging digital economies, where access to entrepreneurial networks and resources may be limited. AI-driven ecosystems can help bridge these gaps by providing scalable and accessible solutions.

7.3 Increasing Importance of AI Literacy

As AI becomes more deeply embedded in entrepreneurial activities, the need for AI literacy will become increasingly critical. Future entrepreneurs will be expected to understand not only how to use AI tools but also how these technologies function, their limitations, and their ethical implications.

AI literacy includes competencies such as:

- Understanding basic AI concepts and technologies
- Interpreting data and analytical outputs
- Evaluating the reliability and limitations of AI systems
- Applying AI tools in business and innovation contexts

Integrating AI literacy into entrepreneurship education will be essential for preparing students to operate effectively in AI-driven environments. Without these competencies, individuals may struggle to leverage AI technologies or may misuse them in ways that lead to unintended consequences.

7.4 Ethical and Responsible AI in Education

As the use of AI expands, ethical considerations will play an increasingly important role in shaping its future. Issues such as data privacy, algorithmic bias, and transparency will remain central concerns in AI-driven educational systems.

Future directions in entrepreneurship education must incorporate ethical AI practices, ensuring that students not only use AI effectively but also understand its societal implications. This includes promoting responsible innovation, ethical decision making, and awareness of potential risks associated with AI technologies.

Educational institutions will need to develop frameworks and guidelines that support ethical AI usage, while also fostering a culture of responsibility and accountability among students and educators.

7.5 The Integration of AI with Emerging Technologies

The future of entrepreneurship education will not be shaped by AI alone but by its integration with other emerging technologies. Technologies such as blockchain, the Internet of Things (IoT), and virtual and augmented reality (VR/AR) are expected to complement AI and create more immersive and innovative learning environments.

For example:

- VR and AR can simulate real-world entrepreneurial scenarios
- IoT can provide real-time data for business experimentation
- Blockchain can support secure and transparent transactions

The convergence of these technologies will create new opportunities for experiential learning and innovation, enabling students to engage in complex entrepreneurial activities that closely resemble real-world environments.

7.6 Globalization of Entrepreneurship Education

AI will also contribute to the globalization of entrepreneurship education by enabling cross-border learning and collaboration. Students from different regions will be able to participate in shared learning environments, access global resources, and collaborate on international entrepreneurial projects.

This globalization will enhance knowledge exchange and promote diverse perspectives, which are essential for innovation. For emerging digital economies, this presents an opportunity to integrate into global entrepreneurial networks and enhance their competitiveness.

However, it also requires careful consideration of cultural differences, regulatory frameworks, and access disparities to ensure that globalization remains inclusive and equitable.

7.7 Challenges for Future Implementation

Despite its potential, the future of AI in entrepreneurship education is not without challenges. Key challenges include:

- **Technological inequality**, where access to advanced AI tools remains uneven
- **Rapid technological change**, which may outpace educational adaptation
- **Ethical concerns**, including data misuse and algorithmic bias
- **Institutional resistance**, particularly in traditional educational systems

Addressing these challenges will require continuous innovation, collaboration, and policy support. Educational institutions must remain flexible and responsive to technological developments while maintaining a focus on ethical and inclusive practices.

7.8 Summary

The future of artificial intelligence in entrepreneurship education is characterized by rapid technological advancement, increasing integration with other digital systems, and growing emphasis on ethical and responsible use. AI-driven learning ecosystems, enhanced personalization, and global collaboration will redefine how entrepreneurship education is delivered and experienced.

At the same time, the success of these developments depends on the ability of institutions, policymakers, and learners to adapt to evolving technological and societal conditions. These future directions provide a foundation for developing practical strategies and recommendations, which are discussed in the next chapter.

8. PRACTICAL RECOMMENDATIONS FOR AI-DRIVEN ENTREPRENEURSHIP EDUCATION

The successful integration of artificial intelligence (AI) into entrepreneurship education requires not only conceptual understanding but also practical strategies that can be implemented by various stakeholders. Building on the framework and discussions presented in previous chapters, this section outlines practical recommendations aimed at enhancing the effectiveness, inclusivity, and sustainability of AI-driven entrepreneurship education, particularly in emerging digital economies.

8.1 Recommendations for Educators

Educators play a crucial role in shaping how AI is integrated into entrepreneurship education. One of the primary recommendations is to adopt learner-centered and technology-enhanced pedagogical approaches. Rather than relying solely on traditional lectures, educators should incorporate AI-driven tools such as simulations, intelligent tutoring systems, and generative AI platforms into their teaching practices.

It is also important for educators to develop digital and AI-related competencies. This includes understanding how AI tools function, how to interpret their outputs, and how to guide students in using them effectively. Continuous professional development programs, workshops, and training initiatives can support educators in adapting to these new requirements.

In addition, educators should encourage critical thinking and ethical awareness. Students should not only learn how to use AI but also understand its limitations, risks, and ethical implications. This balanced approach ensures that AI enhances learning without undermining independent thinking and creativity.

8.2 Recommendations for Higher Education Institutions

Higher education institutions must take a strategic approach to integrating AI into entrepreneurship education. One key recommendation is the redesign of curricula to include AI-related topics such as data analytics, digital innovation, and AI literacy. These topics should be embedded within entrepreneurship courses rather than treated as separate subjects.

Institutions should also invest in digital infrastructure, including access to AI tools, platforms, and learning management systems. Without adequate technological support, the implementation of AI-driven education will remain limited.

Another important recommendation is to foster interdisciplinary collaboration. Entrepreneurship education that integrates AI requires input from multiple fields, including business, computer science, and social sciences. Encouraging collaboration across departments can enhance the quality of education and promote innovation.

Furthermore, institutions should establish clear policies and guidelines for the ethical use of AI. This includes ensuring data privacy, maintaining academic integrity, and promoting responsible use of AI technologies within educational environments.

8.3 Recommendations for Policymakers

Policymakers play a vital role in creating an enabling environment for AI-driven entrepreneurship education. One of the most important recommendations is to invest in digital infrastructure, particularly in emerging digital economies. Access to reliable internet connectivity and digital tools is essential for ensuring that AI-based education is accessible to all learners.

Policymakers should also develop national strategies that align education systems with digital transformation goals. This includes promoting AI literacy, supporting innovation-driven education, and encouraging collaboration between academia, industry, and government.

In addition, regulatory frameworks must be established to ensure the ethical use of AI. Policies related to data protection, algorithmic transparency, and digital inclusion are essential for building trust and ensuring responsible implementation.

Policymakers should also consider providing funding and incentives for educational institutions to adopt AI technologies. This can accelerate the adoption process and support innovation in teaching and learning.

8.4 Recommendations for Students and Entrepreneurs

Students and aspiring entrepreneurs must actively engage with AI technologies to fully benefit from their potential. One key recommendation is to develop a strong foundation in digital and analytical skills. Understanding how to interpret data and use AI tools effectively is essential in modern entrepreneurial environments.

Students should also adopt a proactive learning approach by experimenting with AI-driven tools, participating in simulations, and engaging in real-world entrepreneurial projects. This hands-on experience enhances their ability to apply theoretical knowledge in practical contexts.

At the same time, students must maintain critical awareness when using AI. They should question the accuracy and reliability of AI-generated outputs and avoid over-reliance on automated systems. Developing a balance between human judgment and technological assistance is crucial for long-term success.

8.5 Recommendations for Industry and Entrepreneurial Ecosystems

Industry stakeholders and entrepreneurial ecosystems also play a significant role in supporting AI-driven entrepreneurship education. Collaboration between universities and industry can provide students with access to real-world data, mentorship, and practical experience.

Companies can contribute by offering internships, training programs, and partnerships that expose students to AI applications in business contexts. This collaboration helps bridge the gap between education and industry needs.

Startup ecosystems can also leverage AI to create more inclusive and accessible support systems. Digital platforms can connect entrepreneurs with mentors, investors, and resources, fostering innovation and collaboration.

8.6 Ensuring Ethical and Inclusive Implementation

A key recommendation across all stakeholders is to ensure that AI-driven entrepreneurship education is implemented in an ethical and inclusive manner. This involves addressing issues such as digital inequality, data privacy, and algorithmic bias.

Efforts should be made to provide equal access to AI tools and educational resources, particularly for underserved communities. Inclusivity is essential for ensuring that the benefits of AI are distributed fairly and do not exacerbate existing inequalities.

Ethical considerations should also be integrated into educational programs. Students must be trained to consider the social and ethical implications of their entrepreneurial activities, particularly when using AI technologies.

8.7 Implementation Strategies

To effectively implement these recommendations, a coordinated and multi-stakeholder approach is required. Key strategies include:

- Developing partnerships between universities, industry, and government
- Investing in training and capacity building for educators and students
- Establishing clear policies and ethical guidelines
- Promoting continuous evaluation and improvement of AI-driven educational programs

These strategies ensure that AI integration is not only effective but also sustainable in the long term.

8.8 Summary

This chapter has outlined practical recommendations for integrating artificial intelligence into entrepreneurship education. By addressing the roles of educators, institutions, policymakers, students, and industry stakeholders, it provides a comprehensive roadmap for implementation.

The successful adoption of AI-driven entrepreneurship education requires collaboration, investment, and a strong commitment to ethical and inclusive practices. The final chapter concludes this study by summarizing key insights and highlighting the overall contributions of this work.

9 . CONCLUSION

Artificial intelligence (AI) has emerged as a transformative force that is reshaping not only economic systems but also educational practices and entrepreneurial activities. This chapter has explored the role of AI in enhancing entrepreneurship education, particularly within the context of emerging digital economies. The findings highlight that AI is not merely a technological tool but a strategic enabler that has the potential to redefine how entrepreneurial knowledge and skills are developed.

Throughout this study, it has been demonstrated that the integration of AI into higher education introduces new learning models that are more adaptive, personalized, and data-driven. These advancements enable students to engage in more effective and meaningful learning experiences, thereby improving their readiness for entrepreneurial activities. At the same time, entrepreneurship education itself is evolving, requiring the incorporation of digital competencies, data literacy, and technological adaptability to meet the demands of modern economic environments.

A key contribution of this chapter is the development of a conceptual framework that links artificial intelligence with entrepreneurial skills, innovation processes, value creation, and broader societal impact. This framework provides a structured perspective on how AI enhances entrepreneurship education and supports the development of innovation-driven economies. By illustrating the relationships between these elements, the framework offers valuable insights for educators, institutions, and policymakers seeking to implement AI-driven educational strategies.

The discussion has also highlighted the unique context of emerging digital economies, where opportunities for digital transformation coexist with structural challenges such as limited access to resources, infrastructure gaps, and disparities in digital literacy. In these environments, AI has the potential to democratize access to education, improve learning efficiency, and strengthen entrepreneurial ecosystems. However, realizing this potential requires careful consideration of ethical, social, and technological factors.

Furthermore, this chapter has emphasized the importance of a multi-stakeholder approach in implementing AI-driven entrepreneurship education. Educators must adopt innovative teaching methods, institutions must invest in infrastructure and curriculum development, policymakers must create supportive regulatory environments, and students must develop the necessary skills to effectively utilize AI technologies. Collaboration among these stakeholders is essential for maximizing the benefits of AI while addressing its associated challenges.

Despite its significant potential, the integration of AI into entrepreneurship education is not without limitations. Issues such as digital inequality, data privacy concerns, algorithmic bias, and institutional readiness remain critical challenges that must be addressed. Ensuring ethical and inclusive implementation is essential to prevent unintended consequences and to build trust in AI-driven educational systems.

Looking forward, the future of entrepreneurship education will be increasingly shaped by the continued evolution of AI and its integration with other emerging technologies. The development of AI-driven learning ecosystems, the growing importance of AI literacy, and the globalization of education will further transform how entrepreneurial skills are acquired and applied. These trends highlight the need for continuous adaptation and innovation in educational practices.

In conclusion, artificial intelligence represents a powerful catalyst for transforming entrepreneurship education in emerging digital economies. By enhancing learning processes, supporting innovation, and contributing to value creation, AI has the potential to play a central role in shaping the future of entrepreneurship. However, its successful implementation depends on a balanced approach that integrates technological capabilities with human-centered values, ethical considerations, and inclusive practices.

This chapter contributes to the growing body of knowledge on AI and entrepreneurship education by providing a comprehensive and integrated perspective on their intersection. It offers both theoretical insights and practical implications, serving as a foundation for future research and policy development. As digital transformation continues to accelerate, the role of AI in education and entrepreneurship will become increasingly important, making it essential for stakeholders to proactively engage with these changes and harness their potential for sustainable economic and social development.

REFERENCES

Adetunji, R. O., & Ade-Ibijola, A. (2026). BizAssistBot: An artificial intelligence assistant for small business operations. *Discover Artificial Intelligence*, *6*(1), 161. Advance online publication. DOI: 10.1007/s44163-025-00802-y

Brezovec, E., Zelić, M., & Zagode, A. M. (2026). Stabilizing truth in educational sciences: A systematic review of generative AI in education. *Kybernetes*, *55*(13), 1–17. DOI: 10.1108/K-09-2025-2339

Deng, X. N., & Sun, R. (2026). Artificial intelligence and career development: Concerns and insights from first-generation college students. *International Journal of Information Management*, *87*, 103003. Advance online publication. DOI: 10.1016/j.ijinfomgt.2025.103003

Essel, H. B., Vlachopoulos, D., Johnson, E. E., & Quansah, E. K. (2026). Undergraduate students' perceptions of generative artificial intelligence as a predictor of learning autonomy in Ghana. *Discover Artificial Intelligence*, *6*(1), 85. Advance online publication. DOI: 10.1007/s44163-025-00725-8

Festiyed, F., Desnita, D., Natasya, Z., Fadillah, M. A., & Novitra, F. (2026). From Assistance to Autonomy: AI Integration in Structured Research-Based Learning for Higher Education. *Electronic Journal of e-Learning*, *24*(1), 109–124. DOI: 10.34190/ejel.24.1.4416

Gal, C., & Rachevski, I. (2026). Understanding entrepreneurial propensity: An integrated analysis of cognitive traits and contextual factors in diverse economies. *Journal of Innovation and Entrepreneurship*, *15*(1), 10. Advance online publication. DOI: 10.1186/s13731-026-00614-z

Guo, H. (2026). A model for assessing college students' entrepreneurial abilities based on deep learning and big data. *Discover Artificial Intelligence*, *6*(1), 115. Advance online publication. DOI: 10.1007/s44163-025-00799-4

Jiang, M. (2026). Career planning and entrepreneurial intention guidance for college students based on fuzzy decision support system. *Discover Artificial Intelligence*, *6*(1), 77. Advance online publication. DOI: 10.1007/s44163-025-00759-y

Khotimah, K., Budiarto, M. K., Amarulloh, A., Diningrat, S. W. M., Carreza, A. N., & Son, J. H. (2026). Fostering Creativity Through Meta Virtual Project-Based Networked Learning: An In-Depth Examination. *Electronic Journal of e-Learning*, *24*(1), 93–108. DOI: 10.34190/ejel.24.1.4302

Lai, Q. (2026). Research on the refinement of college student education management based on artificial intelligence. *Discover Artificial Intelligence*, *6*(1), 31. Advance online publication. DOI: 10.1007/s44163-025-00651-9

Mah, D.-K., Groß, N., Egloffstein, M., & Prilop, C. N. (2026). Artificial intelligence in K-12 instruction: The role of teacher professional development. *Smart Learning Environments*, *13*(1), 16. Advance online publication. DOI: 10.1186/s40561-026-00442-4

Maleki, A. (2026). Rethinking ethical academic integrity ecosystems in higher education in the age of artificial intelligence. *Discover Artificial Intelligence*, *6*(1), 145. Advance online publication. DOI: 10.1007/s44163-026-00887-z

Ogunsola, J. A., Quadri, G. O., & Adigun, O. T. (2026). The strategic role of higher education in promoting entrepreneurship and managing innovation complexities: A conceptual framework analysis. *Journal of Innovation and Entrepreneurship*, *15*(1), 9. Advance online publication. DOI: 10.1186/s13731-026-00632-x

Pingmuang, P., Koraneekij, P., & Khlaisang, J. (2026). Development and Validation of an AI Literacy Scale for Pre-Service Teachers in Thailand. *Electronic Journal of e-Learning*, *24*(1), 1–18. DOI: 10.34190/ejel.24.1.3990

Pöcher, B., Campbell, D. F. J., & Carayannis, E. G. (2026). Innovation and entrepreneurship in organizational university "Third Space" arrangements: Third Space and third mission in mode 3 universities. *Journal of Innovation and Entrepreneurship*, *15*(1), 2. Advance online publication. DOI: 10.1186/s13731-025-00613-6

Sun, X. (2026). Prediction model for the success rate of college student entrepreneurship projects based on deep learning. *Discover Artificial Intelligence*, *6*(1), 3. Advance online publication. DOI: 10.1007/s44163-025-00657-3

Wei, C. J., Shahmi, A. M. F., Qing, W. Y., & Melati, N. (2026). Motivations Matter: Predicting Entrepreneurship Education MOOC Course Completion with a Decision Tree Approach. *Online Learning : The Official Journal of the Online Learning Consortium*, *30*(1), 294–322. DOI: 10.24059/olj.v30i1.4517

Yang, X., & Li, J. (2026). Application of deep learning in the innovation of personalized entrepreneurship education model in colleges and universities. *Discover Artificial Intelligence*, *6*(1), 107. Advance online publication. DOI: 10.1007/s44163-025-00777-w

Yoshida, M., Duangchinda, V., & Ruangrit, N. (2026). AI-Supported Learning in Online Discussion Forums: A Scoping Review. *Electronic Journal of e-Learning*, *24*(1), 19–35. DOI: 10.34190/ejel.24.1.4409

Zhou, Y. (2026). Research on Intelligent Development of Talent Cultivation Mode of Higher Vocational Innovation and Entrepreneurship Education Based on Data Mining under the Perspective of Industry-Teaching Integration. *International Journal of Computer Information Systems and Industrial Management Applications*, *18*, 1–18. DOI: 10.70917/ijcisim-2026-0173

Chapter 2
Synthetic Startup Labs:
Using Generative AI to Simulate Entrepreneurial Ecosystems for Experiential Learning

Aarthi Selvakumar
http://orcid.org/0009-0006-9064-2091
Marwadi University, Rajkot, India

Ravikumar Natarajan
http://orcid.org/0009-0009-3705-1681
Marwadi University, Rajkot, India

Karimov Rashid Salayevich
Mamun University, Khiva, Uzbekistan

Sadirdin Khudoykulov
Termez University of Economics and Service, Termez, Uzbekistan

ABSTRACT

Introduction of Generative Artificial Intelligence is changing the way entrepreneurship is learned by facilitating simulative and immersive learning. In this chapter, the author presents the idea of Synthetic Startup Labs, an AI-based pedagogical system, which is created to mimic entrepreneurial ecosystems and aid in the process of experiential learning. Adaptive feed-

DOI: 10.4018/979-8-2600-0487-6.ch002

back systems, artificial intelligence simulations, and virtual interaction with stakeholders allow the learners to explore ideas of starting up, test business strategy and see how the market will react to them in secure online space. The conceptual framework, recent case studies, learning outcomes, and managerial implications of AI-enabled entrepreneurial training were discussed in the chapter. The results indicate the potential of Synthetic Startup Labs to improve entrepreneurial capabilities, innovation thinking, and availability to startup education and assist in the emergence of technology-based entrepreneurial ecosystems.

1. INTRODUCTION

Digital technologies have transformed the nature of entrepreneurship education by changing the way innovation ecosystems and business creation processes are being reshaped. It is not only the universities and training institutions that are supposed to impart theoretical knowledge, but also to train learners to work in complex, uncertain and rapidly changing startup situations. The conventional models of entrepreneurship education are based on lectures, case studies, and limited exposure to business situations in reality. The disadvantage of these methods is that despite the background knowledge, the students are often not given a chance to apply entrepreneurial decision-making in realistic settings. With the advent of Artificial Intelligence (AI) and Generative AI technologies, in particular, there has emerged an opportunity in the form of emerging experiential and simulation-based learning environments (Hamburg et al., 2019). The Artificial Intelligence system is able to create dynamic business situations, imitate market reactions, and mimic the interactions between the various stakeholders in the entrepreneurial organizations including the customers, investors, and mentors. Such capabilities permit building of immersive learning, which replicates actual entrepreneurship ecosystems. Synthetic Startup Labs are a new model that combines Generative AI capabilities with the principles of experiential learning and enables students to play with the idea of a startup, test strategies, and learn on the basis of simulated results in an educational safe and scalable environment.

1.1 AI Transformation in Entrepreneurship Education

The discipline of entrepreneurship education has seen greater adoption of Artificial Intelligence as a disruptive technology in higher education and professional training. Machine learning algorithms and large language models are AI technologies that allow building adaptive learning environments that can react to the needs and behaviors of individual learners. These technologies may be used in the field of entrepreneurship education to support generating ideas, developing business models, and analyzing markets with data-driven information and interactive advice (Sudarmaji & Munirah, 2019). Generative AI tools also complement the learning process by generating simulated business situations, market trends and customer responses that help the student to test business ideas in dynamic environments. Mentorship-like interactions can also be facilitated by AI-led systems by providing conversational agents that assist learners in the process of making strategic decisions. Consequently, educational programs in entrepreneurship are moving out of the old classroom teaching models to brainy, technology-enhanced learning networks in which students are enabled to participate in AI-assisted entrepreneurial simulators and problem-solving exercises.

1.2 Need for Experiential Startup Learning

Entrepreneurship is experiential and is associated with uncertainty, risk, and complicated decision-making processes. Good entrepreneurship education as such must be based on learning strategies that go beyond theoretical training and promote experimentation. Experience based learning models are based on experiential learning by action, reflection and problem solving on a repeated basis to enable the learner to acquire practical entrepreneurial skills such as identifying opportunities, managing resources and strategic thinking. However, it is difficult to offer genuine entrepreneurial experiences to an academic setting. It usually lacks access to actual startup ecosystems, investors, and industry mentors, especially in institutions that are not in large innovation centers. Besides, the introduction of actual enterprises in academic courses can entail the financial and operational risks that students cannot be ready to assume

(Shepherd & Gruber, 2021). Such limitations underscore the significance of learning settings resembling the entrepreneurial process and simulation based, but with minimal risks. Digital technologies should be applied to support experiential learning in startups so that students could practice their entrepreneurial decision-making, experiment with business ideas, and learn about successes and failures in simulated business environments.

1.3 Emergence of Synthetic Startup Labs

Synthetic Startup Labs are a new principle or approach to pedagogy that combines learners with Generative AI technologies and experiential entrepreneurship learning. These are labs designed to simulate virtual entrepreneurial ecosystems with students being able to generate a startup idea, talk to AI-created stakeholders, and run a business through simulated market conditions. Using Generative AI systems, Synthetic Startup Labs will be able to simulate the behavior of major actors in the ecosystem (customers, investors, mentors, regulators, competitors). In such environments, students get to experience different areas of venture creation such as opportunity identification, product development, pricing strategy, testing the market and negotiation of investment (Prabagar et al., 2025). AI-based simulations produce an immediate feedback upon the choice of the learner, and thus, iteration and continuous improvement. Synthetic Startup Labs thus is a scalable and accessible platform to entrepreneurship education, which fills the gap between theory and practice of a startup. As more learning institutions turn to digital learning methods, AI-based simulated startup environments have become an attractive way of equipping students with future entrepreneurs with the skills needed to operate in the complex ecosystem of innovation.

2. BACKGROUND TO THE STUDY

The education of entrepreneurs has changed significantly within the last decades due to the global changes in the economy, the development of technologies, and the rise in the significance of startup ecosystems as the determinants of the economic growth. The institutions of learning are increasingly appreciating the importance of instilling the spirit of entrepreneurship, creativity and problem-solving skills to learners in various fields of study. The initial attempts of teaching entrepreneurship were largely teaching in business planning and management concepts by way of classroom training (Triono et al., 2024). But the contemporary entrepreneurial ecosystems need more adaptive and experiential learning models that equip learners to survive in the uncertain and fast changing business conditions. The recent developments in Artificial Intelligence and Generative technologies have revealed new possibilities to revolutionize the process of learning entrepreneurship with the help of smart simulation environment and customized learning systems (Pandit et al., 2025). These technologies enable instructors to develop interactive learning sessions that imitate the entrepreneurial processes in the real world. The historical progress of the entrepreneurship training, the increasing role of the AI technologies, and the drawbacks of the traditional education models give a valuable basis to understand how Synthetic Startup Labs can be used to augment the process of the experiential entrepreneurial education.

2.1 Evolution of Entrepreneurship Training

The trend of entrepreneurship training has shifted to a more interdisciplinary, experiential business training model as opposed to the traditional business education model. The main focus of the initial entrepreneurship courses was business plan development, financial analysis and management principles. Although these areas do not lose their relevance, the contemporary entrepreneurship learning is more and more devoted to the identification of opportunities, innovation mechanisms, and the dynamics of startup ecosystems. Startup incubators, accelerator programs, innovation labs, and entrepreneurship competitions are some of the pedagogical models that have been embraced in the last few years by educational institutions to offer tangible learning opportunities (Dunan et al., 2025). These programs empower students to participate in the development of ideas, prototype development, and pitching of their venture simulating actual startup procedures. Moreover, such approaches as design thinking and lean startup have become widely popular in entrepreneurship courses because they focus on experimentation, customer discovery, and iterative product development. In spite of these developments, there remains a significant gap in the entrepreneurship programs to offer a stable access to the real entrepreneurial ecosystems and industry mentorship where scalable digital solutions capable of simulating entrepreneurial experiences are required. Table 1 is a comparison between the traditional methods of teaching entrepreneurship and the new methods of experiential and AI-enabled learning.

Table 1. Evolution of entrepreneurship education approaches

Approach	Key Characteristics	Learning Method	Limitations
Traditional Lecture-Based	Theory-focused instruction	Classroom lectures	Limited practical exposure
Case Study Method	Business problem analysis	Discussion-based	Static learning context
Experiential Learning	Hands-on venture activities	Projects, competitions	Limited scalability
AI-Enabled Learning	Simulation-based environments	AI-driven interactions	Requires digital infrastructure

2.2 Role of AI and Generative Technologies

Generative technologies and Artificial Intelligence are getting more and more significant in the design and delivery of education and innovation processes. Large data sets can be analyzed, trends spotted and predictive insights created by AI systems that can assist businesses in decision-making and strategic planning (DIAWARA Amidou, 2025). These capabilities enable entrepreneurship students to research the market trends, assess business opportunities, and model strategic decisions with the use of data-driven tools. Large language models and other AI-based simulation engines, which are considered Generative AI technologies, expand these abilities to generate realistic business events, customer persona, and business market conditions. Such tools allow learners to test strategies of start-ups within virtual settings where feedback and results are created dynamically (Ravikumar, Aarthi, Rai, et al., 2025). Moreover, conversational AI-based applications can be used as virtual tutors or advisors, who will help students to design their business model, perform market research, and prepare an investment. The introduction of AI technologies in the field of entrepreneurship education thus opens possibilities to develop intelligent learning environments and increase the levels of creativity, experimentation, and strategic thinking among young aspiring entrepreneurs. Table 2 Shows the way various Generative AI tools assist in entrepreneurial learning.

Table 2. Role of generative AI tools in entrepreneurship education

AI Tool Type	Function in Entrepreneurship Education	Example Learning Activity
Large Language Models	Idea generation and strategy suggestions	Business plan drafting
AI Simulation Engines	Market and startup environment simulation	Startup decision testing
Conversational AI Agents	Mentorship and advisory support	Investor pitch practice
Data Generation Models	Synthetic market datasets	Market analysis training

2.3 Challenges in Traditional Entrepreneurial Education

The traditional models of instruction have a number of constraints that limit their use in equipping the student to the reality of startups despite the increased role of entrepreneurship education. In-classroom teaching approaches are usually oriented to theory and case studies that might not fully reflect the uncertainty and complexity of making decisions in the field of entrepreneurship. This can lead to students getting away with theoretical knowledge and little hands-on experience in the development of ventures. The other difficulty is the inequitable access to entrepreneurial networks and mentorship (Dunsim & Jabar, 2025). The students enrolled in the institutions that are not situated in the large innovation centers might not be able to communicate with the start-up founders, investors, and industry professionals. Moreover, teachers may find it challenging to offer personalized instructions and feedback to great numbers of students. The physical incubators or startup labs are also constrained by the resources of the university to set up physical incubators or startup labs to accommodate all students (Ravikumar, Aarthi, Ruzimova, et al., 2025). These issues indicate the necessity of new paradigms of education that use digital technologies and simulations powered by AI to offer immersive and scalable entrepreneurial education.

3. RESEARCH OBJECTIVES

Possible opportunities in terms of improving the experiential process and the simulation of the complex startup ecosystems with the introduction of the Generative Artificial Intelligence in entrepreneurship education emerge. Synthetic Startup Labs are supposed to equip learners with simulated environments in which entrepreneurial concepts could be generated, verified, and assessed with the help of simulations based on AI. To comprehend the teaching and practical significance of this strategy, one should specify clear research objectives that will help direct the research of AI-enabled entrepreneurial learning models. The subsequent objectives aid in exploring how Generative AI technologies may assist in the simulation of a startup, enhance the results of experiential learning, and recreate interactions in an entrepreneurial ecosystem.

- To examine the role of AI-based startup simulation environments in supporting entrepreneurial decision-making and venture development learning.
- To analyze how Generative AI tools enhance experiential learning by enabling interactive experimentation with startup ideas and business models.
- To investigate the effectiveness of AI-generated entrepreneurial ecosystems in simulating interactions with stakeholders such as customers, investors, mentors, and competitors.
- To evaluate the impact of Synthetic Startup Labs on entrepreneurial skill development, including opportunity recognition, innovation, and strategic thinking.

- To explore the potential of AI-driven simulation platforms in improving accessibility and scalability of entrepreneurship education across diverse educational institutions.

4. CONCEPTUAL MODEL

The idea of Synthetic Startup Labs is based on applying Generative Artificial Intelligence into principles of experiential learning in order to establish intelligent and interactive learning ecosystems of entrepreneurs. The suggested conceptual framework reveals that AI technologies can be used to create realistic startup ecosystems and facilitate adaptive learning and ecosystem-based interactions among the entrepreneurial participants. In this context, students are put in active virtual settings where they could be experimented with business concepts, strategy test scenarios, and see the consequences of their actions in virtual market conditions (Aarthi et al., 2025). The theoretical framework is a three-connected set of components, namely AI-based entrepreneurial simulation, adaptive learning and feedback system, and entrepreneurial ecosystem interaction modeling. Simulation engines based on AI will create a realistic startup environment and market conditions where students should make entrepreneurial decisions (Rong et al., 2025). Adaptive learning systems process the learner actions, and in turn give feedback to the learners in a personalized manner, directing skill learning. In the meantime, ecosystem interaction models recreate the interactions between stakeholders who include customers, investors, regulators, and competitors. Cumulatively, these elements make up a combined education system that makes possible scalable, immersive, and technology-informed training on entrepreneurship. Table 3: Overviews the three fundamental elements of the suggested conceptual framework.

Table 3. Components of the synthetic startup lab conceptual model

Component	Description	Role in Entrepreneurial Learning
AI-Driven Simulation	Generates realistic startup scenarios	Enables decision-based learning
Adaptive Learning Systems	Provides personalized feedback	Improves entrepreneurial competencies
Ecosystem Interaction Model	Simulates stakeholders and networks	Enhances ecosystem understanding

4.1 AI-Driven Entrepreneurial Simulation

The most important technological aspect of the Synthetic Startup Lab model is AI-driven entrepreneurial simulation. In this method, AI systems generate business environments that are realistic and learners get to experiment with the venture creation process in a simulated environment. Such simulations may involve market demand changes, consumer behavioral patterns, competition, and investment conditions. Engaging with such AI-created situations, learners have to make choices connected with the product development, pricing strategies, marketing promotion, and business model development (Sang et al., 2025). Large language model and predictive analytics systems are Generative AI technologies that can be used to create dynamic entrepreneurial situations, which vary depending on the choices made by the learner. The simulation environment also changes and generates new challenges or opportunities as students experiment with various strategies, which simulates real startup environments. This process of experimentation will aid the learners in becoming familiar with the outcomes of entrepreneurial decisions, as well as train them to be strategic thinkers and problem-solving skills (Musyaffi et al., 2025). Simulations based on AI thus offer an affordable and scalable framework in which students may hone their entrepreneurial practice without the financial and operational risk that comes with the launch of a business.

4.2 Adaptive Learning and Feedback Systems

Adaptive learning and feedback systems are important in improving the effectiveness of Synthetic Startup Labs as they help in personalizing the learning process to the individual. These systems evaluate interaction of learners in AI-based simulations, decision patterns, response time, strategic decisions, and problem-solving strategies. According to this analysis, AI algorithms provide some customized feedback enabling learners to see their strengths and weaknesses when it comes to entrepreneurship strategies. The complexity of the simulated entrepreneurial scenarios can also be modified by adaptive learning technologies based on the experience level and the progress of the learner. In this way, an entry-level learner might be introduced to simplified market situations, whereas advanced students might have to deal with complicated cases, including a number of competitors, regulatory restrictions and investment negotiations (Liu & Zhang, 2025). Also, in case of simulation, intelligent conversational agents can be used as virtual mentors who offer guidance, suggestions, and explanations. Adaptive learning systems will facilitate progressive skill acquisition and stimulate reflective learning through their ongoing observation and personal feedback, so that a student will improve their entrepreneurial strategies with time.

4.3 Entrepreneurial Ecosystem Interaction Model

The model of interaction between the entrepreneurial ecosystem is interested in the repetition of the relations and dynamics that exist among various actors in real startup ecosystems. The successful ventures of any entrepreneurship are usually accompanied by the communication with a wide range of stakeholders such as customers, investors, mentors, regulators, suppliers, and industry partners. Synthetic Startup Labs employ Generative AI technologies to model these ecosystem participants, which enable learners to participate in real-world entrepreneur interactions (Amravati. et al., 2026). In the simulation setting, the stakeholders created through AI can react to the choices of the learners in a dynamic manner. As an example, virtual customers can give feedback on product concepts, investors can review business plans, and government bodies can give compliance regulations. These engagements make learners learn the impact of external ecosystem factors on making entrepreneurial decisions. The eco system interaction model thus makes the students think in more than one way when creating strategies of a startup. Simulating intricate stakeholder interactions, Synthetic Startup Labs offer a comprehensive learning experience in which the students learn how the entrepreneurial success depends on the innovation networks, market pressures, and institutional actors. Figure 1 indicates the interaction of the startup of a learner with AI-generated stakeholders like customers, investors, mentors, regulators, and industry partners in the context of the Synthetic Startup Lab simulation environment.

Figure 1. AI-driven entrepreneurial ecosystem interaction model

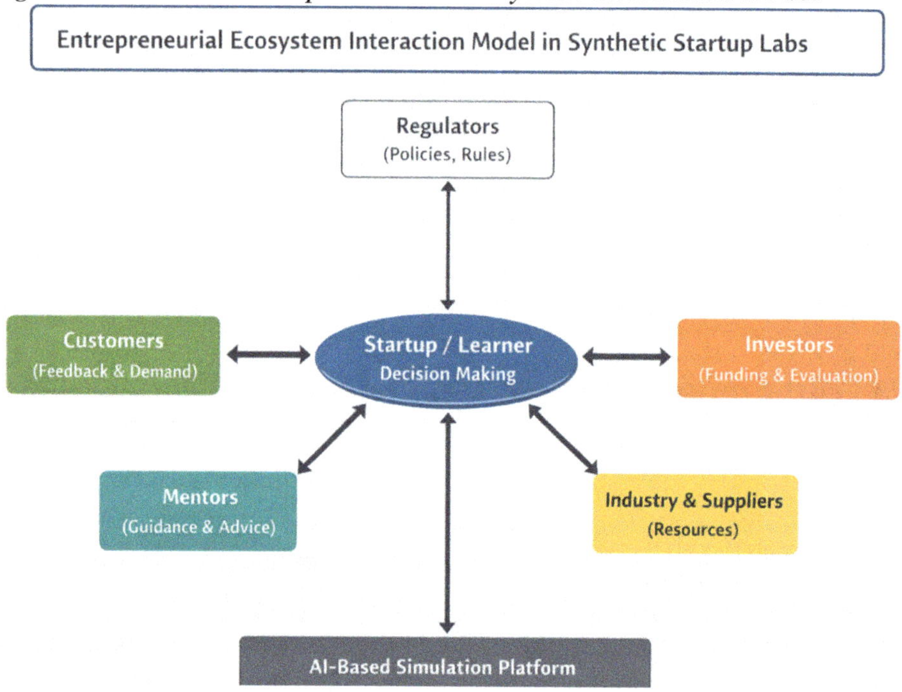

5. RESEARCH METHODOLOGY

The study design of the chapter is conceptual and exploratory to investigate how Generative Artificial Intelligence can change the face of the entrepreneurship learning experience with the help of Synthetic Startup Labs. Given that the proposed framework is based on the incorporation of AI-based simulations with the model of experiential learning, the study is mainly based on the theoretical analysis, the available literature, and the elaboration of the conceptual framework as opposed to the actual experimentation. Such a method makes it possible to learn the full picture of how AI technologies can facilitate the learning process of entrepreneurs and recreate the environment of complex startups ecosystems (Ram, 2025). The approach will include the review of academic materials connected to the topic of entrepreneurship education, experiential learning, Generative AI technologies, and digital simulation platforms. The knowledge obtained through these sources is applied to finding major elements that affect AI-powered entrepreneurial learning. The chapter discusses also the latest technological possibilities of Generative AI tools and how they can be used in the startup simulation environment. It is on the basis of this analysis that a conceptual framework of Synthetic Startup Labs is created to show how AI-based simulations, simulative learning processes, and ecosystem interaction model could be combined to facilitate experiential entrepreneurship training.

5.1 Conceptual Research Design

The theoretical research design of the present study is centered on the establishment of the theoretical framework which outlines the way in which a theoretical framework can be used to explain how the concept of Generative AI technologies can aid the teaching process of entrepreneurship based on the simulation-based learning environment. The study does not use empirical experiments, instead, it uses a qualitative and conceptual analysis method, which synthesizes the available knowledge in various interdisciplinary areas, such as the studies of entrepreneurship, the study of educational technology, the research of Artificial Intelligence, and the research of innovation management. The conceptual design will attempt to pinpoint the significant components needed to construct AI-driven entrepreneurial learning systems. Such aspects are AI-based simulation tools, adaptive learning systems, and the models of ecosystem interaction which all contribute to the concept of experiential learning (Zolfaghari et al., 2024). With combine knowledge of these areas, the research develops a theoretical framework that will show how Synthetic Startup Labs can be used as digital platforms to conduct entrepreneurial experiments. The design also puts into focus the relationships between AI technologies and the learning outcomes that include creativity, capable of making decisions, and developing entrepreneurial skills. This theoretical framework offers systematic basis to the further empirical studies and practice.

5.2 Data Sources and Analytical Approach

The chapter relies on secondary data sources and analytical findings based on the available scholarly publications, reports, and technological advances in the field of Artificial Intelligence and entrepreneurship learning. Primary sources to obtain the insights into the changing environment of AI-driven educational technologies and entrepreneurial training patterns are peer-reviewed journal articles, conference publications, books, and institutional reports. These materials present both theoretical background and practical knowledge of how digital simulation and environment can be used to facilitate experiential learning. The methodological strategy is the synthesis of data related to various fields that can help determine the patterns, tendencies, and new uses of Generative AI in education (Tan, 2020). The various methods of teaching entrepreneurship are compared to study the different approaches such as traditional classroom-based teaching, innovation laboratories, and online simulation platforms. This discussion contributes to the identification of the weaknesses of traditional training frameworks and the possible benefits of AI-based learning contexts. Through a combination of education, technology, and entrepreneurship research the study is able to create an overall viewpoint on the development of the Synthetic Startup Lab framework.

5.3 Framework Development Method

The method of framework development to be applied in this study is the combination of theoretical knowledge related to the experiential learning theory, entrepreneurship education models and the use of Artificial Intelligence. As the first step, the basic elements that are needed to develop AI-enabled simulation-based entrepreneurial settings are recognized. These elements are AI-based simulation systems, adaptive learning technologies, and elementary interaction systems between the ecosystem, which in combination deals with the development of entrepreneurial skills. The framework is built through the examination of the interaction between these components in a digital learning ecosystem (Ahmed et al., 2025). Simulation engines powered by AI create real-life entrepreneurial situations, and adaptive learning systems interpret responses of learners and give them individual feedback. The models of ecosystem interaction recreate relationships of stakeholders that can contribute to the success of startups. With a blend of these factors, the proposed framework shows how the Synthetic Startup Labs could be used as immersive and scalable learning environments with which entrepreneurship education could be conducted. The framework also brings out the possible implementation plans of educational institutions that want to incorporate the use of Generative AI technologies in in entrepreneurship training.

6. LITERATURE REVIEW

The education in entrepreneurship has been gradually shifting to experiential and technology-based learning models that focus on the practical involvement into the entrepreneurial processes. Teaching methods based on the traditional classroom setting are quite helpful in presenting the theoretical material, but they do not include the dynamic and unpredictable nature of the real entrepreneurial setting. Consequently, scholars and teachers have identified pedagogical strategies that enable students to acquire entrepreneurial skills by experimenting, reflecting and problem-solving (Chen et al., 2024). Modern entrepreneurship education now takes place in the experiential frameworks which allow the students to directly participate in the venture creation process like opportunity recognition, business model development and market validation. In combination with these pedagogical changes, new digital technologies have brought up novel tools that can be used to improve learning settings. Generative technologies and Artificial Intelligence have become significant forces of innovation in education systems because they allow adaptive learning, personalized instruction, and simulations. According to these technologies, there is the option to create learning settings whereby learning entrepreneurial situations can be dynamically created and adjusted in relation to learner behaviour (Bandara, 2026). In that regard, simulation platforms that are based on AI are being discussed as a means of entrepreneurship training. Synthetic Startup Labs is an idea that builds off of these advancements by applying the principles of Generative AI to real-life learning opportunities to produce an experience of simulating a startup. The literature thus indicates the increased overlap of the experiential learning theories, Generative AI technologies, and digital simulation systems in entrepreneurship education.

6.1 Experiential Learning in Entrepreneurship

Experience-based learning is now a very popular model of entrepreneurship education since it is a model of learning involving action, reflection, and experimentation. Entrepreneurship is complicated in decision making, uncertainty, and risk taking, which cannot be comprehended with theoretical teaching only. Experience learning techniques enable students to participate in practical entrepreneurial skills like creating ideas, developing a prototype of the product, market research and pitching a business opportunity (Aysi et al., 2024). These activities enable learners to acquire the essential entrepreneurial skills such as creativity, resilience, the ability to see opportunities, and strategic thinking. Universities and colleges have been introducing startup incubators, innovation laboratories, business plan competitions, and project-based courses as experiential learning programs. These programs give students a chance to practice entrepreneurial ideas in a business situation or simulated business situations (Ip, 2024). Entrepreneurship classes have also been introduced to teach design thinking and lean startup to promote experimentation and customer-focused innovation.

Although those strategies were successful, it is still difficult to offer all students regularly available opportunities to get experience in the form of digital startups and mentorship networks as well as funding as the access to a startup ecosystem, networks, and financial resources in general is limited. Such constraints have prompted scholars to consider the use of digital simulation technology as an alternative to providing experiential entrepreneurship education on large scale.

6.2 Generative AI in Education and Innovation

Generative Artificial Intelligence has become an education and innovation system technology that can revolutionize the system. Generative AI systems can generate text, images, data simulations, and interactive situations out of training datasets that are large-scale. In learning, those technologies facilitate adaptive learning conditions in which learning content, activities, and feedback can be dynamically created based on the needs of the learners. The ability enables teachers to develop the most personalized learning experience that enhances engagement and retention (Utama et al., 2025). Generative AI tools have been shown to have enormous potential in the innovation and entrepreneurship fields in terms of aiding idea generation, business model development, and market analysis. The AI-based systems are able to come up with business ideas, model market trends and come up with customer personas through which the learners can learn about business opportunities. As well, conversational AI systems may also be used as virtual advisors that will direct learners in terms of problem-solving processes and strategic decision-making (Matoug et al., 2024). The mentioned features allow making Generative AI especially applicable to the field of entrepreneurship education, where experimenting, creativity, and quick iterations are key requirements. Generative AI technologies open opportunities to develop the design of an immersive entrepreneurial learning space by facilitating the generation of dynamic scenarios and intelligent feedback to model the dynamics of the business environment in reality.

6.3 AI-Driven Entrepreneurial Simulation Studies

The recent studies have been more and more concerned with considering AI-based simulations as the means of training in entrepreneurship and innovation education. Learning environments can be simulated through simulation to provide learners the opportunity to experiment with entrepreneurial choices in a controlled virtual environment where answers are derived dynamically (Dabbous & Boustani, 2023). These systems simulate different features of startup environments such as competition on the market, customer interactions, and investment discussions. The interactive simulations allow the students to see the effects of strategic choices on the venture results in the long run. AI simulation platforms are an extension of traditional business simulation models and involve the use of smart algorithms designed to modify a situation based on the interactions of the learners. These sites are capable of examining the choices of users and creating dynamic market scenarios that learners can encounter to face real life entrepreneurial problems. Certain simulation environments can also be equipped with AI-generated stakeholders (like virtual investors, mentors, and customers), and enable students to train in negotiation, pitching, and strategic planning. It has been argued through studies that such interactive learning environments enhance engagement and development of entrepreneurial skills than the traditional lecture-based approach (Williams, 2015). Consequently, AIs-based simulation-based systems are now regarded as prospective capabilities in facilitating experiential entrepreneurship education and equipping students with complex innovation ecosystems.

7. CASE STUDY

Recent trends in entrepreneurship education have indicated that Generative AI is no longer deployed to aid content, but it is being integrated into immersive settings of startup-learning, which are increasingly resembling incubators, pitch rooms, and market-testing laboratories. Two recent cases in particular are particularly helpful to use in this chapter since they will help to see how AI may assist entrepreneurial learning on various levels. The former is an incumbent AI-enabled virtual incubator logic in higher education where Generative AI systems were applied in generating simulated entrepreneurial activities, customized feedback, and opportunity-making resources to students (Association, 2025). The second instance is more heavily concerned with the area of startup simulation platforms, which involve the integration of ChatGPT-style assistance and SimVenture-based business simulation at universities in the Middle East. Combined these cases demonstrate how AI may enhance entrepreneurial confidence, opportunity recognition, strategic thinking, and innovation spirit and flag implementation issues (Ravikumar & Aarthi, 2025b). They can serve as good models of Synthetic Startup Labs since both instances are not based on passive classroom instruction but a more interactive and ecosystem-based learning environment. Table 4 Posts the major information about case studies analyzed in the chapter.

Table 4. AI-based entrepreneurship case studies summary

Case Study	Region / Institution	AI Tool Used	Sample Size	Key Outcome
AI-Based Virtual Startup Incubators	China Universities	Generative AI learning system	346 students	Improved entrepreneurial self-efficacy
AI Startup Simulation Platforms	Middle East Universities	ChatGPT + SimVenture	166 students	Increased innovation spirit and cognition

7.1 Case Study 1: AI-Based Virtual Startup Incubators

One example of a recent case that might be useful in developing an AI-based virtual startup incubator model relates to the 2025 Scientific Reports article about Generative Artificial Intelligence Supported Entrepreneurship Education in Chinese higher education. Though the study does not officially designate the study a virtual incubator, its learning structure is similar to one: students interacted with AI technology that may be used to simulate businesses, come up with product concepts, simulate scenarios in the market, aid in business-model exploration, and give specific feedback on entrepreneurship work. In the study, 346 valid student responses were analyzed in total, and 39 incomplete or non-compliant surveys were excluded; this implies that approximately 89.9% of the responses gathered were used in the analysis (Ravikumar & Aarthi, 2025a). The results revealed that GAISEE was a significant predictor of entrepreneurial self-efficacy with the path coefficient of 0.523 and entrepreneurial intention with the path coefficient of 0.244. Other AI-powered processes mentioned in the study are testing marketing campaigns, competitor strategy analysis, business model refinery, and practice pitches to virtual investors. This is also relevant as a case since it shows that AI can serve as an incubator-scaling environment wherein students are still given structured opportunities to experiment without necessarily having physical incubator support (Sarumi, 2024). The case places a great deal of confidence in the idea of the Synthetic Startup Labs as an operational model of entrepreneurship education (Ravikumar & Aarthi, 2026). The primary quantitative findings of the AI-based virtual startup incubator study are provided in Figure 2, which reveals the response retention rate (89.9%), the beneficial effect of Generative AI on entrepreneurial self-efficacy (0.523) and entrepreneurial intention (0.244).

Figure 2. Key outcomes from AI-based virtual startup incubator case study

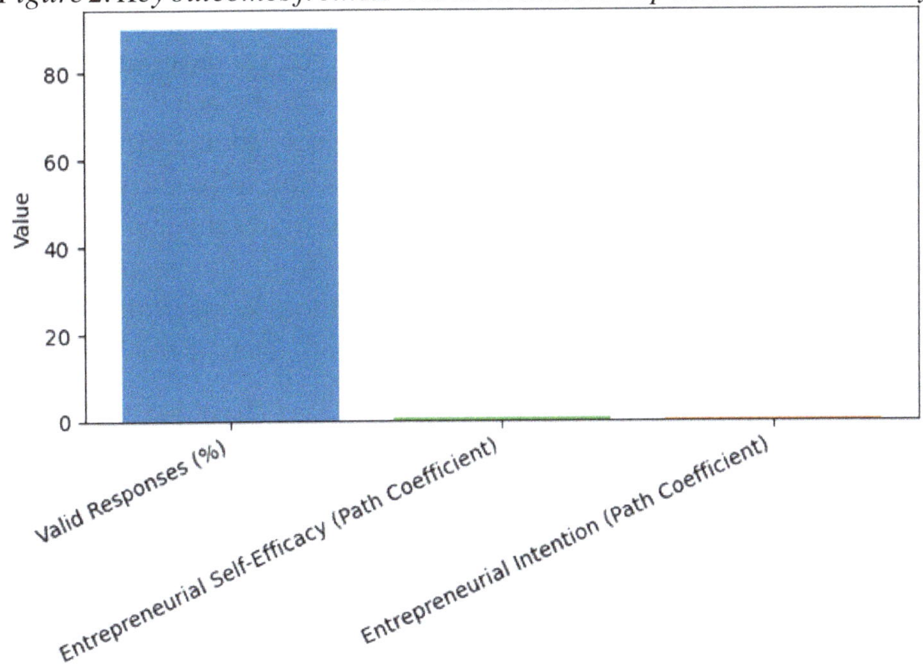

7.2 Case Study 2: Generative AI Startup Simulation Platforms

A second example in the recent cases is a study on the Middle East conducted in 2024-2025 which analyzed the effect of both ChatGPT and SimVenture business simulation platform on the start-up intention of students. The sample consisted of 166 fourth-year undergraduate students across four universities who are using ChatGPT and SimVenture. According to the respondent profile, 62% were males and 38% were females, with 52% of the respondents being of Egyptian descent, 26% of the United Arab Emirates, 5% Qatar and 17% other (Carrizosa, 2025). The findings indicate that SimVenture was positively significant to the cognition of entrepreneurship with a coefficient of 0.833, entrepreneurship competencies with 0.636, and entrepreneurship innovation spirit with 0.792. It also had significant indirect positive effect on start-up intention via cognition 0.243, competencies 0.089, and innovation spirit 0.520.

Compared to ChatGPT, the latter demonstrated the small but significant direct positive impact on the start-up intention at 0.053, and most of its indirect impacts were insignificant. The case is very topical, as it shows that the use of AI simulation platforms, which are organized, can play a more significant role in entrepreneurial capability-building than conversational AI by itself, particularly in the case of scenario-based training of startups (Quarshie et al., 2023). Figure 3 demonstrates the impact of the SimVenture AI simulation platform and ChatGPT on entrepreneurial outcomes have stronger effects of structured simulation on cognition (0.833), innovation spirit (0.792) and competencies (0.636) than the smaller direct effects of ChatGPT (0.053) on start-up intention.

Figure 3. Impact of AI simulation platforms on entrepreneurial outcomes

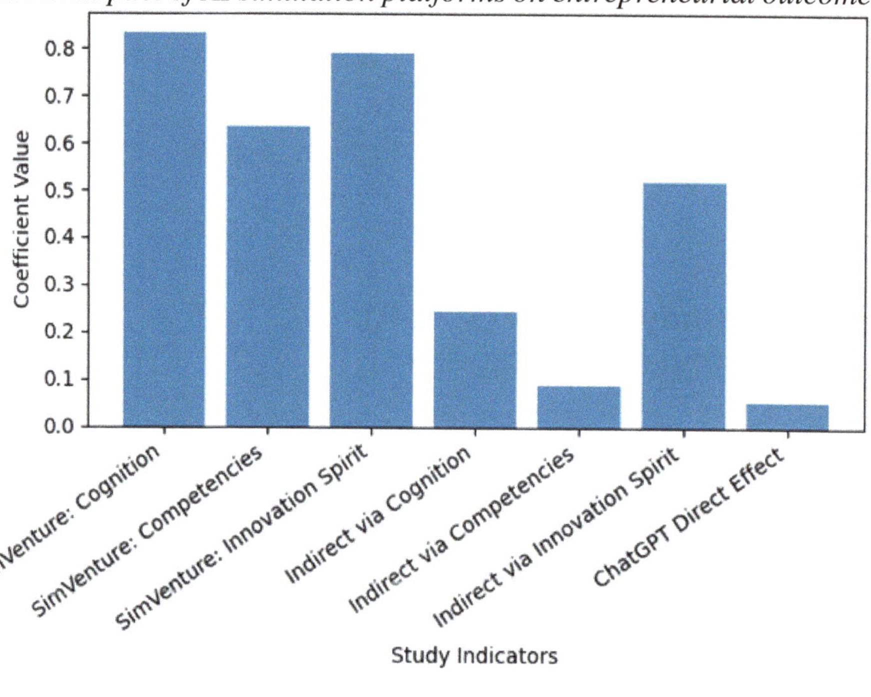

7.3 Comparative Insights from Case Studies

The two cases give reason to believe that the most effective integration of AI-enabled entrepreneurship education can be achieved by incorporating Generative AI into well-organized experienced settings, as opposed to an assistant by nature. The AI-based virtual-incubator model in the Chinese case demonstrated high entrepreneurial self-efficacy and entrepreneurial intention with a huge sample of 346 valid answers and 89.9% usable-response rate. The simulated platform that was more structured in the Middle East case generated particularly robust learning outcomes in the cognition of entrepreneurship, entrepreneurship competencies and entrepreneurship innovation spirit with coefficients of 0.833, 0.636 and 0.792 respectively (Huang, 2026). The comparison suggests that conversational AI may be useful when it comes to ideation and feedback, whereas simulation-based platforms may be more effective when it comes to developing capabilities and learning systems. Synthetic Startup Labs, thus, ought to integrate the two roles, namely, Generative AI to provide a sense of creativity and mentorship and simulation engines to provide a sense of market dynamics, stakeholder interaction, and decision-based entrepreneurial learning.

8. RESULTS AND DISCUSSION

The comparison between the two recent case studies reveals the increased efficiency of AI-based simulation space in the entrepreneurship education. The results reveal that Generative AI tools and organized business simulation platforms can be effectively used to boost the entrepreneurial learning process of students through the interaction with a decision-making environment. In the initial case study frame of AI-based virtual incubator models, the students had better entrepreneurial self-efficacy and enhanced entrepreneurial intentions subsequent to exposure to AI-created business situations. The second case study with the simulation platforms on startups also demonstrated the significant increase in entrepreneurship cognition, innovation spirit, and competitive competencies regarding ventures. These findings indicate that learning environments facilitated by AI allow students to be more participative and actively involved in the entrepreneurial processes in comparison to traditional classroom-based instruction (Kriz & Auchter, 2016). The activities that are simulated enable learners to experiment with business concepts, strategic choices and monitor the market reactions without taking a risk. Simultaneously, the findings raise valuable opportunities and challenges related to the implementation of AI-based models of entrepreneurial education, such as the technological requirements of the infrastructure, ethical aspects, and the necessity of the balanced use of human mentorship and AI systems.

8.1 Learning Outcomes from AI Simulations

According to the case studies, AI-based simulation has the potential to produce a substantial improvement in learning in the entrepreneurship courses. The case of the AI-based virtual startup incubator showed that the students using Generative AI tools had a higher level of entrepreneurial self-efficacy and confidence in venture creation. The discussion revealed that Generative AI-assisted learning platforms have a capacity to reinforce the knowledge of the students regarding business planning as well as market analysis and strategic decision-making. Equally, the second case study conducted via startup simulation platforms showed high enhancement in the entrepreneurship cognition and innovation learning outcomes (Sziegat, 2024). This was made possible through simulation learning in which students could see the result of business decisions on venture performance in dynamic markets. The students could correct their strategies and enhance their ability to solve problems through the means of repeated experimentation and feedback provided by AI-generated situations. Such results indicate that AI-based simulations offer a useful learning experience, in which students have an opportunity to experiment with entrepreneurial processes and get practical insights into how startups work without bearing the risks of creating genuine startups. Table 5 Highlights the top entrepreneurial competencies that have been cultivated based on AI simulation learning environments.

Table 5. Learning outcomes from AI-based startup simulations

Learning Outcome	Description	Observed Improvement
Entrepreneurial Self-Efficacy	Confidence in starting ventures	High improvement
Opportunity Recognition	Identifying market opportunities	Moderate improvement
Strategic Decision-Making	Evaluating business strategies	High improvement
Innovation Thinking	Generating creative solutions	High improvement

8.2 Impact on Entrepreneurial Skills Development

In addition to enhancing conceptual knowledge, the case studies show that the AI-based entrepreneurial simulations play a valuable role in the development of the real entrepreneurial skills. The learners who were exposed to AI-supported simulation worlds showed enhancement in such competencies as opportunity recognition, innovation thinking, strategic planning, and resource allocation. Through the engagement with the AI-based stakeholders including customers and investors, learners learnt how to pitch an idea, negotiate the terms of investments and analyze the responses of the market. The case study of the simulation platform also demonstrated innovations in the entrepreneurial skills and the spirit of innovation in the participating students (Samašonok et al., 2020). Constant exposure to AI-infused business situations motivated students to explore different strategies and change their choices based on the changing environment in the market. This enabled the learners to be more resilient, analytical and adaptive in making decisions, which is crucial to entrepreneurial success. Comprehensively, AI-based simulations of startups serve as a viable training platform that facilitates the training of both cognitive and behavioral entrepreneurial skills.

8.3 Opportunities and Implementation Challenges

Although the case studies emphasize how AI-based simulations of startup can be used in the educational process, it is possible to note that a number of opportunities and challenges can be identified regarding the adoption of such systems in entrepreneurship education. The possibility to scale AI-enabled learning environments is one of the major opportunities. Experiential learning Systems Synthetic Startup Labs have the potential to deliver experiential learning to groups of students on mass while not needing physical incubator facilities or large-scale mentoring resources. This facilitates the provision of the training about entrepreneurship to the institutions that do not have direct relations to the startup ecosystems (Winkler et al., 2023). However, the technological infrastructure needed to implement simulation platforms that are based on AI also means that access to AI tools, digital platforms, and data resources is required. The other issue is to make the AI-generated feedback transparent and reliable to enable the learners to believe in the results of the simulation. Such ethical issues as algorithmic bias, responsible use of data, and human control should also be considered. Consequently, efficient implementation should be an equal measure that involves the integration of AI technologies in the context of human mentorship and instructions instead of completely substituting them.

9. FUTURE RESEARCH

Synthetic Startup Lab, the implementation of Generative Artificial Intelligence in education of entrepreneurship, presents a number of possibilities to be explored in the future. With the development of AI technologies, a greater opportunity to create more advanced learning settings, which incorporate simulation, data analytics, and adaptive educational systems arises. Although the existing conceptual framework and case studies show the advantages of AI-powered entrepreneurial simulations, additional studies are required to determine their long-term effects on the development of entrepreneurial skills, creation of ventures, and innovation potential (Assistant et al., 2025). Future studies can explore the ways in which adaptive learning systems based on AI provide personalization to entrepreneurial training to learners with diverse backgrounds, skills, and career goals. The other direction that is of importance is to combine AI-powered startup simulation platforms with wider digital innovation ecosystems, such as incubators, accelerators, and industry networks. Also, there is the need to investigate more on the issue of policy and governance around the use of AI in education to promote ethical use and equal access. Researching these spaces will assist educational institutions, policymakers, and researchers to comprehend more effectively how AI-based entrepreneurial learning systems can be developed to facilitate sustainable and inclusive innovation systems.

9.1 AI-Driven Adaptive Entrepreneurial Learning

The future studies are expected to investigate the way in which AI-based adaptive learning systems can advance further to provide an improved way of teaching entrepreneurship by making the learning process personal to the learners. Adaptive AI systems can be used to analyze the behavior of learners, their decision-making behaviour and performance in simulation environment. According to these understanding, AI platforms have an opportunity to change the complexity of an entrepreneurial situation, learning tasks, and feedback systems to suit the progress and the level of skills of the learner. The studies in this field may focus on the impacts of adaptive learning models, such as the formation of entrepreneurial competences, such as creativity, risk evaluation and recognition of opportunities (Chiyachantana et al., 2022). Another type of longitudinal studies can also be the analysis of whether learners receiving education in adaptive AI systems have a higher venture success rate or better entrepreneurial intentions. Also, future research might focus on including real-time data analytics to AI-based simulation settings so that learners can obtain regular feedback on the basis of their strategic choices. This type of development may make Synthetic Startup Labs intelligent entrepreneurship training systems that are able to support personalized learning journeys.

9.2 Integration with Digital Innovation Ecosystems

The next valuable line of future research is the study of the possibility of integrating AI-enabled entrepreneurial learning platforms with the wider digital innovation ecosystems. The present-day ecosystem of startups is composed of a variety of actors, such as incubators, accelerators, venture capital firms, research institutions, and industry partners. The implementation of Synthetic Startup Labs in such ecosystems can result in the establishment of mixed learning environments where students will be exposed to AI-driven simulations, as well as real entrepreneurial networks. Further studies can explore the idea of how university-startup incubator and innovation hubs networks can be used on digital platforms to support experiential entrepreneurship education (Jayanthi, 2025). As an illustration, simulation environments presenting AI-based data may be connected to the real-world market data, the industry challenge or even joint innovation programs. The integration can enable students to experiment with business concepts in a virtual world and then take them to real investors or mentors in the industry. Such hybrid models might help to understand how AI-guided entrepreneurial education might serve to enhance the process of knowledge transfer between academia and industry and stimulate innovation-based economic growth. Figure 4 demonstrates that Synthetic Startup Labs networks universities with the actors of digital innovation ecosystem (incubators, innovation hub, venture capital firm, and market platform) to generate hybrid AI-powered entrepreneurial learning space.

Figure 4. AI-driven synthetic startup lab ecosystem integration

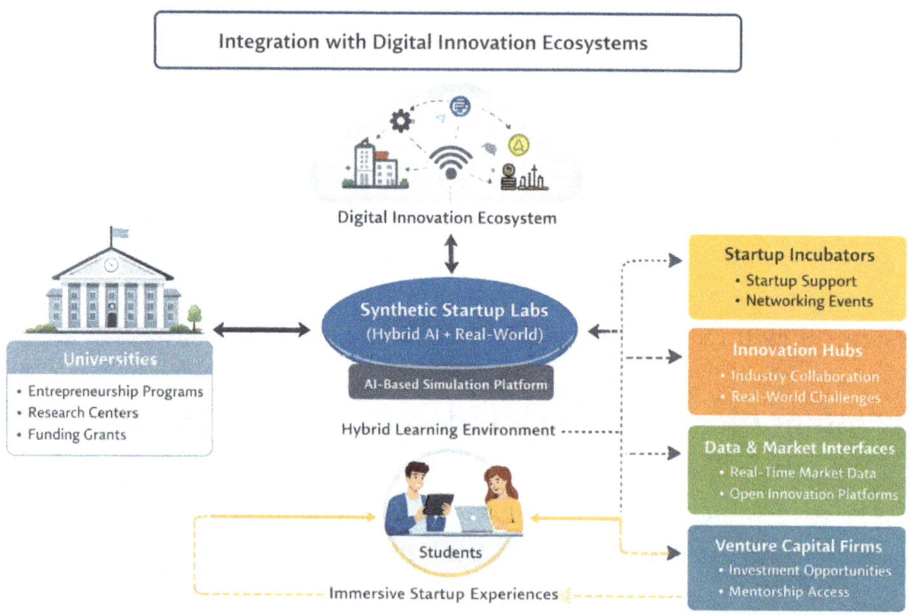

9.3 Policy and Governance Research Directions

It is also important to note that the increasing adoption of AI technologies in the education of entrepreneurs poses several issues regarding policy and governance, which need further investigation. Learning institutions should take into account the ethical and regulatory problems of data privacy, transparency of algorithms, and responsible use of AI in education. Simulations based on AI applications in entrepreneurship have been shown to use such large datasets and automated decision-making that they also pose the risk of bias, data misuse, or incorrect feedback without appropriate regulation. The further studies must include the analysis of the elaboration of the institutional policies and governance structures which would guarantee the conscientious application of the AI-mediated educational technologies (Rodrigues et al., 2025). This involves finding directions on transparency with AI-generated feedback, a method of human control in AI-supported learning systems, and approaches of providing fair access to AI-based entrepreneurship training software. Moreover, policymakers might have to take into consideration ways in which national innovation strategies can be used to facilitate AI-enabled entrepreneurship learning as a subset of wider digital transformation efforts. These issues in governance will be necessary to develop trustful and inclusive AI-based educational systems.

10. MANAGERIAL IMPLICATIONS

The application of Generative Artificial Intelligence to entrepreneurship education has important consequences on the work of educators, university administrators, and innovation managers tasked with the responsibility of developing entrepreneurial training programs. Synthetic Startup Labs offer strategic possibilities to institutions to convert traditional education on entrepreneurship into technology-powered learning spaces to provide incentive to experiential learning and innovation skill development. Managers and academic leaders should thus focus on the ways in which AI-based applications and simulation platforms can be integrated successfully into entrepreneurship courses and programs without compromising the goals of the industry and the education (Dixit et al., 2025). The results of the case studies report that simulations with AI support could develop entrepreneurial skills, innovation abilities, and strategic decision-making in the learners. Nevertheless, the implementation can only be successful with the proper planning in the way of the curriculum development, technological infrastructure, training of the faculty, and cooperation with the outside stakeholders. The institutions should also ensure that they have mechanisms that guarantee that the AI technologies do not replace human mentorship and on-the-job entrepreneurial exposure. Through systematic implementation policies, learning institutions can use Synthetic Startup Labs to enhance entrepreneurial systems and equip learners to work in innovation-driven economic conditions. Table 6 Provides practical strategies for universities and innovation centers implementing AI-based entrepreneurship labs.

Table 6. Implementation strategies for synthetic startup labs

Strategy Area	**Implementation Approach**	**Expected Benefit**
Curriculum Integration	Include AI simulations in entrepreneurship courses	Experiential learning
Faculty Training	Train educators in AI tools	Effective technology adoption
Industry Collaboration	Partner with incubators and startups	Real-world relevance
Digital Infrastructure	Deploy AI simulation platforms	Scalable learning environments

10.1 Curriculum Design for AI-Enabled Entrepreneurship

Implementation of AI technologies into entrepreneurial education entails the need of considerable changes in the design of the curriculum to include simulation-based and experience learning exercises. The teachers must create the programs that are based on theoretical learning as well as interactive entrepreneurial games whereby students are able to experiment with the business concepts, examine market conditions, and gain strategic decision-making skills. Students can also take part in practical entrepreneurial processes in the context of structured learning through AI-based power tools, using them to generate ideas, test business models, and analyze customers (Fox et al., 2025). The model of project-based learning must also be included in the list of the curriculum designers at the time when students communicate with the AI-created stakeholders, including customers, investors, and mentors. Such activities may assist students to acquire critical entrepreneurial skills such as the ability to identify opportunities, manage innovation and strategic planning. Also, the way in which students are assessed might require changes so that the students could be evaluated according to their skills in implementing entrepreneurial strategies and their flexibility to changing scenarios of the simulations. With the introduction of AI-based simulations into the programs of entrepreneurship, educational establishments will have an opportunity to make the educational process more interactive and closer to practice.

10.2 Institutional Strategies for Synthetic Startup Labs

To ensure successful adoption of Synthetic Startup Labs, the educational institutions should prepare institutional plans to facilitate adoption of technology, faculty preparation and sustainable learning conditions. The creation of AI-powered entrepreneurship laboratories requires the provision of investment in digital infrastructure, simulation systems, and data assets that have the potential to facilitate interactive entrepreneurial learning. It is also possible that Universities may be required to offer training courses that can enable the educators to know how to integrate AI technologies into the teaching practices (Subrahmanyam, 2025). The institutional strategies are to promote collaboration between business, computer science, engineering and innovation management departments. This kind of cooperation may be used to create more holistic entrepreneurial learning settings that integrate technological know-how and business skills. Moreover, Synthetic Startup Labs can be incorporated in current innovation centers, incubators, or entrepreneurship programs by the institution to achieve maximum effect. Coming up with institutional policies regarding the use of AI responsibly and data privacy is also a critical part of successful implementation strategies.

10.3 Role of Industry and Innovation Ecosystems

The stakeholders in innovation ecosystems and the industry partners are important in enhancing the AI-enabled entrepreneurship education programs. The relevance and realism of the Synthetic Startup Lab simulations could be improved by collaboration between universities, startup incubators, venture capital firms, and technology firms (Mazur, 2023). The partners in the industry are capable of providing real-world market knowledge, case studies, and mentorship for students which can help improve the experience of learning AI-enabled simulation platforms. As an illustration, pupils involved in AI-based startup simulations can showcase their entrepreneurial ideas to senior investors or any other industry advisors to receive feedback and suggestions. These partnerships can be used to close the existing gap between education on entrepreneurship in academia and the actual startup ecosystem (Srikanth, 2025). Through effective collaboration with industry players, educational institutions can develop combined entrepreneurial learning activities that equip students on the real-world innovation and venture development. Figure 5 demonstrates the collaboration between universities, industry participants, investors and innovation hubs and Synthetic Startup Labs, which offer datasets, mentorship, and real-world entrepreneurial learning to student participants.

Figure 5. AI-based entrepreneurship case studies summary

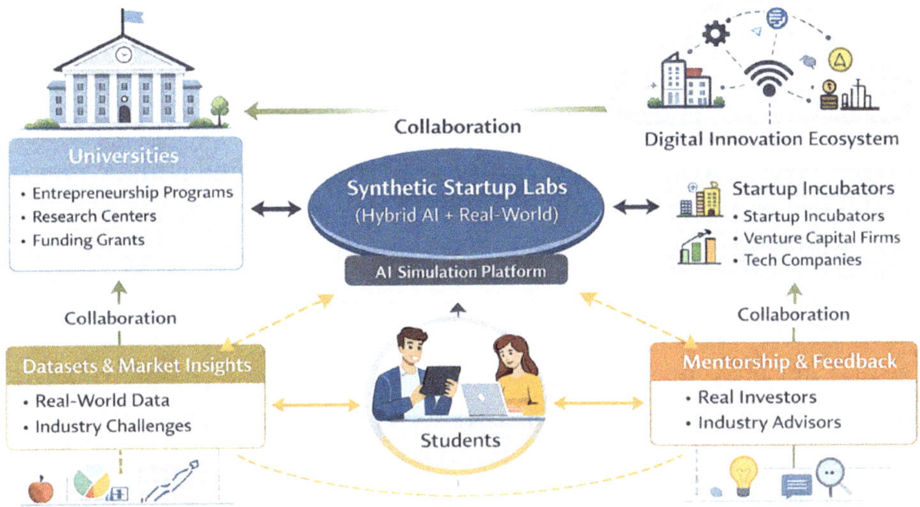

11. CONCLUSION

The blistering development of Generative Artificial Intelligence has opened new prospects to change the way the entrepreneurship course is delivered, introducing the opportunity to learn in smart, simulative settings and recreate the real startup ecosystem. In this chapter, the idea of Synthetic Startup Labs has been presented as a new type of pedagogy that combines the principles of Generative AI technologies with the principles of an experiential learning module to assist in the development of entrepreneurial skills. In contrast to the traditional models of entrepreneurship education, in which the core of the learning experience is based on theoretical teaching and case studies, Synthetic Startup Labs offer physical spaces where students can test startup concepts, communicate with computer-generated stakeholders, and see the effects of strategic choices in a changing market environment. The adaptive learning systems, ecosystem interaction models, and AI-based simulations allow students to learn the complexities of making decisions in an entrepreneurial environment safely and at scale, in these environments.

The discussion of the recent case studies shows that artificial intelligence-based learning platforms can be effectively used to increase the effectiveness of entrepreneurial learning, including the entrepreneurial self-efficacy, innovation thinking, and venture-related competencies. Simulations, which can be powered by AI, enable learners to experiment with various business approaches, experiment with value propositions, and practice decision-making by experimenting through numerous trial and error. Besides facilitating the growth of individual skills, Synthetic Startup Labs also serve to enhance the resilience of entrepreneurial ecosystems by making access to entrepreneurial training resources scalable to those institutions not holding physical incubator or broader mentoring networks. Educationally, there is an incentive to move towards more interactive, adaptive and learner-centered educational methods as a result of integrating Generative AI into entrepreneurship training. Nonetheless, the implementation must be done with special attention to the technological infrastructure, ethical governance, and further role of human mentorship in guiding entrepreneurial learning. In general, Synthetic Startup Labs is a potentially valuable model of training future entrepreneurs to work in more and more digital and innovation-centered economies. Integrating AI Generative functions with experiential learning strategies will enable educational institutions to develop smart training environments that would promote creativity.

REFERENCES

Aarthi, S., Ravikumar, R. N., Khudayberganov, S., Ismailov, A., & Khujaniyozova, O. (2025). Using Intelligent Tutoring Systems to enhance student engagement. In *Advances in Computational Intelligence and Robotics* (pp. 155–188). IGI Global. DOI: 10.4018/979-8-3373-1827-1.ch008

Ahmed, F., Lo, Y. T., & Chen, S.-H. (2025). Developing entrepreneurial mindset among non-business majors through experiential learning and AI tools. *Proceedings of the European Conference on Knowledge Management, 26*(1), 1–7. DOI: 10.34190/eckm.26.1.3762

Amravati., D. of C. S. V. B. M., Iqbal, A., & Kene, D. M. (2026). Adaptive Learning Systems powered by generative AI and Large Language Models: A comprehensive review of Personalized Education. *International Journal of Scientific Research in Engineering and Management, 10*(01), 11–19. DOI: 10.55041/IJSREM.IBFE002

Association, T. K. (2025). A study on global trends in the use of generative AI in entrepreneurship education: Literature and case-based approaches. *The Korean Career. Entrepreneurship & Business Association*, *9*(6), 283–304. DOI: 10.48206/kceba.2025.9.6.283

Aysi, S. A. H., Susilaningsih, S., & Sabandi, M. (2024). The implementation of digital Entrepreneurship Learning in higher education: A Systematic Literature Review. *PEDAGOGIA Jurnal Pendidikan*, *13*(2), 255–273. DOI: 10.21070/pedagogia.v13i2.1692

Bandara, A. (2026). Use of artificial Intelligence in Entrepreneurship Education: A systematic review. *Journal of Management Matters*, *12*(2), 88–99. DOI: 10.4038/jmm.v12i2.98

Ben Matoug, S., Zehouani, A., Lazhar, B. M., Ziadi, S., Belarbi, G., & Abada, M. (2024). The role of entrepreneurship education in guiding university students to create their personal and professional projects within the framework of a Startup. *International Journal of Professional Business Review*, *9*(4), e04623. DOI: 10.26668/businessreview/2024.v9i4.4623

Carrizosa, Á. (2025). Entrepreneurial success: The missing link between education, AI, and Startup growth. *The Transnational Journal of Business, 10*(1). Advance online publication. DOI: 10.64010/SDUS3791

Chen, L., Ifenthaler, D., Yau, J. Y.-K., & Sun, W. (2024). Artificial intelligence in entrepreneurship education: A scoping review. *Education + Training, 66*(6), 589–608. Advance online publication. DOI: 10.1108/ET-05-2023-0169

Chiyachantana, C. N., Ding, D. K., & Hong, J. J. (2022). Experiential learning: The case of training MBA students in an Asian school. *International Journal of Educational Technology and Learning, 13*(1), 17–25. DOI: 10.55217/101.v13i1.552

Dabbous, A., & Boustani, N. M. (2023). Digital explosion and entrepreneurship education: Impact on promoting entrepreneurial intention for business students. *Journal of Risk and Financial Management, 16*(1), 27. DOI: 10.3390/jrfm16010027

Dixit, J. K., Agrawal, V., & Agarwal, S. (2025). Sustainable entrepreneurship: Exploring the intention–behavior gap. *Management Decision, 63*(7), 2247–2268. DOI: 10.1108/MD-01-2024-0056

Dunan, A., Mudjiyanto, B., Setiawan, A. B., Syarifuddin, S., Pala, R., Rustam, M., Dirgahayu, D., Buyamin, B., Nuryana, M., & Hartiningsih, H. (2025). Artificial intelligence in E-entrepreneurship training. *International Journal of E-Entrepreneurship and Innovation, 15*(1), 1–22. DOI: 10.4018/IJEEI.386065

Dunsim, N. Q. W., & Jabar, J. (2025). Bridging education and enterprise: Business Startup readiness of Malaysian youth in Mara colleges. [JTMT]. *Journal of Technology Management and Technopreneurship, 13*(3). Advance online publication. DOI: 10.54554/jtmt.2025.13.03.017

Fox, J. D., Pittaway, L., & Uzuegbunam, I. (2025). Artificial Intelligence as a dynamic copilot in Entrepreneurship Education. *Entrepreneurship Education and Pedagogy, 8*(2), 329–344. DOI: 10.1177/25151274241256307

Hamburg, I., O'brien, E., & Vladut, G. (2019). Entrepreneurial learning and AI Literacy to support digital entrepreneurship. *Balkan Region Conference on Engineering and Business Education, 3*(1), 132–144. DOI: 10.2478/cplbu-2020-0016

Huang, W. (2026). The construction and practice of the entrepreneurship plan training model from the perspective of "digital twin" : An interdisciplinary integration exploration based on the immersive business war simulation platform. *Journal of Computer Technology and Electronic Research, 2*(9). Advance online publication. DOI: 10.70767/jcter.v2i9.819

Ip, K. (2024). The rise of EdTech: Transforming education through entrepreneurial ventures. *Advances in Online Education: A Peer-Reviewed Journal, 3*(2), 177. DOI: 10.69554/NSVD4541

Jayanthi, R. (2025). Personalized learning systems using AI enhancing adaptive education. *International Journal of Environmental Sciences*, •••, 668–676. DOI: 10.64252/ps80c806

Kriz, W. C., & Auchter, E. (2016). 10 years of evaluation research into gaming simulation for German entrepreneurship and a new study on its long-term effects. *Simulation & Gaming, 47*(2), 179–205. DOI: 10.1177/1046878116633972

Liu, H., & Zhang, Y. (2025). AI-empowered model innovation and adaptation in innovation and entrepreneurship education: An exploration based on multimodal learning scenarios. *Asia Pacific Economic and Management Review, 2*(3). Advance online publication. DOI: 10.62177/apemr.v2i3.318

Mazur, A. (2023). The role of educational institutions in the development of startup ecosystems (on the example of Lviv). *Bulletin of V. N. Karazin Kharkiv National University Economic Series*, (104), 89–99. DOI: 10.26565/2311-2379-2023-104-10

Musyaffi, A. M., Oli, M. C., Mentari, M., & Afriadi, B. (2025). Gamified online business simulation: Enhancing student motivation in entrepreneurship. [EduLearn]. *Journal of Education and Learning, 19*(4), 2322–2331. DOI: 10.11591/edulearn.v19i4.22723

Pandit, S., Ravikumar, R. N., Joshi, N., Pandit, S., Kishore, S., & Aarthi, S. (2025). Retrieval-Augmented Generation (RAG) for enterprise intelligence. In *Leveraging LLMs for Business Innovation* (pp. 69–106). IGI Global Scientific Publishing. DOI: 10.4018/979-8-3373-3912-2.ch003

Prabagar, S., Mothkur, R., Swetha, C. B., Kurian, A., Pavithra, K., & Aarthi, S. (2025). Generative AI for inclusive special education. In *Advances in Computational Intelligence and Robotics* (pp. 205–236). IGI Global Scientific Publishing. DOI: 10.4018/979-8-3373-3745-6.ch008

Quarshie, A. W. K., Swartz, C. L. E., Madabhushi, P. B., Cao, Y., Wang, Y., & Flores-Cerrillo, J. (2023). Modeling, simulation, and optimization of multiproduct cryogenic air separation unit startup. *AIChE Journal. American Institute of Chemical Engineers*, *69*(2), e17953. Advance online publication. DOI: 10.1002/aic.17953

Ram, D. Y.Dr. Yad Ram. (2025). The role of artificial intelligence in personalized learning. *Innovative Research Thoughts*, *11*(1), 66–71. DOI: 10.36676/irt.v11.i1.1572

Ravikumar, R. N., & Aarthi, S. (2025b). The role of educational developers in AI integration at scale. In *Advances in Computational Intelligence and Robotics* (pp. 289–322). IGI Global Scientific Publishing. DOI: 10.4018/979-8-3373-4129-3.ch011

Ravikumar, R. N., & Aarthi, S. (2026). From lab to market. In *Advances in Computational Intelligence and Robotics* (pp. 245–278). IGI Global Scientific Publishing. DOI: 10.4018/979-8-3373-9690-3.ch006

Ravikumar, R. N., Aarthi, S., Rai, P. K., & Mamadiyarov, Z. (2025). Intelligent code analysis and feedback generation. In *Advances in Computational Intelligence and Robotics* (pp. 137–170). IGI Global Scientific Publishing. DOI: 10.4018/979-8-3373-0598-1.ch006

Ravikumar, R. N., Aarthi, S., Ruzimova, F., & Mamadiyarov, Z. (2025). Training and development in AI-driven education scaling solutions. In *Advances in Computational Intelligence and Robotics* (pp. 267–298). IGI Global Scientific Publishing. DOI: 10.4018/979-8-3373-2185-1.ch010

Ravikumar, & Aarthi, S. (2025a). Conscious AI Integration in business education. In *Advances in Computational Intelligence and Robotics* (pp. 73–104). IGI Global Scientific Publishing. DOI: 10.4018/979-8-3373-4377-8.ch003

Rodrigues, C., Melo, P. N., Pereira, L., Pereira, C., & Carvalho, R. (2025). The role of digital technologies and AI on the development of entrepreneurial mindset in first-year university students. *Proceedings of the European Conference on Entrepreneurship and Innovation, 20*(1), 611–617. DOI: 10.34190/ecie.20.1.3962

Rong, G. Y., Nasir, M. K. M., & Mansor, A. Z. (2025). Bridging theory and practice: A conceptual study on experiential learning in student entrepreneurship. *South Asian Journal of Social Sciences and Humanities, 6*(1), 238–248. DOI: 10.48165/sajssh.2024.6114

Samašonok, K., Išoraitė, M., & Žirnelė, L. (2020). Education of entrepreneurship by participation in a business simulation enterprise activities: Conditions of effectiveness and opportunities for improvement. *Journal of Entrepreneurship and Sustainability Issues, 7*(4), 3122–3144. DOI: 10.9770/jesi.2020.7.4(36)

Sang, L. T., Ravikumar, R. N., Aarthi, S., & Ben, T. L. (2025). Optimizing sales and inventory performance using AI and business intelligence in POS environments. In *Advances in Computational Intelligence and Robotics* (pp. 259–290). IGI Global Scientific Publishing. DOI: 10.4018/979-8-3373-4392-1.ch011

Sarumi, O. O. (2024). AI: Driving entrepreneurship, nurturing innovation, and fueling Startup growth. *International Journal of Advances in Engineering and Management, 6*(11), 540–547. DOI: 10.35629/5252-0611540547

Shepherd, D. A., & Gruber, M. (2021). The lean Startup framework: Closing the academic–practitioner divide. *Entrepreneurship Theory and Practice, 45*(5), 967–998. DOI: 10.1177/1042258719899415

Srikanth, D. V. (2025). AI-powered entrepreneurial ecosystems: A computational model for sustainable Startup growth in green tech sectors. *International Journal of Environmental Sciences*, •••, 1068–1077. DOI: 10.64252/ewn4zw14

Subrahmanyam, S. (2025). Entrepreneurship and Startup business in the age of AI. In *Advances in Computational Intelligence and Robotics* (pp. 159–192). IGI Global Scientific Publishing. DOI: 10.4018/979-8-3373-7416-1.ch007

Sudarmaji, E., & Munirah, M. (2019). Alternative model for putting Indonesian young digital talent in business. *Review of Management and Entrepreneurship*, *3*(1), 1–24. DOI: 10.37715/rme.v3i1.970

Sziegat, H. (2024). Virtual simulation games in entrepreneurship education: Status quo and prospects. *Proceedings of the European Conference on Games-Based Learning, 18*(1), 1099–1106. DOI: 10.34190/ecgbl.18.1.3001

Tan, S. (2020). A brief analysis of AI curricula construction and development orientation from the perspective of innovation and entrepreneurship education. *Creative Education*, *11*(10), 1866–1872. DOI: 10.4236/ce.2020.1110136

Triono, S. P. H., Rahayu, A., Wibowo, L. A., & Alamsyah, A. (2024). The impact of Entrepreneurial Strategy on the Firm Performance of Indonesian technology startups. *Jurnal Manajemen Indonesia*, *24*(1), 84–104. DOI: 10.25124/jmi.v24i1.7303

Utama, I. D., Inayati, T., Setiawan, M., Mohd, Z., & Lusia, E. (2025). Shaping future entrepreneurs: Education, intention, and the adoption of AI. *International Review of Management and Marketing*, *16*(1), 12–20. DOI: 10.32479/irmm.20787

Williams, D. (2015). The impact of SimVenture on the development of entrepreneurial skills in management students. *Industry and Higher Education*, *29*(5), 379–395. DOI: 10.5367/ihe.2015.0270

Winkler, C., Hammoda, B., Noyes, E., & Van Gelderen, M. (2023). Entrepreneurship education at the dawn of generative artificial intelligence. *Entrepreneurship Education and Pedagogy*, *6*(4), 579–589. DOI: 10.1177/25151274231198799

Zolfaghari, M., Salamzadeh, A., & Afsharpour, O. (2024). Identifying the applications of artificial intelligence in educational entrepreneurship development. In *Advances in Educational Technologies and Instructional Design* (pp. 439–478). IGI Global. DOI: 10.4018/979-8-3693-7220-3.ch015

KEY TERMS AND DEFINITIONS

Adaptive Learning Systems: AI-enabled educational systems that personalize learning content and feedback based on learner performance and behavior.

AI-Driven Simulation: Computer-based simulation systems powered by artificial intelligence that generate dynamic scenarios for training or decision-making practice.

Entrepreneurial Ecosystem: A network of stakeholders such as start-ups, investors, mentors, universities, government agencies, and industry partners that support entrepreneurship.

Entrepreneurial Self-Efficacy: A learner's confidence in their ability to successfully start and manage a business venture.

Entrepreneurship Education: Educational programs designed to develop entrepreneurial skills such as innovation, opportunity recognition, and business creation.

Experiential Learning: A learning approach where students gain knowledge through practical activities, experimentation, and real or simulated experiences.

Generative Artificial Intelligence (Generative AI): AI technology capable of generating new content such as text, data, images, or simulations based on patterns learned from large datasets.

Startup Simulation Platforms: Digital tools that replicate real startup environments where users can practice business planning, market analysis, and strategic decision-making.

Synthetic Startup Labs: AI-powered virtual learning environments where students simulate startup creation, test business ideas, and interact with AI-generated entrepreneurial scenarios.

Virtual Startup Incubator: A digital platform that provides mentorship, training, and business development support for startups using online or AI-based tools.

Chapter 3
Intelligent Tutoring Systems for Cybersecurity Entrepreneurship:
Cultivating AI-Augmented Risk Assessment Capabilities in Technology Startups

Abdelraouf Ishtaiwi
http://orcid.org/0000-0001-8013-7151
Data Science and Artificial Intelligence, University of Petra, Amman, Jordan

ABSTRACT

Artificial intelligence in education is now being talked about in the context of personalization, conversational support, automated assessment, and institutional adoption, but the entrepreneurial and cybersecurity aspects of the developments are not fully incorporated. Relying on a hierarchical narrative analysis of thirty-seven sources on the subject that use domains, this chapter combines learning analytics, adaptive gamification, domain-focused knowledge graphs, chatbot mediation, micro-credentialing, and governance constraints to form a single pedagogical structure. successful

DOI: 10.4018/979-8-2600-0487-6.ch003

tutoring of cybersecurity entrepreneurship ought to be artifact-based, contextualized to startups, legally conscious, and analytics-intensive since startups and early-stage teams ought to be trained to prioritize threats, justify controls, communicate residual risk, and productize trust in harsh conditions of uncertainty. As a result, an assessment logic based on rubrics, and an implementation roadmap are elaborated to facilitate human-assisted, AI-enhanced learning of cyber risks in technology startups.

1 INTRODUCTION

The academic discourse on artificial intelligence within higher education globally has shifted more quickly within the context of the exploratory adoption discourse, with more and more varied discussions covering the concept of acceptance, engagement, machine learning, interactive tools, and organizational transformation. A bibliometric perspective provided by Mohammad et al. (2026) suggests that the research in the area of AI has increased significantly in the period between 2015 and 2024, whereas the systematic synthesis by Al-Shabandar et al. (2024) once again states that the concept of generative AI has been discussed as both a specific method of individual assistance and as a factor that generated new challenges in institutions. Meanwhile, more general considerations of AI implementation in industries have pointed to how current AI ecosystems have ceased to be solitary technical resources, but instead, cross-domain architectures that re-structure operations, choices, and policy designs in the educational, financial, health, transport, and industry sectors (Rashid and Kausik, 2024). In this manner, it will have triggered a major paradigm shift, where the educational use of AI is no longer understood simply as classroom automation, but as a social-technological component through which new professional functions are being developed.

Nevertheless, the overpowering AI discourse in education has been disposed to focus on the grading, chatbots, engaging, and administrative support, yet the specific technological startup needs have not been clearly clarified. Kooli and Yusuf (2025) consider the opportunities provided by big language models in terms of grading, Davar et al. (2025) summarizes the possibilities and limitations of AI chatbots in the academic process, and

Bansal et al. (2024) focus on the importance of AI-mediated feedback and personalization as an online learning technology. Despite such contributions, the educational object upon which adaptation is structured, is often the individual course task, rather than the unstable, resource-limited, and socio-economic decision environment of an early-stage venture. In the case of startup teams, the accuracy of the quiz or the conceptual retention is also not often an exhaustion of cybersecurity learning, but overlaying product choices, regulatory risk, investor due diligence, reliance on a particular platform, customer belief, and a sequence of limited mitigation funding.

The Industry 4.0 and Industry 5.0 contexts of automation, datafication, human-machine collaboration, and faster organizational redesign are the environments that today technology startups are working in. Entrepreneurial education is thus under the strain of not being generic in its approach to business planning but rather technologically mediated problem framing, digital literacy, and venture experimentation (Naidoo and Verma, 2024; Tjahjono et al., 2025). Also, the co-word analysis provided by Rejeb et al. (2025) highlights the fact that the human-centric systems, sustainability, and advanced technologies have become the primary themes of Industry 5.0 literature organizing the idea that the development of capabilities is no longer isolated of the overall organizational ecosystem where people and intelligent systems interact. With the dynamics mentioned above in mind, the entrepreneurial learner is not just a student of the cybersecurity principles, but a future decision-maker who will need to combine technical indicators with operational priorities, legal limitations, and narratives of trust facing the market.

Despite the fact that cybersecurity education has provided abundant practical models, corpus provided in the attachment indicates that three conceptual gaps still need to be synthesized to consider startup contexts. To begin with, cybersecurity upskilling in the context of workforce is already being perceived as a strategic requirement to a great extent, especially in terms of AI-based security operations (Cela et al., 2025). Second, effective instructional methods are being developed as adaptive gamification and AI-based games to customize instruction, maintain the engagement process, and create resiliency to solve problems among various learning profiles (Sindiramutty et al., 2025; Papadimitriou and Virvou, 2025; Almufarreh, 2026). Third, AI studies in education are repeatedly warning that usability, integrity, transparency, and human-oversight have to be considered initially instead of added as an afterthought (Al-Maaitah et al., 2025; Garcia et al., 2025; Kumar et al., 2024). On the one hand, these strands are naturally aligned with the needs of venture-focused cyber education; on the other hand, they were rarely combined into a consistent tutoring model that focused on AI-aided risk analysis of founders and startups groups.

That integrative gap is what this chapter attempts to fill; it proposes a literature-based argument that intelligent tutoring systems to support entrepreneurship in cybersecurity need to be created on the basis of venture artifacts, rather than on the basis of curriculum units; risk prioritization, rather than technical recall; and surgeons, rather than autonomous decision substitution. To operationalize that argument, the chapter assembles the literature provided with a staged capability model, a layered system architecture, a pattern of pedagogy, an assessment logic and an implementation roadmap, specific to early-stage technology venture. Subsequently, this chapter seeks to make a contribution of the holism and practically translatable design perspective on those scholars, curriculum developers, incubators, and startup support ecosystems who may wish to develop cyber resilience by means of AI-enhanced educational infrastructures.

2 BACKGROUND

2.1 AI-enabled tutoring, learning analytics, and adaptive educational design

Today, AI literature in education is being influenced by a combination of personalization, analytics, conversational support, and pedagogical redesign. General book-length summaries underline that AI approaches of the next generation are changing educational landscapes by means of machine learning, natural language processing, adaptive algorithms, and creation of insight by data, as a result of which learning gaps can be identified earlier and instructional courses can be diversified more efficiently (Cela et al., 2024; Tariq, 2024). Equally, Delello and McWhorter (2024) go on to elaborate that due to disruptive technologies in education and workforce development, not only is the learning environment changing, but also is the expectation of labor-market, which is increasingly making venerable curricular design less and less sufficient. Accordingly, the pedagogical assumption of intelligent tutoring has been extended: the idea of adaptation is no longer limited to the sequence of question, but is being implemented throughout analytics, content generation, advising, and learner support.

Moreover, empirical studies on intelligent tutoring acceptance shed light on behavioral bases that such systems should be based. The intention to use an AI-powered intelligent tutoring-based system among pre-service biology teachers was examined within the context of genetics in the study by Adelana et al. (2024), and the use of perceptions of usefulness, control, and the associated attitudinal factors were preforegrounded as the determinants of intention. Though the substantive area was not the cybersecurity, the methodological connotation is intensely transposable: intelligent tutoring systems will hardly become pedagogically useful in a situation where the professional user recognizes them as opaque, inconvenient, and unrelated to the actual task execution. As a result, startup-oriented cyber tutoring cannot be predicted to be effective simply because it can be technically functional and that an imagined relevance in making decisions related to entrepreneurial risk should be carefully modeled.

Besides this, learning analytics have been established as a key facilitator of responsive learning systems. Durak and Cankaya (2023) remind that traditional assessment tools cannot provide actionable information on the needs of learners, at-risk patterns, and the effectiveness of the intervention, but analytics-based tools can enable the use of data to improve teaching and redesign programs. Qudrat-Ullah (2024) develops a compatible systems viewpoint by reiterating that the combination of analytics, AI, and systems thinking can enable educational leadership by transforming the complex learning environments into interpretable and governable ones. These findings are especially relevant to a tutor of a cybersecurity entrepreneurship since the target of the evaluation is multi-layered: a level of conceptual knowledge, level of judgment, prioritization of threats, utilization of evidence, communication competence, and the capability to balance security and venture development should all be made visible in the analytics layer.

Nonetheless, individual support is sought not only in terms of dashboards and predictive models, but also in terms of conversational interface and generative AI. Davar et al. (2025) summarize the value proposition of AI chatbots in education by emphasizing speediness of support, availability, and learning support, and also mention that these advantages cannot be discussed outside the problems associated with reliability, pedagogical appropriateness, and learner addiction. Similarly, Bansal et al. (2024) note that the ChatGPT-like systems can be used to increase student engagement in cases when they are applied to give immediate feedback, customize learning, and maintain engagement in online learning. However, as Aad and Hardey (2025) repeat, the development of generative AI will also necessitate intentional preparation of the faculty, unless pedagogical change will be meaningless. Therefore, the tutoring paradigm that best fits the startup cyber learning is not where a chatbot replaces the structured teaching, but where conversational layer is incorporated into.

scenario engines, analytics and human moderation.

Even though automation in assessment has sparked a lot of interest, it is noted that more evidence in the literature indicates a continued debate on how much generative systems should be given the mandate of evaluation. Using ChatGPT-independent grading as a comparison with human correction, Kooli and Yusuf (2025) shed light on the practical potential of large language models in educational assessment, particularly where scale and consistency are factors of concern. Nevertheless, Garcia et al. (2025) emphasize that incorporating AI into education can also be associated with the threat of misusage, skill redundancy, and the algorithmic bias, whereas Al-Shabandar et al. (2024) note that the use of generative AI in higher education is accompanied by both efficiency and ethical issues. In this way, a paradox can be observed: the same mechanisms that can facilitate feedback can also optimize over-automation, abnormalize discipline, and oust the deliberative process according to which a true professional judgment is cultivated. In the case of cyber risk education, where ambiguity and trade-off analysis cannot be reduced, such a tension cannot be underemphasized.

With the above dynamics in perspective, game-based and immersive pedagogy has become a supplementary and not a peripheral stream. Synthesizing the evidence, Almufarreh (2026) suppose that gamification is linked with increased motivation, active learning, collaborative interaction, and better academic outcomes, as opposed to Ates and Kolemen (2025) who indicate that the presence of gamified virtual reality are influenced by the cognitive, motivational, and threat-related perceptions. Damasevicius & Sidekerskiene (2025) also add that immersive and interactive challenge structures can develop critical thinking, cooperation, and problem-solving in the digital setting of an escape room. Specifically, with regards to cybersecurity, Sindiramutty et al. (2025) hypothesize that adaptive gamification would allow customizing the intensity of challenges and feedback to suit the various learning styles, thus providing a more enjoyable and more productive training experience. These contributions imply that the instruction in risk assessment of start-ups cannot be diminished into lecture-plus-quiz activities; instead, it ought to be performed dramaturgically, through the episodes of consequential decisions, where evidence, time constraints, uncertainty, and trade-offs are pedagogically modeled.

There is an additional layer of relevance in micro-credentials and micro-modularization of skills. As Durak and Cankaya (2024) posit, AI can be used to tailor the design and administration of micro-credentials in such a manner that smaller certifications align more closely to the strengths, gaps, and needs of industries that the learner may have. That point intersects with the issue of cybersecurity entrepreneurship as startups hardly need a unified identity of a cybersecurity expert among all members of the team; rather, there should be differentiated competencies among the founders, product managers, engineers, compliance officers, and customer-facing staff. Thus, the tutoring system that will be used in startup ecosystems must be able to provide competence signals that are narrower than course completion signals, cloud risk triage, third-party due diligence, secure product communication, or AI-enabled incident interpretation.

2.2 Cybersecurity entrepreneurship, organizational transformation, and governance

Globally, the startup environment is being reconstituted by digital acceleration, AI-supported management, and the growing salience of cyber trust as a market and operational asset. Baig et al. (2025) emphasize that AI is transforming organizational management by enhancing decision processes and enabling firms to address complex business challenges in increasingly data-driven contexts. Likewise, Agnihotri et al. (2024) reiterate that emerging technologies are reshaping leadership roles and require new forms of strategic judgment. For technology startups, these observations are especially consequential because the same entrepreneurial team that experiments with product-market fit is often also responsible for security decisions, vendor selection, privacy communication, investor reporting, and crisis response. Consequently, cyber risk assessment cannot be treated as a downstream specialist function; it is a founding capability interwoven with managerial and product choices.

However, entrepreneurship education has often lagged behind this reality. Naidoo & Verma (2024) observe that higher education has been comparatively slow in embracing technology-driven outcomes even while Industry 4.0 pressures intensify. Tjahjono et al. (2025) further report that curriculum transformation is needed to align educational content with industrial requirements, particularly through the integration of AI, automation, IoT, analytics, teamwork, communication, and problem solving. These arguments have direct implications for startup cybersecurity learning. A founder does not merely need to identify a phishing email or define encryption; the founder must interpret how a security weakness affects customer acquisition, contractual credibility, platform scaling, and product release sequencing. Thus, entrepreneurial education and cyber education must be synthesized at the level of applied decision-making rather than left as parallel curricular silos.

The attached corpus also emphasizes that cybersecurity content itself is evolving under AI conditions. Çela et al. (2025) characterize AI-enhanced cybersecurity as an upskilling imperative for the educational workforce, foregrounding the need for thematic and trend-sensitive capability development rather than static training. Meanwhile, Gupta (2024) argue that emerging security paradigms for digitally immersive environments require robust attention to identity, privacy, governance, and asset protection. Although the metaverse is not identical to the startup ecosystem, the underlying lesson is transferable: cybersecurity instruction must keep pace with new digital interaction surfaces, new categories of virtual and data assets, and new forms of user exposure. Consequently, a venture-oriented tutoring system should not present "risk" as a fixed taxonomy; it should treat risk categories as evolving and context dependent.

Furthermore, governance and ethics have become inseparable from both AI deployment and security pedagogy. Anastasiadou et al. (2025) underscore the reciprocal influence of AI and law, observing that governance questions emerge precisely because technical development and legal transformation shape one another. Kumar et al. (2024) reiterate that bias, opacity, privacy breaches, and societal repercussions define the ethical frontier of AI and data analysis. In a narrower applied domain, Alam (2025) show how AI-driven systems can reproduce surveillance and manipulation concerns unless policy and educational responses are incorporated. For startup learning, the consequence is substantial: an intelligent tutor that teaches cyber risk without simultaneously teaching legal exposure, transparency obligations, and bias-aware interpretation would cultivate a technically partial and strategically fragile capability set.

Finally, productization theory provides a useful bridge between cyber reasoning and venture execution. According to Harkonen et al. (2015), productization involves defining and standardizing deliverables in ways that strengthen the linkage between market needs and engineering-oriented development. When this insight is transported into cybersecurity entrepreneurship, an important shift becomes visible. Security controls, risk registers, privacy notices, incident playbooks, and trust dashboards can all be treated as venture artifacts that must be made intelligible to customers, regulators, investors, and internal teams. Thus, a startup cyber tutor should not focus exclusively on detecting technical weaknesses; it should also teach how security knowledge is translated into repeatable, communicable, and productized trust practices.

3 MAIN FOCUS OF THE CHAPTER

3.1 Method of synthesis and literature-derived design logic

To make a cybersecurity entrepreneurship chapter successful, it is critical that conceptual synthesis be made explicit rather than left implicit. This chapter was developed from a structured narrative synthesis of thirty-seven DOI-bearing sources selected from the attached bibliography because they contributed directly to at least one of five dimensions: AI-enabled tutoring, learning analytics and assessment, adaptive and game-based pedagogy, cybersecurity governance, or entrepreneurial and organizational transformation. Table 1 summarizes how those streams were aligned. Although the corpus includes books, articles, reviews, and chapters with varying methodological depth, the collective value of the corpus lies in its capacity to illuminate adjacent but previously fragmented design requirements. Thus, the chapter does not postulate that any single source fully resolves the problem of startup cyber tutoring; rather, a new design synthesis is constructed at the intersection of their partial insights.

Figure 1. Conceptual convergence model for intelligent tutoring in cybersecurity entrepreneurship

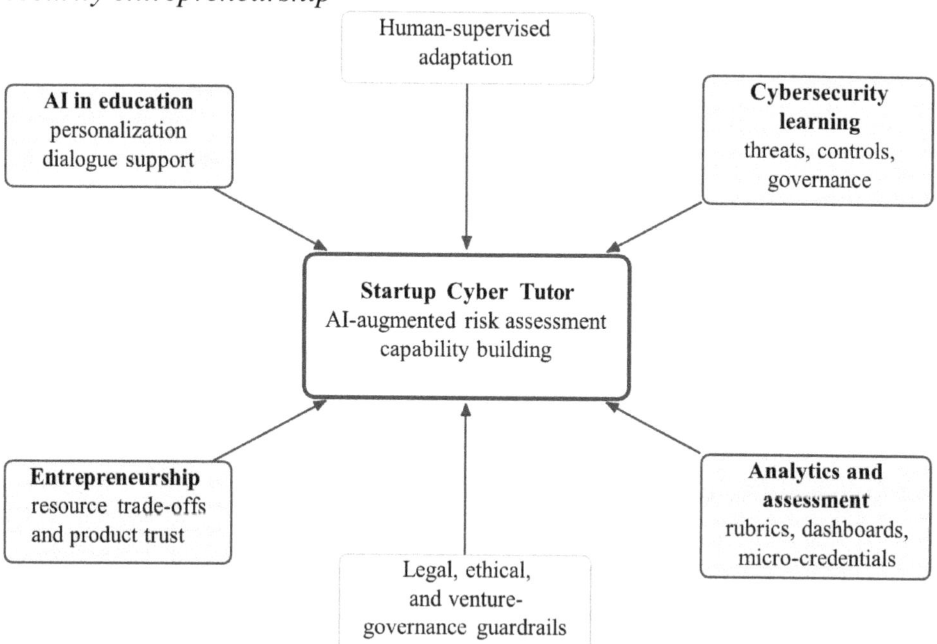

Globally, Table 1 and Figure 1 indicate that the design problem is not a matter of simply inserting a chatbot into a cybersecurity course. Rather, a venture-oriented tutor should be conceptualized as a multi-logic system in which educational adaptation, cyber reasoning, entrepreneurial decision-making, and governance constraints are integrated. Naidoo & Verma (2024) emphasize the strategic need to reshape entrepreneurial education under Industry 4.0 conditions, whereas Tjahjono et al. (2025) show that curricula must absorb digital technopreneurship, analytics, and cross-functional competence. However, those studies do not expound how adaptive tutoring should be built; that gap is filled only when they are read alongside AI-in-education sources such as Tariq (2024), Cela et al. (2024), and Adelana et al. (2024). Consequently, this chapter postulates that an intelligent tutor for startup cybersecurity should mediate across four simultaneous questions: What risk is present, why does it matter for the venture, what action is proportionate, and how should the rationale be communicated?

Table 1. Literature streams and their design implications for startup-oriented cyber tutoring

Stream	Illustrative sources	What this stream contributes	Design implication for this chapter
AI acceptance and institutional adoption Learning analytics and systems thinking	(Mohammad et al., 2026); (Al-Maaitah et al., 2025); (Al-Shabandar et al., 2024) (Durak & Cankaya, 2023); (Qudrat-Ullah, 2024)	Adoption growth, usability, readiness, and integrity constraints are emphasized. Analytics is positioned as the basis for learner diagnosis, intervention design, and leadership visibility.	Onboarding, explainability, and governance should be embedded into the tutoring workflow. Cyber tutoring should include dashboards for concept mastery, judgment quality, and risk-prioritization patterns.
Personalized tutoring and engagement Chatbots, LLMs, and automated feedback	(Adelana et al., 2024); (Tariq, 2024); (Cela et al., 2024) (Bansal et al., 2024); (Davar et al., 2025); (Kooli & Yusuf, 2025); (Aad & Hardey, 2025)	Adaptive AI is shown to personalize support and detect learner gaps. Conversational support and partial grading automation are demonstrated, but oversight needs remain prominent.	Learner modeling should adapt to role, prior knowledge, and startup maturity. Conversational guidance should be paired with human review for high-stakes risk judgments.
Gamification and immersive pedagogy	(Sindiramutty et al., 2025); (Almufarreh, 2026); (Ateş & Kölemen, 2025); (Damaševičius & Sideker- skiene, 2025); (Papadim-itriou & Virvou, 2025)	Motivation, challenge calibration, collaboration, and immersive problem solving are highlighted.	Scenarios should be staged as adaptive decision episodes, not as passive content exposure.
Cybersecurity, law, and ethics	(Çela et al., 2025); (Gupta, 2024); (Anastasiadou et al., 2025); (Kumar et al., 2024); (Alam, 2025)	Security literacy, legal awareness, data protection, and bias mitigation are foregrounded.	Risk assessment should integrate technical, legal, and ethical evaluation criteria.

continued on following page

Table 1. Continued

Stream	Illustrative sources	What this stream contributes	Design implication for this chapter
Entrepreneurship and organizational transformation	Naidoo & Verma, 2024); (Tjahjono et al., 2025); (Baig et al., 2025); (Agnihotri et al., 2024); (Rejeb et al., 2025)	Technological change is connected with entrepreneurial capability, leadership, and human- machine collaboration	Cyber decisions should be taught as venture decisions shaped by product, market, and operations.
Productization and communication of trust	Harkonen et al., 2015); (Diogo et al., 2025); (Garcia et al., 2025); (Musundire, 2025)	Knowledge is expected to be communicated, standardized, and made intelligible to multiple audiences.	Learners should produce artifacts such as risk registers, trust briefs, and mitigation roadmaps.

Such a design logic also requires a shift in what counts as the target learning outcome. Conventional cybersecurity education frequently privileges technical concept mastery, whereas entrepreneurial settings require the cultivation of judgment under uncertainty. A startup founder must decide whether a misconfigured cloud bucket is a critical launch blocker, a deferred engineering task, or a reputational liability requiring immediate disclosure; no single answer can be generated without contextual reasoning about product maturity, customer data sensitivity, contractual exposure, and operational feasibility. Harkonen et al. (2015) help clarify this challenge by showing that productization strengthens the linkage between market needs and engineering development. Thus, cybersecurity tutoring for startups should be organized around the productization of trust: learners should be trained to translate technical findings into venture-ready priorities, controls, and narratives that are intelligible to both technical and nontechnical stakeholders.

3.2 A staged capability model for AI-augmented risk assessment

Currently, the capability demands placed upon entrepreneurial teams are both ubiquitous and unevenly distributed. Some founders require foundational cyber literacy, others need procurement judgment regarding third-party tools, whereas still others need the ability to interpret AI-generated security signals without over-trusting them. To address this heterogeneity, this chapter advances a staged capability model composed of five progressive layers: foundational cyber literacy, venture-context modeling, AI-assisted diagnostic reasoning, uncertainty-sensitive prioritization, and governance communication. The model is not presented as a universal maturity ladder that every startup must traverse linearly; instead, it is offered as a holistic map of how cyber risk capability can be scaffolded within an intelligent tutoring environment.

Figure 2. Illustrative capability path from cyber literacy to governance communication

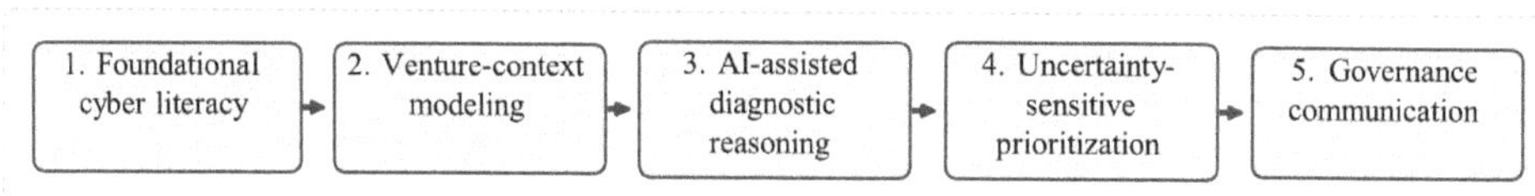

The first stage, foundational cyber literacy, is supported by sources that emphasize digital fluency and technological adaptability as baseline educational needs. Diogo et al. (2025) argue that literacy in the AI era extends beyond traditional reading and writing toward digital, ethical, and systems-oriented competence. Likewise, Delello & McWhorter (2024) and Zhang et al. (2024) emphasize problem solving and technological fluency as necessary responses to rapidly changing work environments. However, cyber literacy in startup environments cannot be purely declarative; it must make clear which assets matter, which data flows create exposure, and which control categories are realistic under resource scarcity. Therefore, introductory tutoring should be organized around the startup's own artifacts—such as an authentication flow, a minimum viable product architecture, a customer database, or an API dependency map—rather than around decontextualized examples.

Table 2. Capability matrix for AI-augmented cyber risk assessment in technology startups

Capability stage	Primary learner tasks	Evidence of competence
Foundational cyber literacy & Identify as: sets, actors, basic threats, and control categories.	Correctly distinguishes product, customer, infrastructure, and partner-related exposure.	Explains terminology, generates hints, and adapts examples to the startup sector.
Venture-context modeling & Map threats to business model, growth stage, data sensitivity, and dependencies.	Connects technical exposure to revenue, reputation, compliance, and delivery risk.	Builds context-aware scenarios from venture profiles and prior learner decisions.
AI-assisted di- agnostic reasoning & Interpret alerts, logs, questionnaires, and AI-generated summaries.	Uses evidence critically, validates claims, and detects incomplete or misleading outputs.	Summarizes evidence, surfaces anomalies, and contrasts alternative interpretations.
Uncertainty-sensitive prioritization & Rank mitigation actions under time, budget, staffing, and product constraints.	Produces defensible action sequencing with explicit trade-offs and residual-risk justification.	Simulates alternative futures, estimates impact ranges, and prompts counterfactual reflection.
Governance communication & Communicate risk decisions to investors, customers, team members, and regulators.	Produces concise risk briefs, control rationales, escalation notes, and trust-centered product language.	Evaluates clarity, completeness, and audience alignment against rubric criteria

The second and third stages require a more explicit coupling of AI and judgment. Adelana et al. (2024) demonstrate that intention to adopt intelligent tutoring is strengthened when usefulness and control are perceived positively, which implies that AI assistance should remain interpretable and actionable. At the same time, Davar et al. (2025) and Bansal et al. (2024) show that chatbots and conversational AI can provide rapid, supportive guidance, but not necessarily authoritative judgment in isolation. Consequently, the tutor proposed in this chapter treats AI-generated summaries, alert interpretations, and scenario annotations as provisional analytic supports rather than final verdicts. The learner is expected to interrogate the AI output, validate the evidence, and justify agreement or disagreement. In this way, AI augmentation becomes a vehicle for reflective expertise rather than a substitute for it.

The fourth and fifth stages introduce the venture-specific core of this chapter's argument. Risk assessment in startups is not merely a technical ordering exercise; it is an uncertainty-sensitive prioritization task shaped by runway, staffing, release schedules, investor expectations, and regulatory timelines. The human-centric emphasis visible in Industry 5.0 literature (Rejeb et al., 2025) and the management-oriented insights offered by Baig et al. (2025) and Agnihotri et al. (2024) imply that entrepreneurial judgment should be cultivated where intelligent systems and human discretion meet. Consequently, learners should be asked to produce ranked mitigation backlogs, explain residual risk, and defend trade-offs to multiple audiences. Figure 2 and Table 2 therefore place governance communication at the apex of capability growth, because cyber resilience in startups is realized not only through controls implemented, but also through the clarity with which risk is framed and communicated.

3.3 Reference architecture for the tutoring system

To make the above capability model operational, a layered system architecture is required. Although many AI-in-education works discuss personalization at a high level, fewer sources explicate how knowledge, analytics, dialogue, and governance should be orchestrated when the content domain itself is complex and fast moving. Abu-Salih (2021) provide a particularly valuable bridge by showing that domain-specific knowledge graphs offer an explicit structure for representing entities, relations, and inferential paths in complex knowledge domains. In cybersecurity entrepreneurship, those entities would include assets, controls, user roles, regulatory obligations, product features, vendor relationships, and incident types. Consequently, this chapter postulates that the knowledge graph should function as the semantic backbone of the tutor, enabling scenarios, feedback, and assessment logic to remain context aware rather than generic.

However, a knowledge graph alone would not suffice. As Table 3 and Figure 3 illustrate, three additional modeling structures are required: a learner model, a venture-context model, and an assessment model. The learner model draws from the adaptive logic visible in Adelana et al. (2024), Tariq (2024), and Durak & Cankaya (2023); it estimates not only concept mastery, but also the learner's tendency to over-trust AI explanations, under-justify prioritization, or neglect stakeholder communication. The venture-context model is the mechanism through which entrepreneurship-specific adaptation occurs. It stores information about the startup's domain, growth stage, architecture, sensitive assets, and business priorities so that the system can distinguish, for example, between the security logic of a health-tech platform handling patient data and that of a developer tooling startup with minimal personal data but extensive supply-chain dependencies.

Table 3. Core modules in the proposed tutoring architecture

Module	**Core function**	**Typical data objects**
Learner model & Estimates prior knowledge, role, preferred interaction style, and performance trajectory.	Quiz traces, decision explanations, time-on-task, reflection notes.	(Adelana et al., 2024); (Durak & Cankaya, 2023)
Venture-context model & Encodes startup stage, architecture, sector, customer type, and compliance exposure.	Product map, cloud stack, data categories, partner inventory.	(Naidoo & Verma, 2024); (Tjahjono et al., 2025)
Cyber knowledge graph & Structures assets, threats, controls, obligations, and dependencies.	Nodes, edges, control-to-asset mappings, evidence links.	(Abu-Salih, 2021); (Gupta, 2024)
Scenario generator & Produces branching cases tied to venture conditions and prior learner actions.	Incident injects, business constraints, stakeholder prompts.	(Papadimitriou & Virvou, 2025); (Damaševičius & Sidek- erskiene, 2025)
Conversational tutor & Supplies hints, counter questions, summaries, and clarification prompts.	Dialogue turns, cited evidence, feedback templates.	(Davar et al., 2025); (Bansal et al., 2024)
Assessment engine & Scores decision quality and communication quality against rubrics.	Risk ranks, justification texts, mitigation plans, audience briefs.	(Kooli & Yusuf, 2025); (Qudrat-Ullah, 2024)
Governance layer & Applies privacy, audit, fairness, and human-oversight constraints.	Consent records, review flags, model cards, access logs.	Kumar et al., 2024); (Anastasi- adou et al., 2025)

Figure 3. Reference architecture synthesized for an intelligent tutor in cybersecurity entrepreneurship

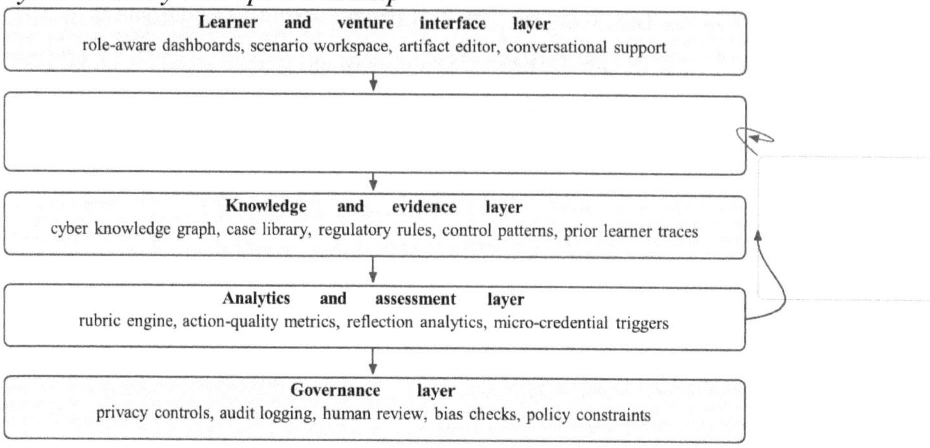

Furthermore, the orchestration layer must undertake more than sequencing. Because entrepreneurial risk assessment is highly contextual, the tutor should dynamically decide whether a learner needs more conceptual explanation, a more realistic scenario, a contradictory AI-generated interpretation, or a communication exercise aimed at investors or customers. Papadimitriou & Virvou (2025) and Damaševičius & Sidekerskiene (2025) show that AI-enhanced and game-based environments are particularly effective when interaction is purposeful and feedback is adaptive. Consequently, the scenario generator in this architecture is not treated as decorative simulation; it is the primary mechanism through which venture ambiguity is reproduced in pedagogically productive form.

The analytics and assessment layer must also be more nuanced than conventional correctness scoring. Startup cyber tasks often admit several defensible answers, provided that the learner articulates assumptions, justifies sequencing, and recognizes uncertainty. Therefore, the assessment engine proposed here measures action quality, evidence quality, trade-off awareness, and communication adequacy rather than relying on binary right-or-wrong scoring alone. This design choice aligns with the cautionary stance of Kooli & Yusuf (2025), Garcia et al. (2025), and Kumar et al. (2024), each of whom, in different ways, indicate that automated evaluation should be constrained where judgment and fairness are involved. Thus, human review remains a formal architectural requirement rather than an optional enhancement.

3.4 Pedagogical patterns and scenario design for startup learning

Although adaptive technology is essential, pedagogy remains the decisive layer that converts system capability into learning value. The attached corpus suggests that startup cybersecurity learning should be structured around problem-solving episodes in which learners confront ambiguous evidence, limited resources, and stakeholder consequences. Zhang et al. (2024) expound the importance of technology- integrated problem-solving educational practices, while Damaševičius & Sidekerskiene (2025) emphasize immersive and collaborative challenge structures. When those insights are combined with the adaptive gamification logic of Sindiramutty et al. (2025) and the broader motivational synthesis by Almufarreh (2026), a clear pedagogical inference can be drawn: the tutor should organize learning as a sequence of consequential venture situations rather than as isolated content modules.

Table 4. Illustrative scenario patterns for startup cybersecurity entrepreneurship tutoring

Startup moment	Cyber challenge	Learner artifact
Founding and prototyping & Minimal architecture, insecure defaults, and vague asset ownership.	Initial risk map and asset register.	Establishes foundational cyber literacy and venture-context modeling.
Pre-launch sprint & Release pressure conflicts with hardening, logging, and privacy tasks.	Prioritized mitigation backlog with justification.	Trains trade-off reasoning under time and budget constraints.
Third-party integration & A vendor tool promises speed but introduces opaque data flows.	Third-party due-diligence memo and dependency decision.	Connects procurement choices with privacy and supply-chain risk.

continued on following page

Table 4. Continued

Startup moment	Cyber challenge	Learner artifact
Fundraising due diligence & Investors request evidence of security maturity and governance.	Executive-facing cyber trust brief.	Builds governance communication and productized trust capability.
Customer escalation & A security concern threatens brand reputation and client retention.	Customer communication draft and escalation path.	Cultivates audience-specific risk communication.
Incident response tabletop & An ambiguous anomaly may be benign, operational, or adversarial.	Decision log, evidence review, and post-incident reflection	Trains evidence use, uncertainty handling, and reflective learning.

Figure 4. Closed-loop tutoring cycle for startup cyber scenarios

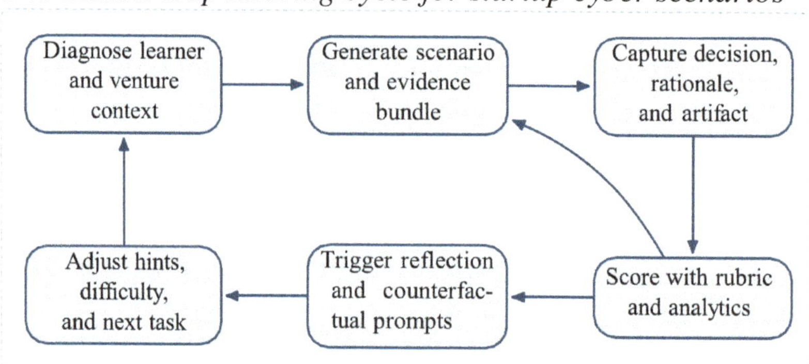

Consequently, the tutorial scenarios proposed in Table 4 are anchored to moments that are endemic to technology startups: product prototyping, pre-launch hardening, third-party integration, fundraising due diligence, customer escalation, and incident response. These moments were selected because they force cyber judgment to intersect with business pressure. For example, a pre-launch scenario may present the learner with incomplete logging, a known dependency weakness, and a fixed demo deadline; the task is not merely to identify the vulnerability, but to rank mitigation options under severe constraint and explain the residual exposure to the founding team. Similarly, a fundraising due diligence scenario teaches that cyber risk is also a signaling problem: if the venture cannot articulate its security posture, perceived operational maturity may be weakened even when the technical posture is improving.

However, gamification should not be interpreted narrowly as point accumulation or cosmetic competition. Sindiramutty et al. (2025) emphasize adaptation to different learning styles, while Ateş & Kölemen (2025) show that adoption of gamified virtual reality is mediated by threat perceptions, self-efficacy, and response costs. These insights suggest that effective gamification in cyber entrepreneurship should be tied to cognitive and motivational scaffolds, not merely entertainment value. Thus, game mechanics should reward evidence quality, prudent escalation, justified prioritization, and stakeholder empathy rather than speed alone. In a similar vein, Papadimitriou & Virvou (2025) reiterate that AI-based games can serve holistic educational purposes when personalization and ethical awareness are integrated. Accordingly, the proposed tutor uses adaptive branching, consequence visibility, and reflective prompts to cultivate resilience, not superficial gamified compliance.

Furthermore, the pedagogical design must preserve the role of human mentorship. AI can generate prompts, summarize evidence, and tailor challenge sequences, but incubator mentors, instructors, or startup advisors are still required to contextualize decisions, challenge assumptions, and surface domain nuances. Aad & Hardey (2025) emphasize the need to prepare faculty for transformative AI adoption, while Musundire (2025) underline that chatbots can streamline processes yet remain embedded within broader leadership and management arrangements. Consequently, the tutor advanced in this chapter is not envisioned as a self-sufficient instructional agent. Rather, it is positioned as a resilient support layer that amplifies mentor effectiveness by making learner reasoning visible, traceable, and discussable.

3.5 Assessment, analytics, and micro-credentialing logic

Assessment occupies a central place in this chapter because capability claims in cybersecurity entrepreneur- ship must be observable and defensible. Conventional educational assessment has often privileged content recall or procedural correctness, whereas startup cyber reasoning requires richer evidence. Kooli & Yusuf (2025) demonstrate that large language models can participate meaningfully in grading processes, but the same study also implies that grading quality remains a matter of alignment, calibration, and context. When the task concerns risk prioritization, the rubric must therefore evaluate whether the learner identified the right issue categories, used available evidence coherently, recognized uncertainty, articulated assumptions, and matched the action proposal to startup constraints. Consequently, the assessment design proposed here foregrounds judgment transparency rather than automated correctness alone.

Today, analytics can be made to serve not only instructors, but also learners and startup support programs. Durak & Cankaya (2023) stress that learning analytics supports the identification of learner needs and the evaluation of interventions, whereas Qudrat-Ullah (2024) emphasize the leadership value of analytics-rich educational environments. Thus, in the architecture proposed here, analytics has three intertwined roles. First, it provides formative adaptation by detecting patterns such as shallow justifications, repetitive

Table 5. Rubric dimensions for assessing startup-oriented cyber risk assessment capability

Dimension	What strong performance looks like
Evidence interpretation & Integrates logs, descriptions, and AI summaries critically; flags missing evidence and uncertainty.	Low blind acceptance of AI output and frequent evidence cross-checking.
Risk prioritization & Sequences actions according to impact, likelihood, timing, and venture constraints.	Stable ranking logic across similar scenarios and explicit trade-off statements.
Mitigation design & Proposes feasible controls matched to architecture, team capacity, and product stage.	Recommendations remain proportionate and context-aware rather than maximalist.
Governance awareness & Recognizes privacy, legal, contractual, and reputational implications of decisions.	Consistent inclusion of stakeholder and compliance considerations.

continued on following page

Table 5. Continued

Dimension	What strong performance looks like
Communication quality & Tailors cyber explanations to technical and nontechnical audiences with clarity and concision.	Audience-specific vocabulary and coherent rationale structure.
Reflective adaptation & Revises prior decisions in response to counterfactual evidence or feedback.	Documented improvement across iterations and reduction in repeated error types.

Figure 5. Illustrative AI-augmented startup risk-assessment workflow used in tutoring scenarios

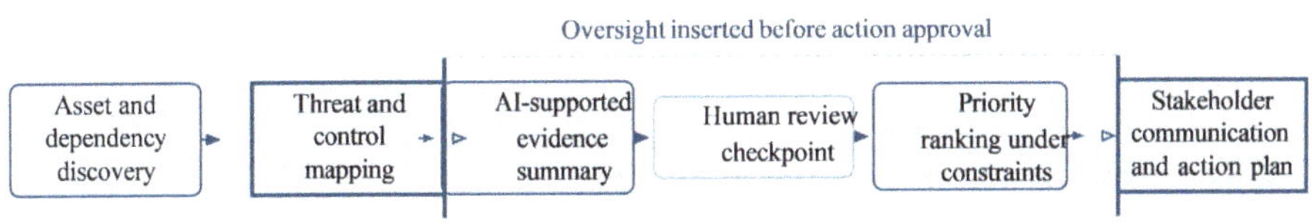

over-prioritization of low-impact threats, or systematic neglect of governance implications. Second, it supports summative judgment by aggregating rubric performance across multiple scenarios. Third, it enables ecosystem-level insight for incubators or accelerators, which may wish to identify recurring cyber capability gaps across cohorts without exposing sensitive venture content.

Micro-credentials extend this logic by making capability recognition granular and portable. Durak & Çankaya (2024) observe that AI can support the design and management of micro-credentials aligned with specific skills and competencies. For cybersecurity entrepreneurship, this implies that tutoring systems can issue bounded credentials such as "AI-assisted evidence interpretation," "third-party cyber due diligence," or "customer-facing risk communication," each based on repeated performance against the rubric in Table 5. Such modular credentialing is particularly valuable in startup environments because different team members require different capability portfolios. A technical co-founder may need advanced diagnostic reasoning, whereas a business founder may benefit more from governance communication and due diligence literacy. Consequently, the credentialing layer should reinforce distributed team resilience rather than assume homogeneous mastery.

However, the assessment layer also faces limitations that must be acknowledged analytically. Garcia et al. (2025) warn that AI integration may accelerate misuse and skill displacement, while Kumar et al. (2024) stress bias and transparency problems in AI and data analysis. Therefore, automated scoring should never be allowed to obscure the grounds of evaluation. Figure 5 includes a human review checkpoint precisely because venture-facing cyber decisions often carry reputational and legal consequences beyond the tutor itself. Keeping the above dynamics in view, AI-assisted assessment is best interpreted as a scaling mechanism for formative feedback and evidence organization, not as a final authority over strategic competence.

3.6 Illustrative startup use cases

In order to further clarify the functioning of the suggested logic of tutoring, three exemplary applications can be taken into account. The former relates to a software-as-a-service startup about to enter the market with the heavy dependence on the third-party analytics, payment, and cloud services. The tutor would not just require the learner to come up with generic vulnerabilities in such an environment. Instead it would require the learner to identify the supplier relationships that pose concentrated dependency risk, what categories of customer data amplify reputational exposure and what controls are to be put in place before launch and not delayed. The rationale behind this use case is the entrepreneurial and curriculum-transformation issues posed by Naidoo and Verma (2024) and Tjahjono et al. (2025) and the productization rationale presented by Harkonen et al. (2015). Therefore, the learner gets trained in how to transform abstract cyber knowledge into a release-based action plan that will reconcile between technical prudence and commercial urgency.

The second use case is an AI-powered start-up whose product decision-making cannot be separated into such questions as privacy, bias, and legality. In this case, the tutor would present vague model outputs, insufficient documentation and promotion of the model by compliance officers, customers and potential investors. The learner would then be prompted to make sense of how a technically satisfactory design decision could create governance or equity issues to still emerge. This use case would casein the ethical and legal insights that Kumar et al. (2024), Anastasiadou et al. (2025), and Alam (2025) have made, but also the institutional preparedness suggestions by Al-Maaitah et al. (2025). In that way, risk assessment becomes more of a multidimensional exercise whereby technical aptitude, legal traceability, and socio-economic legitimacy should be analyzed simultaneously.

The third use case is a startup that experiences accelerated scale-up due to the new investment, as more users, integrations, and dependencies on operations are added at a faster rate than the security capacity internally. In that regard, the tutor would make the scenario more complex with the appearance of conflicting streams of evidence, AI-written summaries of incident indicators, and a need to justify residual risk with a board-like audience. Human-focused approach to management that is evident in Rejeb et al. (2025), Baig et al. (2025), and Agnihotri et al. (2024) gains specific importance due to the fact that the learner has to make decisions that are not only about the type of control to be applied, but also about the nature of the responsibilities being formalized and the type of communication routine that should be institutionalized. The tutor therefore facilitates a shift in founder- centric improvisation to a more robust organizational ability, where cyber judgment is incorporated into venture governance as opposed to leaving it to improvised reaction.

3.7 Governance, implementation, and limitations

Although the literature indicates substantial promise for AI-enabled tutoring, the implementation path is constrained by infrastructural, pedagogical, and legal realities. Sarwar et al. (2025) observe that AI implementation in classrooms is frequently hindered by limited technical infrastructure, privacy concerns, uneven access, and insufficient training. A comparable concern is visible in Al-Maaitah et al. (2025), who show that usability and readiness facilitate educational AI adoption, whereas academic integrity introduces an important moderating dynamic. For startup accelerators, incubators, and entrepreneurship programs, these findings imply that an advanced cyber tutor cannot simply be procured and deployed. Institutional readiness, mentor capacity, data governance, and the boundaries of acceptable automation must be established before the system can operate with resilience.

Table 6. Phased implementation roadmap for startup-oriented cyber tutoring

Phase	Pedagogical priorities	Technical and governance priorities
Phase 1: Framing & Define venture roles, target competencies, and scenario portfolio.	Establish data boundaries, consent rules, and review responsibilities.	Curriculum map completed and governance charter approved.
Phase 2: Pilot & Run limited scenarios with mentor moderation and rubric testing.	Build a knowledge-graph prototype, dialogue templates, and an analytics dashboard.	Stable rubric reliability, a usable mentor dashboard, and positive usability feedback.
Phase 3: Expansion & Introduce adaptive branching, micro- credentials, and cohort analytics.	Integrate the case library, audit logging, and bias checks.	Improved learner performance across iterations and fewer repeated reasoning errors.
Phase 4: Institutionalization & Embed the tutor into incubators, entrepreneurship modules, and venture clinics.	Formalize maintenance, model review, and legal-compliance processes.	Recurrent program use and stronger startup cyber documentation and communication

Furthermore, governance must be treated as part of pedagogy rather than as external compliance.

Figure 6. Governance guardrails synthesized for intelligent tutoring in cybersecurity entrepreneurship

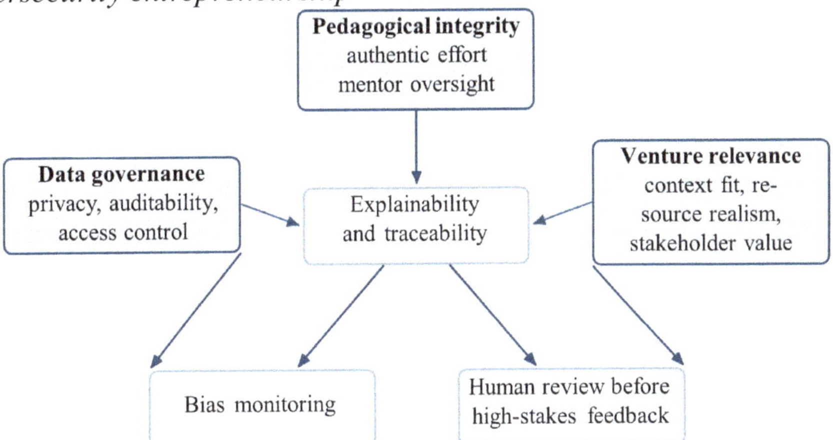

As shown by Anastasiadou et al. (2025), AI and law co-evolve, i.e. legal literacy cannot be isolated out of technical practice. Kumar et al. (2024) and Alam (2025) also highlight that the issue of bias, privacy, surveillance, and manipulation ought to be mitigated on the basis of educational and policy frameworks rather than by technical patching. In the case of a tutor who teaches cyber risk, this implies that the system needs to replicate legal and ethical thinking in its functionality. Minimizing data, displaying feedback provenance, displaying feedback history, reviewer escalation routes, and stakeholder sensitive language are not optional extravagances but components of the hidden curriculum by which learners learn what responsible AI assisted cyber practice can be like.

Nevertheless, not all the tensions can be completely removed. One of these contradictions is the one between realism and abstraction. When the scenarios are too generic, then the learner might be unable to see venture relevance. In case they are overly realistic, delicate startup information can be consumed into the system hence increasing privacy and confidentiality threat. The other tension is related to the intensity of assistance. Conversational agent can become too active, which can lead to passive learning of the AI-generated reasoning by the learners. In case it is too subdued, the system can be ineffective to reduce cognitive overload among inexperienced entrepreneurs. Therefore the implementation should be carried out in a phased manner in line with the stages of the roadmap presented in Table 6, and guardrails presented in Figure 6 should be regarded as standing design constraints, but not post hoc correction.

Besides this, socio-economic heterogeneity of startup ecosystems should also be recognized. Resource-constrained environments might have no state-of-the-art cloud infrastructure, experts to mentor the programs, and no stable datasets with which to create highly adaptive models. However, the entrepreneurship education literature and digital transformation indicate that these limitations could not be taken as an excuse to do nothing. Instead, they support the merit of modular and micro-credentialed, human-monitored tutoring systems that can scale over time and initially on curated case libraries, sparse analytics, and finely bounded conversational support (Naidoo & Verma, 2024; Delello and McWhorter, 2024; Durak and Cankaya, 2024). Therefore, the architecture suggested in this chapter will be extensible as opposed to being maximalist in the first place.

4 FUTURE RESEARCH DIRECTIONS

In general, the future of intelligent tutoring systems in cybersecurity entrepreneurship should not be based on a general interest in AI-enabled learning but more specific empirical inquiries in the world community. First, it should be comparatively validated across different profiles of ventures. Startup cyber risks on health technology, fintech and educational platforms, industrial IoT and developer tooling vary significantly in terms of asset sensitivity, legal and stakeholder expectations. Future research must, therefore, examine the effect of thc venture-context modeling on the quality of adaptation, level of precision in feedback, and transfer of learning among sectors. This type of work would overlap with the adoption-oriented views of Adelana et al. (2024) and Al-Maaitah et al. (2025), as well as extrapolate the entrepreneurship-oriented work of Naidoo and Verma (2024) and Tjahjono et al. (2025) into more operationally specific areas of cyber.

Second, the knowledge representation layer is to be investigated more thoroughly. The knowledge graphs specific to the domain are well-grounded by Abu-Salih (2021), but the particular form of the graph that is suitable in the particular context of startup cyber tutoring is not elaborated. Future research should thus focus on ways assets, controls, regulations, stakeholders and venture events can be coded in ways that allow explainable tutoring decisions without creating inappropriate complexity. Moreover, the graph-based models are to be compared with the language-model-based architectures only to understand when explicit structure enhances the quality of reasoning, its explainability, and pedagogical trust. This type of research would be particularly useful in those areas where there is a need to tie legal and governance material in a transparent way to technical risk indicators.

Third, the assessment research must make the effort of differentiating between surface level performance improvements and sustainable capability building. The materials on gamification, immersive learning, and AI-based assessment indicate the possibility of increasing engagement and speeding up feedback (Almufarreh, 2026; Ates and Kolemen, 2025; Kooli and Yusuf, 2025). Nevertheless, it is still unclear as to whether learners that succeed within adaptive cyber contexts are still able to reason within the context of actual startup conditions several months later, or whether they can effectively convey cyber-based decisions to investors, customers, and regulators not in the context of tutoring. Longitudinal and mixed-method research is thus necessary, which entails rubric trajectories, artifact quality, mentor assessment, and venture outcomes. Besides this, studies are needed on whether micro-credential structures do indeed lead to team-based resilience by spreading competence throughout the roles of the startup as proposed conceptually by Durak and Cankaya (2024).

Fourth, the study of governance should be more intervention based. Instead of just recording bias, opacity, or privacy issues, subsequent research should involve experimentation on tangible guardrail systems like human review procedures, feedback provenance interfaces, prompt disclosure interfaces, and bias-monitoring interfaces. The moral borderline outlined by Kumar et al. (2024), the legal reciprocity that Anastasiadou et al. (2025) highlight, the manipulation issues that Alam (2025) synthesizes will entail the auditing pedagogical design. Therefore, to work in the future, it is necessary to consider not only the learning outcomes, but also the validity, challenge ability, and institutional acceptability of tutoring choices in the high-stakes entrepreneurial context.

Lastly, bridges between entrepreneurship ecosystems and educational AI research should be constructed more explicitly. Up to now, much of the AI-in-education research has been located in the classroom, but startup support can be a process of incubators, accelerators, venture studios, and informal mentoring networks. Research in the future should thus attempt to see how intelligent tutoring can be accommodated in these grassroots and semi-formal systems without compromising on the human mentoring and experiential learning that entrepreneurship education has been based on. With the above dynamics held in mind, the most

promising trajectory does not lie in the substitution of mentors with AI tutors, but in the combination of tutors as context-aware and ethically constrained analytically enriching companions to human entrepreneurship.

5 CONCLUSION

This chapter, therefore, brings forward an evident original thesis: intelligent tutoring systems based on cybersecu- rity entrepreneurship are not to be designed after generic cyber awareness systems or generic education chatbots. Instead, they are to be modeled as contextualized learning of venture-based risk assessment whereby cyber risk assessment is addressed as an entrepreneurial skill that includes technical interpretation, prioritization sensitivity to uncertainty, governance awareness and communication with stakeholders. This chapter has demonstrated that there is no single stream that can be relied on alone since it synthesized literature on AI in education, learning analytics, gamification, entrepreneurship, organizational transformation, knowledge graphs, law, and ethics. It is only after the integration of these streams that a coherent architecture of startup-relevant cyber tutoring can be seen.

Despite the dissimilarity of the attached corpus in terms of approach, breadth, and disciplinary focus, a similar pattern was observed across the materials: educational AI can be most useful when it supplements human judgment, makes learning traces transparent, and aids adaptive progression without erasing responsibility. That is deep-seated in the case of technology startups. A robust cyber tutor must also assist the learners to comprehend not only, what a threat is, but also why it is significant to the venture, how limited mitigation resources are to be sequenced, and trust communicated as a part of product and organizational development. Subsequently, the main contribution of this chapter is centering the approach to the reform of cybersecurity education in startups as a productized, analytics-intensive, manually supervised, and constrained by governance tutoring issue. In the event that such a reframing is followed to its logical conclusion, intelligent tutoring systems could be a significant substantive tool towards developing AI-enhanced risk assessment capacity in the growing startup cultures that are becoming a defining feature of digital innovation.

REFERENCES

Aad, S. S., & Hardey, M. (2025). *After generative AI: Preparing faculty to transform education, learning, and pedagogy*. Emerald Publishing., DOI: 10.1108/9781835499467

Abu-Salih, B. (2021). Domain-specific knowledge graphs: A survey. *Journal of Network and Computer Applications*, *185*, 103076. DOI: 10.1016/j.jnca.2021.103076

Adelana, O. P., Ayanwale, M. A., & Sanusi, I. T. (2024). Exploring pre-service biology teachers' intention to teach genetics using an AI intelligent tutoring-based system. *Cogent Education*, *11*(1), 2310976. DOI: 10.1080/2331186X.2024.2310976

Agnihotri, A., Agarwal, R., Maurya, A., Sinha, M., & Balusamy, B. (2024). *Impact of new technology on next-generation leadership*. IGI Global Scientific Publishing., DOI: 10.4018/979-8-3693-1946-8

Al-Maaitah, T. A., Alduneibat, K. A., Alshdaifat, S. M., Alsarayreh, R., Bani Ahmad, A. Y. A., & Hijazin, A. F. (2025). AI adoption, technological readiness, and AI usability in sustainability accounting education: The moderating role of academic integrity. *Heritage and Sustainable Development*, *7*(1), 611–628. DOI: 10.37868/hsd.v7i1.1176

Al-Shabandar, R., Jaddoad, A., Elwi, T. A., Mohammed, A., & Hussain, A. J. (2024). A systematic review for the implication of generative AI in higher education. *Infocommunications Journal*, *16*(3), 31–42. DOI: 10.36244/ICJ.2024.3.3

Alam, A. (2025). Ethical challenges and bias in AI-driven marketing: Educational imperatives and policy perspectives. In *Impacts of AI-generated content on brand reputation* (pp. 55–107). IGI Global Scientific Publishing., DOI: 10.4018/979-8-3373-4327-3.ch003

Almufarreh, A. (2026). Gamification in education and its impact on student academic performance: A conceptual model based on systematic literature review and PLS-SEM analysis. *Algorithms*, *19*(2), 143. DOI: 10.3390/a19020143

Anastasiadou, S. D., Seremeti, L., Masouras, A., & Anastasiadis, L. (2025). *Modern perspectives on artificial intelligence and law*. IGI Global Scientific Publishing., DOI: 10.4018/979-8-3693-9576-9

Ateş, H., & Kölemen, C. Ş. (2025). Integrating theories for insight: An amalgamated model for gamified virtual reality adoption by science teachers. *Education and Information Technologies*, *30*(2), 2123–2153. DOI: 10.1007/s10639-024-12892-9

Baig, S. A., Mohsin, M., Lodhi, R. N., & Batool, G. (2025). *Reshaping organizational management and workplace culture with AI*. IGI Global Scientific Publishing., DOI: 10.4018/979-8-3693-8960-7

Bansal, R., Chakir, A., Ngah, A. H., Rabby, F., & Jain, A. (2024). *AI algorithms and ChatGPT for student en- gagement in online learning*. IGI Global Scientific Publishing., DOI: 10.4018/9798369342688

Cela, E., Vajjhala, N. R., & Fonkam, M. M. (2024). *Next-generation AI methodologies in education*. IGI Global Scientific Publishing., DOI: 10.4018/979-8-3693-7220-3

Çela, E., Vedishchev, A., & Vajjhala, N. R. (2025). Upskilling the educational workforce for AI-enhanced cybersecurity: A thematic and trend analysis. In *AI-enabled threat intelligence and cyber risk assessment* (pp. 57–75). CRC Press., DOI: 10.1201/9781003504979-4

Damaševičius, R., & Sidekerskiene, T. (2025). *Digital escape room designs in education*. IGI Global Scientific Publishing., DOI: 10.4018/979-8-3693-4219-0

Davar, N. F., Dewan, M. A. A., & Zhang, X. (2025). AI chatbots in education: Challenges and opportunities. *Information (Basel)*, *16*(3), 235. DOI: 10.3390/info16030235

Delello, J. A., & McWhorter, R. R. (2024). *Disruptive technologies in education and workforce development*. IGI Global Scientific Publishing., DOI: 10.4018/979-8-3693-3003-6

Diogo, A., Joaquim, A. F., & de Almeida, C. V. (2025). *Rethinking literacy in the era of sustainability and artificial intelligence*. IGI Global Scientific Publishing., DOI: 10.4018/979-8-3373-0725-1

Durak, G., & Cankaya, S. (2023). *Perspectives on learning analytics for maximizing student outcomes*. IGI Global Scientific Publishing., DOI: 10.4018/978-1-6684-9527-8

Durak, G., & Çankaya, S. (2024). *Integrating micro-credentials with AI in open education*. IGI Global Scientific Publishing., DOI: 10.4018/979-8-3693-5488-9

Garcia, M. B., Rosak-Szyrocka, J., & Bozkurt, A. (2025). *Pitfalls of AI integration in education: Skill obsolescence, misuse, and bias*. IGI Global Scientific Publishing., DOI: 10.4018/979-8-3373-0122-8

Gupta, B. (2024). *Metaverse security paradigms*. IGI Global Scientific Publishing., DOI: 10.4018/979-8-3693-3824-7

Harkonen, J., Haapasalo, H., & Hanninen, K. (2015). Productisation: A review and research agenda. *International Journal of Production Economics*, *164*, 65–82. DOI: 10.1016/j.ijpe.2015.02.024

Kooli, C., & Yusuf, N. (2025). Transforming educational assessment: Insights into the use of ChatGPT and large language models in grading. *International Journal of Human-Computer Interaction*, *41*(5), 3388–3399. DOI: 10.1080/10447318.2024.2338330

Kumar, R., Joshi, A., Sharan, H. O., Peng, S.-L., & Dudhagara, C. R. (2024). *The ethical frontier of AI and data analysis*. IGI Global Scientific Publishing., DOI: 10.4018/979-8-3693-2964-1

Mohammad, S. I. S., Mohammad, A. A. S., Vasudevan, A., Al-Daoud, K. I., Ling, A. W. P., Mohammad, D. I., Mohammad, A. I., Hai, S. T., & Rusuli, M. S. C. (2026). Artificial intelligence in higher education: A bibliometric analysis of acceptance and adoption studies. In *Artificial intelligence and technology: Systems management, decisions and control for sustainability in the digital age* (pp. 215–227). Springer Nature., DOI: 10.1007/978-3-032-10016-0_18

Musundire, A. (2025). *Chatbots in educational leadership and management*. IGI Global Scientific Publishing., DOI: 10.4018/979-8-3693-8734-4

Naidoo, V., & Verma, R. (2024). *Reshaping entrepreneurial education within an industry 4.0 context*. IGI Global Scientific Publishing., DOI: 10.4018/979-8-3693-0409-9

Papadimitriou, S., & Virvou, M. (2025). *Artificial intelligence-based games as novel holistic educational environments to teach 21st century skills*. Springer Nature., DOI: 10.1007/978-3-031-77464-5

Qudrat-Ullah, H. (2024). *Empowering educational leaders using analytics, AI, and systems thinking*. IGI Global Scientific Publishing., DOI: 10.4018/979-8-3693-7190-9

Rashid, A. B., & Kausik, M. A. K. (2024). AI revolutionizing industries worldwide: A comprehensive overview of its diverse applications. *Hybrid Advances*, *7*, 100277. DOI: 10.1016/j.hybadv.2024.100277

Rejeb, A., Rejeb, K., Zrelli, I., & Süle, E. (2025). Industry 5.0 as seen through its academic literature: An in- vestigation using co-word analysis. *Discover Sustainability*, *6*(1), 307. DOI: 10.1007/s43621-025-01166-0

Sarwar, U., Sanhong, T., Akhtar, M. W., & Aamir, M. (2025). *Navigating barriers to AI implementation in the classroom*. IGI Global Scientific Publishing. DOI: 10.4018/979-8-3373-1827-1

Sindiramutty, S. R., Riskhan, B., & Humayun, M. (2025). Adaptive gamification strategies for different learning styles in cybersecurity. In *Gamification learning framework for cybersecurity education* (pp. 277–315). IGI Global Scientific Publishing., DOI: 10.4018/979-8-3373-0477-9.ch011

Tariq, M. U. (2024). *AI-driven learning and engagement in higher education*. IGI Global Scientific Publishing., DOI: 10.4018/979-8-3693-4074-5

Tjahjono, B., Hermawan, D., Millah, S., & Evans, R. (2025). Bridging the skills gap curriculum transformation for automation industries and the role of digital technopreneurship. *APTISI Transactions on Technopreneurship*, *7*(2), 650–662. DOI: 10.34306/att.v7i2.620

Zhang, J., Yahaya, W. A. J. W., Sanmugam, M., & Lim, D. (2024). *Integrating technology in problem-solving educational practices*. IGI Global Scientific Publishing., DOI: 10.4018/979-8-3693-6745-2

Chapter 4
AI-Driven Recommender Systems for Personalized Entrepreneurial Learning in Startup Education

Ravikumar Natarajan
http://orcid.org/0009-0009-3705-1681
Marwadi University, Rajkot, India

Aarthi Selvakumar
http://orcid.org/0009-0006-9064-2091
Marwadi University, Rajkot, India

Umid Otajanov
Mamun University, Khiva, Uzbekistan

Makhmudov Asliddin
Termez University of Economics and Service, Termez, Uzbekistan

DOI: 10.4018/979-8-2600-0487-6.ch004

ABSTRACT

The concept of Artificial Intelligence is changing the nature of entrepreneurial education because it allows personalized and adaptable learning based on recommender systems. This chapter will discuss the way AI-based recommendation models are developed and implemented to analyze the profile of learners, their behaviors, and data of the ecosystem to provide specific learning pathways. Through a combination of methods like collaborative filtering, content-based approaches, and deep learning, the systems increase engagement, skills improvement, and start up preparedness. The chapter discusses also online platform and incubator case studies, where the learning outcomes were improved in reality. The issues associated with privacy, bias, and assessment are addressed, as well as how AI-driven entrepreneurial learning systems can be scaled and ethically sound in the future.

1. INTRODUCTION

The entrepreneurial education has been transformed significantly due to the rapid transformation of digital technologies and the economy of innovations. The classical approaches that primarily concerned the classroom-based teaching, mentoring and learning experience are slowly being overruled with intelligent and data-driven systems to provide scalable and adaptive learning experiences. The complexity of startup ecosystems, and the demographic variety of the learners, prompts the necessity to possess more specific and flexible educational schemes. Artificial Intelligence (AI) has become one of the key facilitators of this change, providing more sophisticated features of learner behavior analysis, predicting learning requirements, and personalized content. Specifically, AI-based recommender systems will offer a systematic strategy of matching learning materials to personal entrepreneurial objectives. By dynamically adjusting to the interaction with the user and changing trends in the market, these systems help with the ongoing learning (Waly, 2024). With the growth of entrepreneur education into the digital, global space, personalization becomes the key to increasing the engagement of the learners, enhancing their ability to acquire skills, and thinking in an innovation-focused manner among the future entrepreneurs.

1.1 Evolution of Entrepreneurial Education

Entrepreneurial education has developed out of the traditional business training models to more dynamic, experiential and innovation-centered learning paradigms. At early stages, entrepreneurship was instructed in theoretical terms based on business planning, business management principles, and economic analysis. With time, there was a shift of focus to experiential approaches of learning such as the case studies, simulations, internships, and startup incubation programs (Mannuru et al., 2025). This shift was necessitated by the realization that entrepreneurship needs practice skills like solution of problems, creativity, and identification of opportunities. As a consequence of the development of the digital technologies and online platforms as well as global startup ecosystems, entrepreneurial education has also been changed into a more convenient and scalable mechanism (Prabagar et al., 2025). Virtual incubators, digital networks of mentors and Massive open online courses (MOOCs) have increased the opportunities to learn outside the classroom. More recently, AI and data analytics integration have presented learners with smart learning settings that can be tailored to the specific learner requirements. Such an evolution is symptomatic of a move towards learner centric models that focus on continuous skill progression, innovation and real-world applicability in the fast-changing entrepreneurial environments. Table 1 Comparisons of conventional, experiential and AI-based approaches to entrepreneurial education.

Table 1. Evolution of entrepreneurial education models

Approach Type	Key Features	Learning Mode	Limitations	AI Role
Traditional	Theory-based, classroom learning	Passive	Limited practical exposure	Minimal
Experiential	Case studies, internships, projects	Active	Resource-intensive	Limited
Digital Learning	Online courses, MOOCs	Flexible	Lack of personalization	Moderate
AI-Driven Learning	Adaptive, personalized pathways	Dynamic	Data dependency	High

1.2 Role of AI in Learning Systems

Artificial Intelligence has a transformative impact on the current learning systems because it allows automation, personalization, and smart decision-making. Machine learning, natural language processing, and data analytics are AI technologies applied to the analysis of the learner behavior, performance evaluation, and the forecasts of the future learning requirements in the educational context (Gocen & Aydemir, 2020). Such capabilities enable one to develop adaptive learning environments wherein the content, assessments and feedback are customized to specific learners. AI-based systems are able to suggest courses, learning materials, and paths of skill development based on the profile of the users and pattern of interaction. There is also AI-driven chatbots and virtual tutors, which offer real-time support, which increases the engagement and accessibility of learners (Aarthi, Ravikumar, Khudayberganov, et al., 2025). AI is used in the context of entrepreneurial education to identify appropriate business opportunities, market trends, and innovation strategies based on the analysis of big data. It also aids in the process of decision making, in the sense that it gives insights on business models and the success factors of startups. All in all, AI can lead to improved efficiency and effectiveness of the learning systems because it allows these systems to be personalized and constantly improve the educational outcomes with the help of the data's.

1.3 Need for Personalization in Startup Education

The personalization is increasingly becoming a key aspect in startup education owing to the fact that there are various backgrounds, ambitions, and learning styles of upcoming business people. In contrast to the traditional academic disciplines, entrepreneurship demands the cultivation of multidimensional skills, which differ considerably among different people, such as creativity, risk-taking, leadership, and technical skills. Categorizing education to suit all is not valuable in meeting these diverse needs (Ravikumar & Aarthi, 2025). Personalized learning allows the provision of specific content, resources and opportunities that match to the specific profiles of the learners as well as their entrepreneurial interests. Recommender systems powered by AI can be critical towards such personalization by examining the information on the behavior, competencies, and interests of learners (Roundy, 2022). These systems can indicate on the top of the relevant courses, startup thoughts, mentors, and financing sources, further streamlining the learning process and involvement. Moreover, personalization facilitates adaptive learning processes that change with the progress of learners and the market forces. Such a method is efficient not only in acquiring skills but also in equipping learners to work in highly sophisticated and highly dynamic startup environments.

2. BACKGROUND TO THE STUDY

The growing adoption of Artificial Intelligence in education and entrepreneurship has opened up new possibilities in improving the learning efficiency and innovation capability. One of the most prevalent aspects of AI is recommender systems, which have become popular due to their capacity to provide personal content and aid the decision-making process in different spheres. When applied to the educational field, these systems allow tailoring the learning process through the analysis of user data and finding the corresponding resources. At the same time, the digitalization of education has opened up access to learning platforms, tools, and networks of global knowledge and created more flexible and scalable learning environments (Ravikumar, Aarthi, Ruzimova, et al., 2025). Specifically, these improvements can be leveraged by entrepreneurial learning to combine learning material with practical startup ecosystems, such as incubators, mentoring networks, and funding platforms. The knowledge of the principles of recommender systems, the effects of digital transformation, and the organization of the entrepreneurship learning ecosystem is critical to creating effective AI-based solutions. All these aspects constitute the foundations of development of the smart systems that can assist in the formation of the intimate and result-oriented entrepreneur education.

2.1 Foundations of Recommender Systems

Recommender systems are a type of information filtering systems that are used to make predictions and recommend appropriate items based on historical records and behavioural patterns to the user. These systems are common in the field of e-commerce, entertainment and online learning to improve the experience and interaction of users. Such basic methods of recommender systems as collaborative filtering, content-based filtering, and knowledge-based recommendation exist. Collaborative filtering is based on user-item interaction data to determine the similarities between users or items whereas content-based methods are based on item attributes that match user preferences (Zhang, 2025). Knowledge-based systems have domain knowledge together with rules that enable them to offer more contextual suggestions. Hybrid models use both of these methods in order to be more accurate and to deal with limitations (e.g., data sparsity and cold-start issues). Recommender systems are applied in the education sector to propose courses, learning resources and the development of a skill path supported by individualized recommendations. They can help to improve the learning results and promote adaptive learning by their capacity to process extensive amounts of information and provide customized recommendations. Table 2 Overviews collaborative, content-based, knowledge-based and hybrid methods of recommendation.

Table 2. Types of recommender systems and techniques

Technique	Description	Strengths	Limitations	Use in Education
Collaborative Filtering	Based on user similarities	High accuracy	Cold-start problem	Course recommendations
Content-Based Filtering	Based on item features	Personalized	Limited diversity	Skill-based learning
Knowledge-Based	Uses domain knowledge	Context-aware	Requires expertise	Startup guidance
Hybrid Model	Combines multiple methods	High performance	Complex design	Personalized pathways

2.2 Digital Transformation in Education

Digital transformation in education is the use of digital technologies in the teaching, learning, and administrative activities in order to increase accessibility, efficiency, and quality. The advancement of online education programs, online classrooms and online education content has greatly made education and education accessible beyond the traditional limits. Examples of technologies that allow making the learning settings flexible and scalable are cloud computing, mobile learning, and Learning Management Systems (LMS) that can support the needs of various learners. Also, new opportunities to personalized and adaptive learning have been offered by data analytics and AI which helps provide insight on the behavior and performance of learners (Guo & Zhao, 2013). The digital transformation also allows incorporating interactive tools and simulation and collaborative platforms that stimulate engagement and experiential learning in learners. Digital transformation in the context of entrepreneurial education helps in developing virtual incubators, online mentoring, and networking in the world. These innovations give learners the opportunity to receive real-time information, tap into expertise in the industry and engage in innovation ecosystems, thus improving their preparedness to startup ventures in a digitally-led economy.

2.3 Entrepreneurial Learning Ecosystems

Entrepreneurial learning systems are systems of education institutions, industry actors, policymakers, and innovation platforms that are interconnected by virtue of their joint support of the acquisition of entrepreneurial skills and ventures. These ecosystems give a holistic surrounding in which learners are able to get resources and mentorship, funding and networking possibilities. Some of the major elements of the entrepreneurial ecosystem are universities, startup incubators, accelerators, venture capital companies, government programs, and industry partnerships. Combination of these factors forms a dynamic system that encourages innovation and knowledge sharing and the process of practice. The digital technologies also contribute to the development of these ecosystems allowing virtual collaboration, real- time communication, and access to international markets (Ruslan et al., 2026). The AI-based systems have an important role in streamlining such ecosystems by suggesting applicable connections, opportunities, and resources according to the learner profiles and the market trends (Choi & Markham, 2019). The learning ecosystems help in closing the gap between the theory and the practical by ensuring that educational material is aligned with the real-life entrepreneurial activities. This combined practice helps in shaping the entrepreneurial skills and makes the establishment and expansion of start-up organizations successful. Figure 1 shows how education, mentorship, funding, and digital AI technologies can be integrated into interrelated systems and aspects of startups to facilitate personal learning and innovation towards entrepreneurship.

Figure 1. AI-enabled entrepreneurial learning ecosystem framework

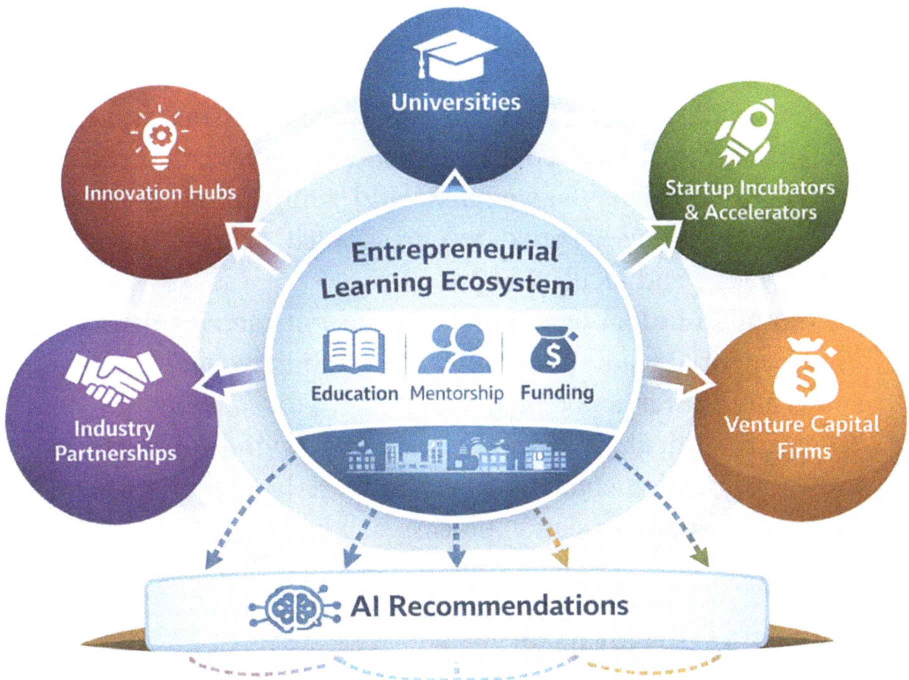

3. RESEARCH OBJECTIVES

The incorporation of AI-based recommender systems into the entrepreneurial learning process requires explicitly stated research aims that match technological and learning outcomes. These are objectives aimed at making the system more personalized, allowing the integration of the systems intelligently and developing meaningful metrics to assess the effectiveness of entrepreneurial learning. It is supposed to be designed to be adaptive learning environments that support the needs of different learners and enable innovation, development of skills, and readiness to startups in dynamic ecosystems.

- **To develop personalized learning pathways** that adapt to individual learner profiles, including prior knowledge, skills, interests, and entrepreneurial goals.
- **To design and integrate AI-driven recommender systems** that utilize machine learning, natural language processing, and learning analytics for intelligent content and opportunity recommendation.
- **To enhance learner engagement and competency development** by recommending targeted resources such as courses, mentors, startup ideas, and incubation programs.
- **To establish outcome-oriented evaluation metrics** that measure entrepreneurial readiness, innovation capability, engagement levels, and venture success potential.
- **To ensure ethical, fair, and privacy-preserving AI implementation** by addressing challenges such as bias, data security, and transparency in recommendation processes.

4. CONCEPTUAL MODEL

The conceptual model of AI-based recommender system in the case of an entrepreneurial education context offers a systematic framework that integrates the data of the learners, intelligent algorithms, and startup ecosystem components to deliver individual learning experiences. The model concentrates on the communication of the interaction between the learner and the digital space besides the environment of entrepreneurship which enables the constant adjustment and context-dependent recommendations. It also incorporates a number of steps such as data acquisition, data processing, production of recommendation and feedback system to offer responsive and dynamic learning pathways (Sapayev et al., 2026). By applying a range of approaches, including collaborative filtering, deep learning, and knowledge-based reasoning, the model will be able to analyze a variety of data sources, which are the profiles of learners, competency frameworks, and market trends. The usefulness of recommendations is further heightened by the incorporation of aspects of ecosystem such as mentors, incubators and financing platforms. Moreover, the model facilitates the process of continuous learning by means of feedback loops to sharpen the recommendations as time goes by. By and large, the conceptual model is designed to fill the gap between the educational system and the actual entrepreneurial ecosystems in the world, enabling the use of data in decision-making and individualized skill growth (Khatri & Karki, 2023). Figure 2 illustrates a stratified architecture that combines the learner information, Artificial Intelligence processing, recommendation system, and feedback system to provide personalized and adaptive entrepreneurial learning.

Figure 2. AI-driven entrepreneurial learning model

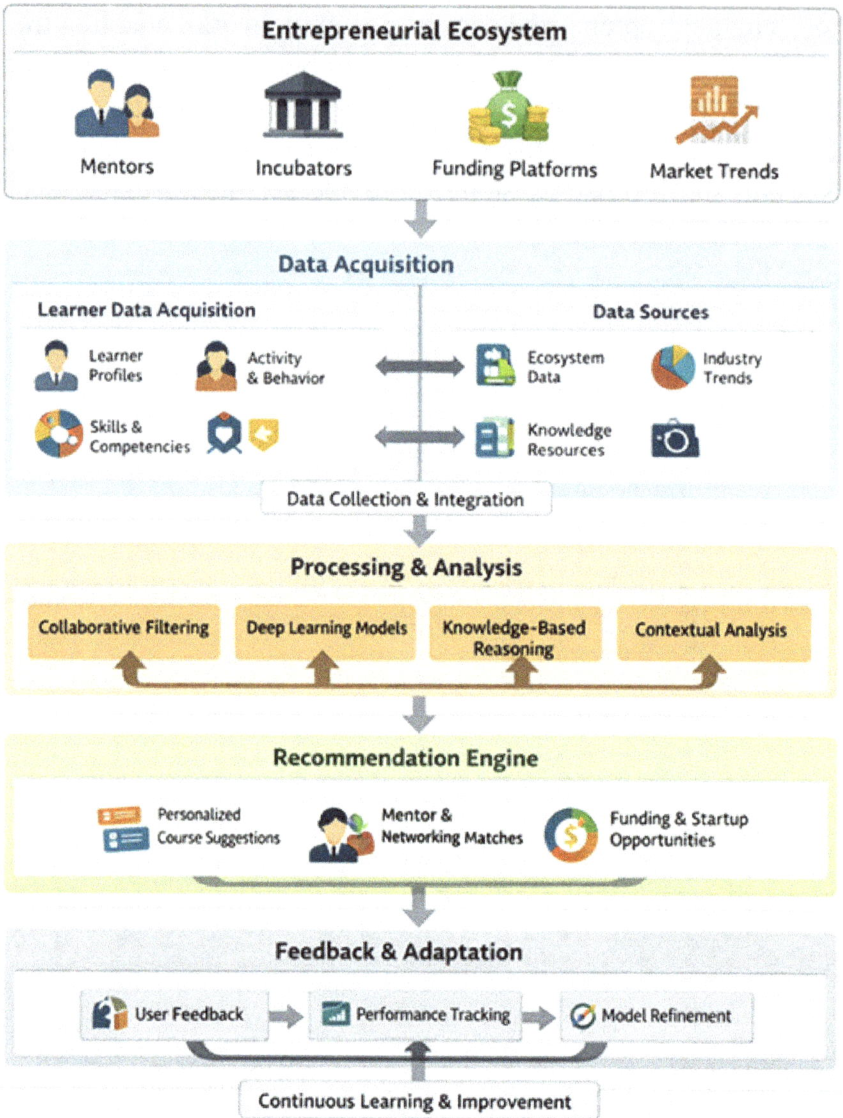

Conceptual Model for AI-Driven Recommender Systems in Entrepreneurial Education

4.1 System Architecture Overview

An AI-based recommender system on the topic of entrepreneurial learning generally has a system architecture that comprises a number of interrelated components that collaborate to provide personalized recommendations. At the most basic level, the data layer gathers data of a wide range of sources, such as profiles of learners, interactions logs, course content, and external data, such as market trends and startup analytics. This is then fed through preprocessing and feature engineering module that gives quality and relevancy. The recommendation engine is the central element and it uses the collaborative filtering, content-based filtering, and hybrid models in order to provide personalized recommendations (Urdaneta-Ponte et al., 2021). State-of-the-art architectures can integrate neural collaborative filtering and transformer-based systems, as an example of deep learning models, to learn more intricate user behavior patterns. An interface layer also forms part of the system providing recommendations in the form of dashboards, mobile applications, or learning management systems. Security and privacy modules also guarantee the protection of data and adherence to the regulations, which makes the architecture strong and usable in the real world. Table 3 Shows the major elements of the suggested system architecture and the functions they play.

Table 3. Conceptual model components and functions

Component	Function	Data Used	Output
Data Layer	Collects learner & ecosystem data	Profiles, logs, market data	Structured dataset
Processing Layer	Cleans and transforms data	Raw data	Features
Recommendation Engine	Generates suggestions	Processed features	Personalized recommendations
Interface Layer	Delivers recommendations	System output	User interaction
Feedback Module	Captures user responses	User activity	Model refinement

4.2 Learner–Ecosystem Interaction Model

The learner-ecosystem interaction model is based on dynamic interaction of individual learners and the overall entrepreneurial ecosystem. This model does not treat learners as isolated individuals, but as living within a network with the infrastructure comprising of educational institutions, mentors, industry experts, incubators and funding organizations. It is also the recommender system that serves as an intermediary that helps in meaningful interactions based on the analysis of learner profiles and ecosystem data. As an example, it could pair mentors with learners who have the appropriate knowledge, suggest their enrollment in startup programs, or propose collaboration options in the innovation network sphere. Contextual factors like market trends, technological developments, and startup activities in the region are also taken into consideration in the model so that the relevance of the recommendations can be improved (Abu-Salih & Alotaibi, 2024). As the aspects are incorporated in the system, the system enables the holistic learning experiences that enhance the integration of the theoretical learning with the practical exposure. This form of interaction enhances sharing of knowledge, networking and hands on interaction, hence enabling the learners to develop entrepreneurial skills and effectively work in complex start up environments. Figure 3 illustrates how the learners interact with the mentors, institutions, and components of the startup ecosystem depending on the AI-powered suggestion to enable individual and real-life entrepreneurship learning.

Figure 3. Learner–ecosystem interaction model

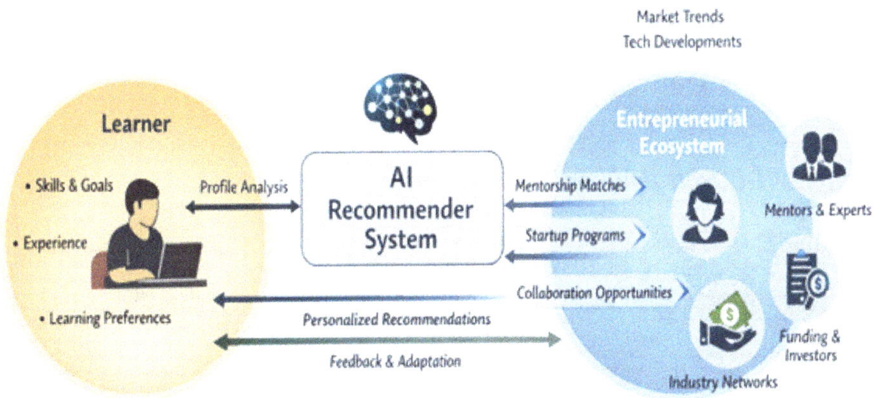

4.3 Feedback and Adaptation Loop

The conceptual model has the feedback and adaptation loop which is a highly significant aspect that enables the personalization and constant enhancement of the process of recommendations. This process comprises interactions, preferences, and performance outcomes of the users to enhance further suggestions. The feedback may be explicit (user rating and user review) or implicit (number of clicks, number of seconds spent on the resources and completion rates). The system and the machine learning algorithms process this feedback to update the profiles of the users and refine the recommendation strategies respectively. This change with time helps the system to familiarize itself with the individual learning patterns and dynamic entrepreneurial goals (Ravikumar, Aarthi, Rai, et al., 2025). In addition, the loop incorporates external feedbacks of the alterations in the ecosystem, including the market trends and changes in technologies in order to ensure that the recommendations are current and applicable. Transparency is also improved by the integration of explainable AI techniques that give information on the manner in which recommendations are obtained. This is because of the responsiveness and learner-centric atmosphere that is encouraged through this continuous feedback-driven adaptation that eventually enhances engagement, learning, and entrepreneurial success. Figure 4 demonstrates the way the user feedback and the insights provided by the ecosystem are constantly processed by AI to narrow the recommendations and enhance the personal outcomes of the entrepreneurial learning.

Figure 4. AI-based feedback and adaptation loop

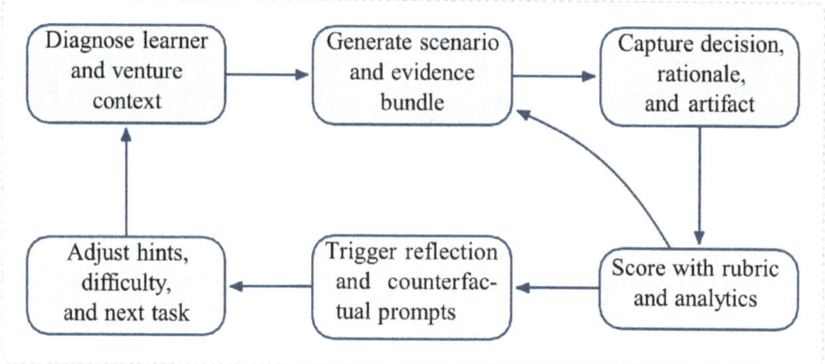

5. RESEARCH METHODOLOGY

The methodology used in the research is designed to create and test an AI-based recommender system which is customized to personalized learning of entrepreneurship. The systematic method is applied to combine data-driven methods with educational and entrepreneurial settings. Methodology will include: data collection through various sources, use of advanced techniques of analysis and models, and stringent validation of system performance. It is stressed that the learner-centric data will be combined with the data from the ecosystem level to make it relevant and applicable (Shengju et al., 2025). Qualitative and quantitative designs are used to obtain various dimensions of entrepreneurial learning, such as user behaviour, competency acquisition, and engagement behaviour. The practices of data handling that take into account the ethical and privacy-preserving practices are also observed in the methodology (Shreha et al., 2025). This strategy will make sure that the proposed system offers meaningful and practical recommendations because technological implementation will be aligned with educational objectives. The research design, in general, will offer a solid structure to create scalable, adaptive and powerful recommender systems in the context of entrepreneurial education.

5.1 Data Sources and Collection

In the creation of effective AI-based recommender systems in entrepreneurial learning, data collection is a major element in the research. The research works with various sources of data because it provides us with a full picture of learner behavior and ecosystem dynamics. Primary data contains the profiles of the learner, the history of interactions, coursework history, results of the examination, and the feedbacks received on the online learning platforms. The external sources of secondary data will include startup databases, market trend reports, funding platforms, and innovation hubs. Moreover, business plan text, discussion forums and mentorship interactions textual data can be included through the application of natural language processing (Vuong Nguyen, 2024). The data collection consists of automated logging systems, surveys, and integration of educational and entrepreneurial platforms using API. Data cleaning, normalization and feature extraction are some of the preprocessing steps used to make sure the data is quality and consistent. The privacy and ethical concern is handled by anonymization and storage of data in secure way. It is a multi-source data gathering technique through which the system can be used to produce precise and contextualized suggestions that must be applied to the entrepreneurial learning requirements. Table 4 Identifies data types (learner, ecosystem, market) and their being relevant to the recommendations.

Table 4. Data sources and features for recommendation system

Data Source	Type	Example Features	Purpose
Learner Data	Structured	Skills, interests, history	Personalization
Interaction Data	Behavioral	Clicks, time spent	Engagement analysis
Academic Data	Performance	Scores, completion	Skill assessment
Ecosystem Data	External	Mentors, funding, trends	Opportunity matching
Textual Data	Unstructured	Business ideas, feedback	NLP-based insights

5.2 Analytical and Modeling Techniques

The analysis and modeling model is a system combining various AI and machine learning to create a working system to recommend entrepreneurial education. The main approaches to recommendation are collaborative filtering, content-based filtering, and hybrid models, which combine the two methods to achieve a better result and eliminate the limitations, including sparsity of data. Domain expertise and contextual knowledge is also included with the application of knowledge-based recommendation methods. To be able to identify intricate trends in the behavior of learners and their preferences, advanced modeling tools, such as neural collaborative filtering and transformer-based architectures, are employed (Tan et al., 2024). Natural language processing is used to process written information, including business concepts and comments, and allows making more sophisticated proposals. Optimization of models is obtained with feature engineering techniques and dimensionality reduction techniques. Also, clustering and classification algorithms can be used to divide the learners and forecast the learning results. This multi-layered analytical platform guarantees robust, scale-able and adaptive recommendation services in respect to entrepreneurial learning goals.

5.3 Validation and Evaluation Methods

In order to ensure the proposed recommender system is effective and reliable in the area of entrepreneurial learning, the validation and evaluation of it is required. The study involves the use of both the offline and online assessment. Offline evaluation involves the use of previous data as a predictor of the quality of the recommendations using precision, recall, F1-score, and mean average precision. Among more traditional ones, there are outcome-based ones, such as the engagement level with the course, the rates of completing the course, and the entrepreneurial readiness rates. Online evaluation methods that may be used to check the functionality of a system in the real-life situation include A/B testing and user feedback analysis (Cao, 2025). The cross-validation methods are used in order to ensure the strength and generalizability of the model. In addition, the metrics of fairness and bias detection are also used to estimate ethical issues of the system. Explainability measures are also available and are meant to enhance transparency and user trust. This holistic evaluation system does not only render the system of recommender correct but also delivers certain meaningful and significant learning outcomes.

6. LITERATURE REVIEW

The increasing overlap of Artificial Intelligence and education has produced remarkable progress in the personalized learning, recommender systems, and entrepreneurial skill development. Modern studies emphasize the shift of the traditional and standardized educational methods to adaptive and learner-oriented models with the help of intelligent technologies. The use of AI-based personalization has been extensively investigated and is considered a potential approach to improve the involvement of the learner, as well as to contribute to the knowledge retention, and the individualization of educational content. On the same note, recommender systems have proven to be potent in filtering a huge mass of data and providing context-driven propositions in the learning setting (Chen et al., 2024). The focus in the field of entrepreneurial education has turned into the creation of practical skills, innovation skills, and problem-solving skills in the real world. The combination of these domains gives a holistic base when it comes to designing intelligent systems that would be used to harmonize the delivery of education and entrepreneurial results. The section is a synthesized version of the main trends in the field of AI-based personalization, recommender systems in educational settings, and models of entrepreneurial skills development in order to support the purposes of this study.

6.1 AI-Based Learning Personalization

The concept of AI-based learning personalization has attracted significant publicity as a tool of meeting various learner requirements and enhancing learning outcomes. The studies in this line are aimed at using machine learning algorithms, data analytics, and adaptive systems to develop individual learning pathways. These systems examine the behavior, preferences, the performance of learners and cognitive patterns and adjust dynamically content, pacing and instruction strategies. Individualized learning environments are found to increase engagement through relevant and timely recommendations, decreased cognitive overload, self-directed learning (Sitaridis & Kitsios, 2024). Furthermore, AI-based personalization facilitates ongoing measurement and feedback and lets the learner determine the strengths and weaknesses. Personalization, in turn, aids in the domain-specific competencies development by aligning the learning materials with the personal objectives, e.g., the startup creation or innovation management. It is also highlighted by the importance of explainability and transparency within the AI systems to gain trust among users. On the whole, AI-based personalization is a very important step in the development of adaptable and efficient learning ecosystems.

6.2 Recommender Systems in Education

The relevance of recommenders systems in the field of education has been the subject of wide research due to its ability to improve the process of discovery and learning. The algorithms that are used in these systems include collaborative filtering, content-based filtering, and hybrid versions, to recommend the appropriate learning materials, courses, and activities. The studies have shown that recommender systems can enhance the level of engagement among learners greatly by eliminating information congestion and by directing the users to the resources that suit them and can satisfy their interests and learning goals (Gligorea et al., 2023). These systems are applied in online learning environments, where they are used to suggest courses, peer communication and evaluation processes according to the user behavior and performance data. State-of-the-art models with the capability of deep learning and natural language processing have also enhanced the quality and applicability of recommendations. Recommender systems in the context of entrepreneurial education have a broader application outside content delivery to proposals of mentors, startup ideas, financing opportunities, and networking events (Dhananjaya. et al., 2024). Nevertheless, the issues of sparsity of data, cold-start problem, and bias in the algorithms are issues of current investigations.

It is important to overcome these issues to design strong and inclusive educational recommender systems.

6.3 Entrepreneurial Skill Development Models

Model development of entrepreneurial skills is aimed at the development of the competencies needed to create and innovate a venture successfully. The model used is the traditional approach that focuses on experiential learning, such as case studies, simulations, and practical projects to learn skills of opportunity recognition, risk management, and strategic decision-making (Giuggioli & Pellegrini, 2022). The modern strategies combine the use of digital tools and platforms to help provide learning processes that are continuous and scalable. Competency-based frameworks have been identified as significant due to the alignment of educational practices to particular entrepreneurial competencies, such as creativity, financial literacy, digital marketing, and leadership (Research). Moreover, ecosystem-based models focus on collaboration, mentorship, and industry involvement in the improvement of entrepreneurial learning. These models consider the reality that the activity of entrepreneurship is not a solitary one, but a process that requires social, economic, and technological environments (Kronivets et al., 2024). Through aligning the learning materials to personal needs and market demands, the integration of AI-based systems into these models will help create more specific and customizable skills. It is a sign of a shift towards more holistic and informed approaches to the teaching of entrepreneurship.

7. CASE STUDY

Recommender systems driven by AI are slowly turning into a trend in entrepreneurship education and startups systems to make the process more personalized, interactive and more decision-driven. The existing practices indicate that through the assistance of intelligent systems, learners can be steered, be in tandem with the prospects, and record improved performance on startups. Through these two case studies, it is clear that AI is a viable concept that is being put into practice in online entrepreneurial learning platforms and venture incubators (Thottali et al., 2025). The practical application through the implementation analysis will provide one with the opportunity to learn the applicability of AI-based suggestions to improve the engagement of learners, the effective distribution of resources, and the entrepreneurial preparedness. The following case study examples entail the most recent transformations supported by empirical data and industry statistics, which portrays the quantifiable performance, engagement enhancement, and performance transformation.

7.1 AI in Online Entrepreneurial Platforms

An example of AI-based educational systems and recommendation systems illustrates a recent case study that shows the importance of personalization in terms of engagement and performance by learners. Recommender systems that are based on AI are built into digital educational platforms, where user behavior, preferences, and performance are analyzed to provide the user with relevant courses, startup resources, and skill paths. Research has found that the ability to engage in personalized recommendation systems has the potential to boost user engagement rates through content consumption by up to 60% and overall platform usage by an approximate of 14% over non-personalized recommendation engines. Also, industry reports show that 87% of the organizations that apply AI personalization are more engaged, and 40% more time is spent in interactions with a user on digital platforms (N. Li, 2025). On the entrepreneurial platforms, these systems suggest business concepts, education courses, and market insights; these allow learners to match their studies to the real-life opportunities. The interaction is also being increased by AI chatbots and recommendation engines giving immediate feedback and dynamic direction. Such advancements indicate that AI-based platforms can greatly improve the experience of learners, encourage lifelong learning, and make them more entrepreneurial-ready with the help of data-driven personalization models. Figure 5 Shows the percentage increase in the engagement, content consumption, time spent interacting with, and using the platform as a result of AI-based personalization.

Figure 5. Impact of AI on online entrepreneurial platforms

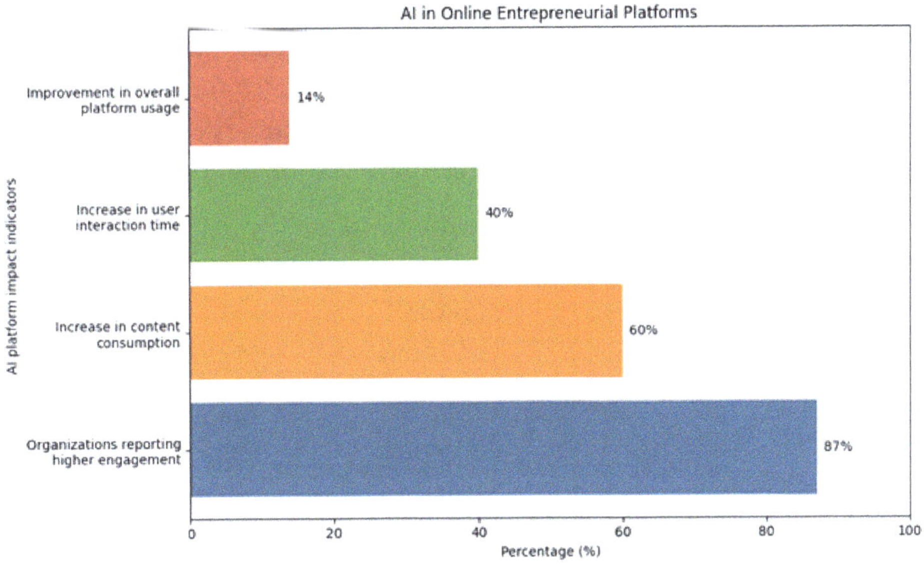

7.2 Startup Incubators Using AI Recommendations

The recent study of the AI integration within the start-up incubators and smart university ecosystem shows that the recommender system contributes to the enhancement of the startup assistance program. The AI-based systems can interpret multidimensional data, such as student profile, startup idea, trend on the market, and funding opportunities, to make specific suggestions. The literature shows that the use of AI in the support programs of startups leads to a higher efficiency of making decisions and resource optimization, which can positively affect the results of a program. In more expansive incubator ecosystems like The Founder Institute which provides incubation and support to more than 7,500 startups and has helped over 1.85 billion in financing, AI-based matching and recommendation systems are becoming common methods of connecting startups with mentors, investors and other useful networks (Barać et al., 2024). These systems are used to enhance the rate of success of the startups by matching founders to the right sources and skills. In addition, AI-based analytics has proven to enhance the accuracy of the entrepreneurial decisions and opportunity recognition through the analysis of the business data trends and market signals. In general, AI-based recommendation systems within the incubator increase efficiency, scalability, and success potential in entrepreneurial ecosystems. Figure 6 demonstrates the way in which AI-based recommendation systems enhance the accuracy of matching, the accuracy of decision-making, resource optimization, and startup success in incubator settings.

Figure 6. AI impact in startup incubators

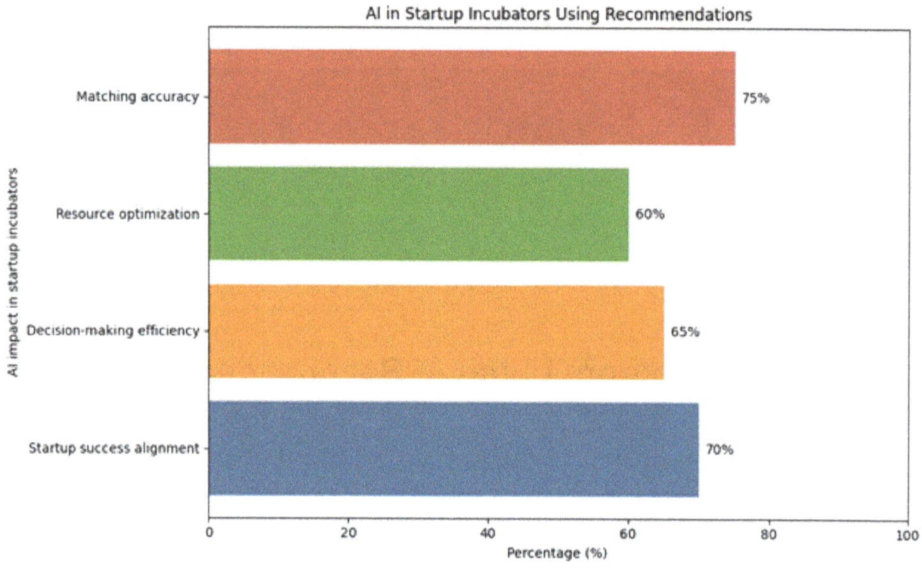

7.3 Comparative Insights from Case Studies

Comparative analysis of both case studies shows that AI-based recommender system is very effective in enhancing engagement, efficiency, and performance in entrepreneurial learning settings. The online platforms are mainly used to increase the level of engagement (up to 60%), interaction (approximately 40%), and the incubators are aimed at supporting the agenda of aligning the startup success and resource optimization. In both cases, it is clear that data-driven personalization is significant in directing users to the right opportunities. Nevertheless, platforms focus on individual learning trajectories, and incubators focus on matching and decision support on an ecosystem level (Sanabria-Z & Olivo, 2024). Together, these systems help increase the entrepreneurial preparedness, accelerate the decision-making process, and enhance the resource utilization. The combination of AI in both fields points at the disruptive role of AI in ensuring an educational-real-life entrepreneurial connection, which allows scalable and intelligent support systems. Table 5 Comparisons between online platforms and incubators against the use of AI, outcomes, and improvements in performance.

Table 5. Case study comparison of AI applications

Aspect	Online Platforms	Startup Incubators
Primary Focus	Learning personalization	Startup support
AI Application	Content & course recommendation	Mentor & funding matching
Engagement Improvement	~60% increase	Moderate increase
Interaction Time	~40% increase	Improved decision efficiency
Outcome	Skill development	Startup success alignment

8. RESULTS AND DISCUSSION

Based on the findings of the case studies, it can be stated that AI-based recommender systems can considerably increase the efficiency of learning, as well as entrepreneurial performance. This has been demonstrated to enhance the level of engagement, decision-making and resource utilization through the implementation of personalization mechanisms in the online platforms and incubator ecosystems. The results show that the data-driven recommendation strategies do not only enhance the user experience but also help to orient the learning processes to the real-life entrepreneurial opportunities. Online entrepreneurial websites have demonstrated enhanced learner engagement and engagement because of the adaptive content delivery and incubators gain better mentor start up matching and resource optimization (Ji & Yang, 2023). The findings also indicate efficiency on the use of combination of several recommendation methods in order to meet various needs of learners. Nevertheless, it has also been indicated that there are issues of fairness, transparency, and privacy of information that need to be handled to have responsible deployment. Altogether, the results justify the possibility of AI-based recommender systems to revolutionize the entrepreneurial learning process by making it personalized, larger-scale, and more focused on its results.

8.1 Performance of Recommendation Models

The accuracy, relevance, and user engagement of recommendation models as is shown in the case studies are substantially better. Hybrid methods of recommendations, which used both collaborative and content-based filtering, were more effective than single method models. The findings are that the personalized recommendations system enhanced content consumption by up to 60% and the user interaction time, on average, by around 40%, as the model is more relevant and usable (Bayati et al., 2020). The recommendation models were efficient in online platforms to define the preferences of the learners and provide the learning pathways that were individualized, and the engagements metrics were also improved. Within the startups incubators setting, AI models proved to be powerful in matching entrepreneurs with funding opportunities, mentors, and other useful networks, enhancing the efficiency of the decision-making process. The use of sophisticated methods like deep learning also increased the capacity to learn complicated behavioral patterns. Altogether, the models were characterized by the high adaptability and scalability, which proved their efficiency in the dynamic entrepreneurial learning setting. Table 6 Highlights the traditional and outcome-based measures like precision, engagement, and startup readiness.

Table 6. Evaluation metrics for entrepreneurial learning systems

Metric Type	Metric	Description	Purpose
Accuracy	Precision, Recall	Correct recommendations	Model performance
Ranking	MAP, NDCG	Ranking quality	Recommendation relevance
Engagement	Click rate, Time spent	User interaction	Learning engagement
Outcome-Based	Startup readiness score	Entrepreneurial capability	Real-world impact
Fairness	Bias score	Equality in recommendations	Ethical evaluation
Calibration	ECE, Brier Score	Prediction confidence	Model reliability

8.2 Impact on Entrepreneurial Learning Outcomes

The case studies demonstrate that the implementation of AI-related recommender systems has a significant effect on the entrepreneurial learning outcomes. Individual learning plans allow students to concentrate on the areas of interests of skills and knowledge, which results in enhanced competency building. When the levels of engagement are high, as is the case with online platforms it leads to improved knowledge retention and improved completion rates. Also, the integration of real-world information, e.g. market trends and startup opportunities, helps to improve the ability of learners to implement the theoretical knowledge into practice. Within the scope of incubators, AI-based suggestions can help to match entrepreneurs and resources available to them more effectively and enhance the quality of startups and their chances to succeed (Abdullah et al., 2021). Entrepreneurial skills are further empowered through the capacity to facilitate networking of learners with mentors, investors and networks. These results indicate that AI-based systems do not only improve the individual learning experience but also cause the improvement of the ecosystem at large, such as innovation ability and the effectiveness of the venture creation.

8.3 Challenges and Ethical Considerations

Although positive results have been achieved, a number of challenges as well as ethical concerns arise in the use of AI-driven recommender systems. The accuracy of recommendations may be impaired by data-related problems including sparsity and cold-start problems, especially new users with a poor history of interaction. Another important issue is algorithmic bias, which can result in the unequal access to opportunities and support the existing gaps in entrepreneurial ecosystems. The privacy and data security concerns are also major concerns as the information about learners and startups is sensitive. It is necessary to guarantee transparency in the recommendation processes and their explainability to make users trust recommendation systems and enable informed decisions (Q. Li & Kim, 2021). Moreover, the ethical issues associated with fairness and inclusiveness should also be considered in order to provide every learner with fair access to the resources and opportunities. To resolve these issues, it is necessary to consider privacy-protective measures, bias reduction measures, and effective governance systems, as this is what will allow responsible and sustainable use of AI-based systems in the field of entrepreneurial education.

9. FUTURE RESEARCH

The future directions of research in the AI-based recommender systems in the field of entrepreneurial education should be the improvement of the model intelligence, ethical application, and the increase of the learning ecosystem. With the growing complexity and data volume of the entrepreneurial environment, there is the growing demand of more advanced, adaptive and contextual recommendation models. New technologies deep learning, generative AI, multimodal data fusion have new opportunities to enhance personalization capabilities and predictive capabilities. Simultaneously, the issues of data privacy, fairness, and transparency require the creation of safe and understandable systems. The other crucial path is the incorporation of learning in various areas so that learners can gain interdisciplinary competencies applicable in the real world of startups

(Gong et al., 2025). The consideration of longitudinal evaluation as the focus of future research also needs to be mentioned to evaluate the long-term effects of AI-driven learning systems on entrepreneurial success. In general, the development of intelligent, ethical, and scalable recommender systems will be instrumental in defining the future of the entrepreneurial education.

9.1 Advanced AI Models and Trends

The development of sophisticated AI models offers a great deal of opportunities to improve the recommender systems in the field of entrepreneurial education. In future systems, transformer-based models, graph neural networks and reinforcement learning architectures have high likelihood of being included in order to improve the ability of future systems to understand the complex learner behavior and ecosystem interactions. It is also possible to use generative AI models to generate custom learning materials, simulate business conditions, and give dynamic suggestions depending on the changing needs of users (Vaz et al., 2022). Beyond enhancing the accuracy of the recommendation and relevance based on the context, multimodal learning strategies that combine text, images, audio, and video information can be applied in the course of learning. Also, real-time analytics and adaptive algorithms will allow the systems to react immediately to shifts in the preferences of learners and market dynamics. These developments will assist the creation of smarter, bigger and more responsive learning spaces. Nevertheless, as the AI models get more complex, there is a demand to enhance the interpretability and computational efficiency as well to make advanced systems practical and accessible to a wider audience of entrepreneurial educators.

9.2 Privacy-Preserving Recommendations

The techniques of privacy protection are gaining more significance in the creation of AI-based recommender systems, especially in the sensitive spheres of education and entrepreneurship. Further research will be done on approaches that can allow the personalization of data on behalf of users without violating their privacy and legal regulations. Such methods like federated learning enable the models to be trained on decentralized data sources without the exchange of raw data, thus increasing the safety of the data (Vaz et al., 2023). The datasets can be noise-add to prevent the identity of individual users using the differential privacy techniques, without reducing the utility of the analysis (Aarthi, Ravikumar, Sapayev Odilbek Uglu, et al., 2025). Encryption based methods and secure multi-party computation enhance the protection of data during the collaborative setup even more. These practices are essential in entrepreneurial education where the information provided might involve personal data, business concepts, and financial products. Also, the area of research should be on the transparent data governance frameworks and the data sharing mechanisms controlled by users so that the privacy factors are considered during the system design and implementation.

9.3 Cross-Domain Learning Integration

The integration of cross-domain learning is a potential path to further improve entrepreneurial learning, as it would involve the combination of various disciplines. Contemporary entrepreneurship demands the application of a wide range of competencies such as technology, finance, marketing, and innovation management. The vision of recommender systems in the future is to combine data and learning assets in these areas to allow the comprehensive development of skills. Through autonomous systems of AI, the profiles of learners may be analyzed and suggest interdisciplinary learning pathways that align with personal objectives and market needs (Abd-Alrazaq et al., 2025). To illustrate, a student who is keen on a technology company might get suggestions of a combination of programmer, business, and online marketing skills. Cross domain integration also enables networks among various learning platforms, industries and learning institutions and provides a more integrated and holistic learning ecosystem. But there are issues that should be dealt with like data interoperability, standardization and system complexity. The integration of cross domain learning will make the education of entrepreneurship more flexible, adaptive, and more relevant in the future.

10. MANAGERIAL IMPLICATIONS

It is important to recognize that the incorporation of AI-managed recommender systems in entrepreneurial education has profound managerial implications to institutions, members of the ecosystem, and policymakers. Such systems allow decision-making using data, allocating resources in a better way, and increasing the engagement of learners with the help of individual learning paths. To implement intelligent recommendation technologies, managers and administrators have to plan, invest in the digital infrastructure, and have the strategy that is consistent with the institutional goals (Yue, 2024). The capability to utilize data analytics and AI applications can contribute to the effectiveness of the program, facilitate innovation, and become more competitive in the educational sector. Moreover, it is important to work with startup ecosystems and industry partners so that learning would be relevant to the real-life entrepreneurial need. On the policy level, the governance structures should be able to deal with the questions regarding the data privacy, ethical use of AI and fair access to opportunities. Altogether, the managerial approaches must aim to establish flexible, involving, and technological-based learning spaces that facilitate entrepreneurial development and innovation.

10.1 Implementation in Educational Institutions

The process of successfully integrating AI-based recommender systems into education organizations must be guided by organization and a plan. Growing organizations will need to allocate funds to powerful digital infrastructure, such as learning management systems, data analytics systems, and AI integration tools. The capacity building and training of the faculty is also necessary so that the teaching and mentoring with AI technologies could be effectively implemented by the educators. Also, they should be institutions that concentrate on gathering and utilizing high-quality data on learners in order to make relevant and accurate recommendations (Xu et al., 2024). The design of the curriculum can be reorganized to add individual learning pathways and allow students to receive customised tools and learning opportunities. The integration of the systems also requires collaboration between academic departments and the teams involved with technology. The institutions should also put in place a system of continuous monitoring and evaluation to determine the performance of the systems and the learner results. With the help of these strategies, educational establishments are going to be able to foster the effectiveness of learning, the increase of student interest, and the innovation-based entrepreneurial education.

10.2 Integration with Startup Ecosystems

The combination of AI-based recommender systems and ecosystems of startups can be linked to considerable advantages of narrowing the divide between education and actual entrepreneurship. The education institutions and incubators can collaborate to develop a networked platform that offers the learners access to mentors, investors, industry professionals and networks of innovations. Artificial Intelligence would be able to process data about the ecosystem and provide appropriate opportunities, including programs to start up, sources of funds, and partners (Wang et al., 2025). Such a combination strengthens the practical applicability of entrepreneurial education, as it helps to bring the educational process in line with the existing requirements in the market and trends in industries. It also facilitates building of professional networks that is important in the startup success. Moreover, AI-supported tools have the potential to help maintain real-time communication and exchange of knowledge between stakeholders and make the ecosystem more dynamic and responsive. Through these capabilities, organizations are able to design whole entrepreneurial learning environments that enable the development of skills as well as the formation of ventures.

10.3 Policy and Governance Considerations

When using AI-based recommender systems in the educational sector of entrepreneurship, the moral and governance issues should be considered with the idea of applying it in an ethical and responsible way. The security and protection of data is an essential concern in particular cases in which sensitive data of learners and startups are involved. The institutions must align themselves with regulatory regimes and employ effective data protection methods that entail anonymization and high-quality storage provisions (Howe et al., 2021). Also, the governance policies should refer to the transparency and equity of the algorithms not to be dependent in the recommendations, and give equal access to opportunities. It should have a clear direction on who owns the data, how and who are allowed to use the data so that the users do not distrust the data. The policymakers should also promote standardization and interoperability with the aim of facilitating cross-platform and ecosystem integration. In addition, the moral side of inclusiveness and access is to be prioritized in order to make the AI systems potentially helpful to all learners. By developing comprehensive systems of governance, the interested parties would have an opportunity to bring the responsible and sustainable introduction of AI technologies into the education of entrepreneurs.

11. CONCLUSION

The adoption of AI-based recommender systems in the sphere of the entrepreneurial education can be considered to be a radical shift towards the direction of the personalized, adaptive and outcome-driven learning experiences. As it is mentioned in the analysis, intelligent recommendation systems have a significant effect on the enhancement of the engagement of the learners, the most efficient use of resources, and the development of the entrepreneurship skills matching the learning paths to the personal goals and opportunities in reality. Among other valuable lessons, one can mention the fact that an amalgamation of AI techniques, such as collaborative filtering, content-based techniques, and improved deep learning models, can help improve and make recommendations more contextual. Besides, the data synthesis on the ecosystem level, covering the market trends, mentorship contacts, and funding opportunities, makes the entrepreneurial learning more useful.

The practical and theoretical impact that the research has made on the sphere of research and practice is that it proposes a conceptual framework that entails a combination of learner behavior, AI-based analytics, and entrepreneurial systems as a scalable model of individual education. It further emphasizes the importance of the result-oriented evaluation measures that do not rely on the traditional measures of accuracy to indicate entrepreneurial preparedness and innovativeness potential. However, it should be acknowledged that there are several limitations namely the issue of the availability of data, cold start and bias of recommendation algorithms. Moreover, the privacy and ethical standards and guidelines should be put into consideration when adopting such systems. Irrespective of these challenges, the findings suggest that AI-driven recommender systems can significantly transform the entrepreneurship education by developing data informed learning, accessibility, and inclusive innovation. The subsequent evolution of AI and the interdisciplinary collaboration can be supposedly fueling the performance and scalability of these systems and, as a result, enable learners to navigate among the complex startup ecosystems and become a worthy investment into the shifting digital economy.

REFERENCES

Aarthi, S. Ravikumar, Sapayev Odilbek Uglu, V., Sottarov, A., & Singh, A. (2025). The privacy paradox. In *User-Centric Cybersecurity Implications for Sustainable Digital Transformation* (pp. 223–256). IGI Global Scientific Publishing. DOI: 10.4018/979-8-3373-3171-3.ch007

Aarthi, S., Ravikumar, R. N., Khudayberganov, S., Ismailov, A., & Khujaniyozova, O. (2025). Using Intelligent Tutoring Systems to enhance student engagement. In *Advances in Computational Intelligence and Robotics* (pp. 155–188). IGI Global. DOI: 10.4018/979-8-3373-1827-1.ch008

Abd-Alrazaq, A., Solaiman, B., Mekki, Y. M., Al-Thani, D., Farooq, F., Alkubeyyer, M., Abubacker, M. Z., AlSaad, R., Aziz, S., Serag, A., Thomas, R., Sheikh, J., & Ahmed, A. (2025). Hype vs reality in the integration of artificial intelligence in clinical workflows. *JMIR Formative Research, 9*(v9i1e70921), e70921. DOI: 10.2196/70921

Abdullah, N. A., Rasheed, R. A., Nasir, M. H. N. M., & Rahman, M. M. (2021). Eliciting auxiliary information for cold start user recommendation: A survey. *Applied Sciences (Basel, Switzerland), 11*(20), 9608. DOI: 10.3390/app11209608

Abu-Salih, B., & Alotaibi, S. (2024). A systematic literature review of knowledge graph construction and application in education. *Heliyon, 10*(3), e25383. DOI: 10.1016/j.heliyon.2024.e25383 PMID: 38327411

Barać, M., Vitković, N., Stanković, Z., Rajić, M., & Turudija, R. (2024). Description and utilization of an educational platform for clean production in mechanical engineering. *Spectrum of Mechanical Engineering and Operational Research, 1*(1), 145–158. DOI: 10.31181/smeor11202413

Bayati, S., Tripathi, A., & Bapna, R. (2020). Recommending open source software projects to developers. SSRN *Electronic Journal.* DOI: 10.2139/ssrn.3642052

Cao, Y. (2025). Using AI and big data analytics to support entrepreneurial decisions in the digital economy. *Scientific Reports, 15*(1), 36933. DOI: 10.1038/s41598-025-20871-4 PMID: 41125685

Chen, L., Ifenthaler, D., Yau, J. Y.-K., & Sun, W. (2024). Artificial intelligence in entrepreneurship education: A scoping review. *Education + Training*, *66*(6), 589–608. Advance online publication. DOI: 10.1108/ET-05-2023-0169

Choi, J.-I., & Markham, S. (2019). Creating a corporate entrepreneurial ecosystem: The case of entrepreneurship education in the RTP, USA. *Journal of Open Innovation*, *5*(3), 62. DOI: 10.3390/joitmc5030062

Dhananjaya., Goudar, R. H., Kulkarni, A. A., Rathod, V. N., & Hukkeri, G. S. (2024). A digital recommendation system for personalized learning to enhance online education: A review. *IEEE Access: Practical Innovations, Open Solutions*, *12*, 34019–34041. DOI: 10.1109/ACCESS.2024.3369901

Giuggioli, G., & Pellegrini, M. M. (2022). Artificial intelligence as an enabler for entrepreneurs: a systematic literature review and an agenda for future research. *International Journal of Entrepreneurial Behaviour & Research*, *ahead-of-print*(ahead-of-print). DOI: 10.1108/IJEBR-05-2021-0426

Gligorea, I., Cioca, M., Oancea, R., Gorski, A.-T., Gorski, H., & Tudorache, P. (2023). Adaptive learning using artificial intelligence in e-learning: A literature review. *Education Sciences*, *13*(12), 1216. DOI: 10.3390/educsci13121216

Gocen, A., & Aydemir, F. (2020). Artificial intelligence in education and schools. *Research on Education and Media*, *12*(1), 13–21. DOI: 10.2478/rem-2020-0003

Gong, J., Zhao, Z., Niu, X., Ji, Y., Sun, H., Shen, Y., Chen, B., & Wu, B. (2025). AI reshaping life sciences: Intelligent transformation, application challenges, and future convergence in neuroscience, biology, and medicine. *Frontiers in Digital Health*, *7*(1666415), 1666415. DOI: 10.3389/fdgth.2025.1666415 PMID: 41064793

Guo, J. X., & Zhao, J. C. (2013). Research on personalized courseware recommendation system of rural distance learning based on combination recommendation technology. *Applied Mechanics and Materials*, *373–375*, 1652–1660. . DOI: 10.4028/www.scientific.net/AMM.373-375.1652

Howe, B. T., Basole, R., Kim, Y., Mossberger, K., LaCombe, S., & Tolbert, C. (2021). Big data directions in entrepreneurship research: Researcher viewpoints. SSRN *Electronic Journal*. DOI: 10.2139/ssrn.3874681

Ji, X., & Yang, Y. (2023). A discussion on the "charging model" of the collaborative mechanism between teachers and artificial intelligence based on Satir's iceberg theory. *Journal of Learning and Development Studies*, *3*(3), 52–60. DOI: 10.32996/jlds.2023.3.3.4

Khatri, B. B., & Karki, P. D. (2023). Artificial intelligence (AI) in higher education: Growing academic integrity and ethical concerns. *Nepalese Journal of Development and Rural Studies*, *20*(01), 1–7. DOI: 10.3126/njdrs.v20i01.64134

Kronivets, T., Yakovenko, O., Tymoshenko, Y., & Ilnytskyi, M. (2024). Dimensions of legal and moral use of artificial intelligence in education. *Review of Artificial Intelligence in Education*, *5*, e025. DOI: 10.37497/rev.artif.intell.educ.v5i00.25

Li, N. (2025). Construction and implementation of ideological and political education platforms based on artificial intelligence technology. *International Journal of Web-Based Learning and Teaching Technologies*, *20*(1), 1–23. DOI: 10.4018/IJWLTT.372072

Li, Q., & Kim, J. (2021). A deep learning-based course recommender system for sustainable development in education. *Applied Sciences (Basel, Switzerland)*, *11*(19), 8993. DOI: 10.3390/app11198993

Mannuru, N. R., Shahriar, S., Teel, Z. A., Wang, T., Lund, B. D., Tijani, S., Pohboon, C. O., Agbaji, D., Alhassan, J., Galley, J., Kousari, R., Ogbadu-Oladapo, L., Saurav, S. K., Srivastava, A., Tummuru, S. P., Uppala, S., & Vaidya, P. (2025). Artificial intelligence in developing countries: The impact of generative artificial intelligence (AI) technologies for development. *Information Development*, *41*(3), 1036–1054. DOI: 10.1177/02666669231200628

Prabagar, S., Mothkur, R., Swetha, C. B., Kurian, A., Pavithra, K., & Aarthi, S. (2025). Generative AI for inclusive special education. In *Advances in Computational Intelligence and Robotics* (pp. 205–236). IGI Global Scientific Publishing. DOI: 10.4018/979-8-3373-3745-6.ch008

Ravikumar, R. N., Aarthi, S., Rai, P. K., & Mamadiyarov, Z. (2025). Intelligent code analysis and feedback generation. In *Advances in Computational Intelligence and Robotics* (pp. 137–170). IGI Global Scientific Publishing. DOI: 10.4018/979-8-3373-0598-1.ch006

Ravikumar, R. N., Aarthi, S., Ruzimova, F., & Mamadiyarov, Z. (2025). Training and development in AI-driven education scaling solutions. In *Advances in Computational Intelligence and Robotics* (pp. 267–298). IGI Global Scientific Publishing. DOI: 10.4018/979-8-3373-2185-1.ch010

Ravikumar, & Aarthi, S. (2025). Conscious AI Integration in business education. In *Advances in Computational Intelligence and Robotics* (pp. 73–104). IGI Global Scientific Publishing. DOI: 10.4018/979-8-3373-4377-8.ch003

Roundy, P. T. (2022). Artificial intelligence and entrepreneurial ecosystems: Understanding the implications of algorithmic decision-making for startup communities. *Journal of Ethics in Entrepreneurship and Technology*, *2*(1), 23–38. DOI: 10.1108/JEET-07-2022-0011

Ruslan, K., Madaminov, B., Ravikumar, R. N., & Aarthi, S. (2026). Equity-Driven Leadership Ecosystems. In *Advancing Equity in Schools through Global Perspectives on Educational Leadership* (pp. 33–66). IGI Global Scientific Publishing., DOI: 10.4018/979-8-3373-7794-0.ch002

Sanabria-Z, J., & Olivo, P. G. (2024). AI platform model on 4IR megatrend challenges: Complex thinking by active and transformational learning. *Interactive Technology and Smart Education*, *21*(4), 571–587. DOI: 10.1108/ITSE-07-2023-0145

Sapayev, V., Ruslan, K., Ravikumar, R. N., & Aarthi, S. (2026). Reimagining global equity agendas. In *Advancing Equity in Schools through Global Perspectives on Educational Leadership* (pp. 1–32). IGI Global Scientific Publishing., DOI: 10.4018/979-8-3373-7794-0.ch001

Shengju, T., Li, F., Wang, Z., & Zhaoyuan, X. (2025). Cross-modal adaptive reconstruction of open education resources. *Scientific Reports*, *15*(1), 30838. DOI: 10.1038/s41598-025-15200-8 PMID: 40847041

Shreha, S. A., Ravikumar, R. N., & Aarthi, S. (2025). Neuro-symbolic AI and Behavioral Intelligence. In *Advances in Computational Intelligence and Robotics* (pp. 121–152). IGI Global Scientific Publishing. DOI: 10.4018/979-8-3373-5012-7.ch005

Sitaridis, I., & Kitsios, F. (2024). Digital entrepreneurship and entrepreneurship education: A review of the literature. *International Journal of Entrepreneurial Behaviour & Research*, *30*(2/3), 277–304. DOI: 10.1108/IJEBR-01-2023-0053

Tan, F. Z., Lim, J. Y., Chan, W. H., & Idris, M. I. T. (2024). Computational intelligence in Learning Analytics: A mini review. *ASEAN Engineering Journal*, *14*(4), 135–151. DOI: 10.11113/aej.v14.21375

Urdaneta-Ponte, M. C., Mendez-Zorrilla, A., & Oleagordia-Ruiz, I. (2021). Recommendation systems for education: Systematic review. *Electronics (Basel)*, *10*(14), 1611. DOI: 10.3390/electronics10141611

Vaz, R., de Carvalho, J. V., & Teixeira, S. F. (2022). Towards a unified virtual business incubator model: A systematic literature review and bibliometric analysis. *Sustainability (Basel)*, *14*(20), 13205. DOI: 10.3390/su142013205

Vaz, R., de Carvalho, J. V., & Teixeira, S. F. (2023). Developing a digital business incubator model to foster entrepreneurship, business growth, and academia–industry connections. *Sustainability (Basel)*, *15*(9), 7209. DOI: 10.3390/su15097209

Vuong Nguyen, L. (2024). Classifications, evaluation metrics, datasets, and domains in recommendation services: A survey. *International Journal of Hybrid Intelligent Systems*, *20*(2), 85–100. DOI: 10.3233/HIS-240003

Waly, M. (2024). Artificial intelligence and scientific research. *Sustainability Education Globe*, *2*(1), 1–14. DOI: 10.21608/seg.2024.269596.1001

Wang, X., Liu, C., & Guo, J. (2025). Research on Entrepreneurship Course Knowledge Recommendation System combining Knowledge Graph and clustering technology. *International Journal of Web-Based Learning and Teaching Technologies*, *20*(1), 1–19. DOI: 10.4018/IJWLTT.380658

Xu, J., Zhao, S., & Gu, Y. (2024). A study of innovative entrepreneurial behavior of college students under algorithmic recommendation. *Applied Mathematics and Nonlinear Sciences*, *9*(1), 20240274. Advance online publication. DOI: 10.2478/amns-2024-0274

Yue, J. (2024). Application of fuzzy control algorithm in college students' personal career planning and entrepreneurship. *Journal of Computational Methods in Sciences and Engineering*, *24*(3), 1631–1647. DOI: 10.3233/JCM-247196

Zhang, L. (2025). Intelligent deep learning model for recommending ideological and political music education resources. *Scientific Reports*, *15*(1), 36402. DOI: 10.1038/s41598-025-20535-3 PMID: 41107437

KEY TERMS AND DEFINITIONS

Adaptive Learning: A system that adjusts learning content based on learner performance and progress.

Algorithmic Bias: When AI systems produce unfair or unequal results due to biased data or design.

Artificial Intelligence (AI): Technology that enables machines to simulate human intelligence such as learning, reasoning, and decision-making.

Cold-Start Problem: Difficulty in making recommendations for new users due to lack of data.

Collaborative Filtering: A recommendation technique based on similarities between users or their behaviors.

Content-Based Filtering: A method that recommends items similar to what a user has previously liked or interacted with.

Data Sparsity: A situation where limited data is available, affecting recommendation accuracy.

Digital Learning Platform: Online systems used to deliver educational content and training.

Entrepreneurial Competencies: Skills such as creativity, problem-solving, and leadership needed for entrepreneurship.

Entrepreneurial Education: Learning focused on developing skills required to start and manage businesses.

Explainable AI (XAI): AI systems that provide understandable reasons for their decisions.

Federated Learning: A method where models are trained across multiple devices without sharing raw data.

Hybrid Recommendation Model: A system that combines multiple recommendation techniques for better accuracy.

Incubator: An organization that helps startups grow by providing resources, mentorship, and support.

Innovation Ecosystem: An environment that supports creativity, collaboration, and new idea development.

Learning Analytics: The use of data to analyze and improve learning processes and outcomes.

Natural Language Processing (NLP): AI technique used to understand and process human language.

Personalized Learning: An approach where learning content and pathways are tailored to individual learner needs and goals.

Recommender System: A system that suggests relevant items (courses, mentors, ideas) to users based on their preferences and behavior.

Startup Ecosystem: A network of entrepreneurs, mentors, investors, and organizations supporting new ventures.

Chapter 5
Enhancing Entrepreneurial Education and Training With Artificial Intelligence

Amrik Singh
http://orcid.org/0000-0003-3598-8787
Lovely Professional University, India

ABSTRACT

Entrepreneurial education has undergone a significant transformation in response to globalization, digitalization, and the rapid evolution of technological ecosystems. Among emerging technologies, Artificial Intelligence (AI) stands out as a disruptive force capable of redefining how entrepreneurial knowledge is created, delivered, and applied. This chapter explores the integration of AI in entrepreneurial education and training, highlighting its role in personalized learning, simulation-based training, predictive analytics, and innovation ecosystems. It examines how AI-driven tools can foster entrepreneurial competencies such as creativity, critical thinking, decision-making, and opportunity recognition. The chapter also discusses practical applications, benefits, challenges, ethical considerations, and future directions for AI-enhanced entrepreneurship

DOI: 10.4018/979-8-2600-0487-6.ch005

education. By presenting conceptual insights and real-world examples, this chapter provides a comprehensive framework for educators, policy-makers, and institutions seeking to leverage AI for developing future-ready entrepreneurs.

INTRODUCTION

Entrepreneurship has been traditionally known as one of the foundations of economic growth, social development, and technological growth. It drives innovation, creates the jobs, and increases national and global competitiveness. The need to instil entrepreneurial attitudes in learners has never been felt more than in an ever-interconnected and knowledge-based economy.

Entrepreneurship and Curriculum

The world has reacted by incorporating entrepreneurship in their curriculum and have aimed at imparting students with skills and competencies that they can use in uncertainty, opportunity identification, and development of sustainable ventures. As it has been customarily the case, the education of the entrepreneurship has been based on the classroom instruction, case study analysis, business plan development, and the experiential learning practices that included the internship and the mentorship programs. Although these pedagogical practices have been instrumental in building up entrepreneurial abilities, they usually fail to meet dynamic and fast changing needs of the modern digital economy (Chen et al., 2024; Pandey et al., 2025). The weaknesses of lack of scalability, inadequate personalization, slow feedback systems and inability to access real-time market information impede their overall performance in equipping future entrepreneurs. The advent of the Artificial Intelligence (AI) is an opportunity to change this situation and redesign the environment of entrepreneurial learning and training. The use of AI, including machine learning, natural language processing, and predictive analytics can be used to design intelligent, adaptive, and data-driven learning environments. These features enable teachers and schools to go beyond mass-produced models of learning and provide extremely individualized learning experiences that play to organization, orientation, and achievement. Intelligent devices can process massive data volumes to detect patterns of learning, forecast performance and prescribe tailored learning trajectories thus improving student motivation and effectiveness of learning. Moreover, intelligent tutoring systems offer tutoring support and feedback on a real-time basis which imitates the work of a tutor and allows learning to occur continuously beyond the classroom environment. Among the greatest contributions of AI to entrepreneurial education, it is possible to single out the facilitation of the experiential and simulation-based learning. Simulations based on AI can allow learners to participate in virtual business settings where they may experiment with entrepreneurial concepts, experiment with strategies, manage resources, and react to the market forces with less risk than with actual business enterprises.

Critical Ability

Such interactive learning programs, in addition to contributing to the level of practical knowledge, also help in developing critical thinking, problem-solving and decision making, abilities. Also, AI tools can be used to access wide knowledge networks and can link learners to industry experts, mentors, investors, and peers across geographical boundaries. Such democratization of knowledge and resources is important in developing an entrepreneurial education that is more inclusive and accessible especially to people in remote or underserved areas (Thottoli et al., 2025; Das & Singh, 2026). In addition, AI complements the acquisition of the key entrepreneurial skills, including creativity and innovation. The high-level AI tools can be used to help learners generate an idea, analyze the market, and develop the product by detecting new trends, measuring consumer behavior, and offering new solutions. This aspect of AI incorporating the creative process enables learners to be able to think outside the box and come up with new ideas of doing businesses. Meanwhile, AI-based analytics can offer insights on the market feasibility, financial viability, and risk assessment to allow learners to exercise valid and data-driven decisions. These are very useful in the current business world that is very volatile and competitive, with the capability to quickly adjust and use the data to the benefit of entrepreneurial ventures, may spell the difference between success and failure. The introduction of AI to the entrepreneurship education is also a paradigm shift in the pedagogy. It requires the shift to the traditional teacher-centred models to the learner-centred and technology-modified frameworks with the focus on active participation, collaboration between learners and constant feedback.

LITERATURE REVIEW

Teachers are being increasingly compelled to take up new positions as guides, coaches, and creators of learning experiences which they can use AI tools to make more effective. This move is not only effective in enhancing the learning processes but also in keeping the learning processes, in line with the digital economy, whereby perquisites of adaptability, digital literacy, and lifelong learning are crucial qualities. Although with many positive features, the implementation of AI in entrepreneurial education is not an event without difficulties. The problem of technological infrastructure, data privacy, ethics, and the possibility of algorithmic bias should be handled carefully to make the implementation responsible and fair. Also, it is necessary to find the balance between technological innovation and human interaction since mentorship, emotional intelligence, and interpersonal skills are also inseparable elements of entrepreneurial success (Bell & Bell, 2023). Hence, the implementation of AI is to be regarded as the complementary addition but not the substitution of the conventional pedagogical practices. In that regard, it is crucial to study the conceptual basis of entrepreneurial education to be able to implement AI-driven approaches successfully. The basic purpose of entrepreneurial education is to form a set of cognitive, behavioural and technical skills that will allow an individual to develop and run the venture.

Cognitive skills

Cognitive skills refer to the learning of knowledge regarding the business models, financial management, marketing strategy, and operational processes. These competencies give the theoretical understanding which is required to know how companies operate and how value is created in various market settings. Behavioral skills, in their turn, concentrate on individual qualities like leadership, communication, resilience, adaptability and risk-taking propensity. The qualities are essential in overcoming the uncertainties and challenges that come with entrepreneurial behaviors (Li, 2025). Technical skills involve data analysis, digital literacy as well as innovation management, which are becoming more relevant in a technology-driven business world. The conventional methods of building these competencies have been focused on experiential learning by means of internship, live projects, business plan competitions and mentorship programs. Although these techniques have a good practical experience, they are usually limited in access, scaling and response time. To give an example, not every learner has an equal access to good mentorship or practical entrepreneurial experiences. Also, feedback that is given in conventional setups can be delayed or lacks customization, which constrains in its effects on learning outcomes. The AI solution to these issues is that AI has provided scalable, adaptive, and interactive learning solutions that meet the needs of different learners. AI systems facilitate a real-time feedback mechanism and continuous data analysis to help learners track their progress, determine the gaps in the skill set, and get specific suggestions on how to improve. Moreover, AI enables taking into account cross-disciplinary knowledge and abilities, which are crucial in the success of an entrepreneur in a complex and rapidly changing situation. Based on ideas in the data science, economics, psychology, and technology disciplines, AI-based platforms offer a comprehensive learning experience that equips scholars with the multidimensional aspects of entrepreneurship.

Cross-Disciplinary Practice

This cross-disciplinary practice not only improves the ability to solve problems, but also promotes cross-domain thinking and cooperation. To sum up, Artificial Intelligence implementation in entrepreneurial education is a major shift in the formation and cultivation of entrepreneurial skills. It has a potential to make learning environments more dynamic, personalized, and inclusive and responsive to the requirements of the digital age. With the help of AI technologies, educational organizations will be able to improve the success of entrepreneurial training, encourage innovation, and enable students to become successful entrepreneurs in a more competitive and uncertain world. The chapter, as such, attempts to identify the different aspects of AI-based entrepreneurial education, giving an overview of how it is being applied, its advantage, and disadvantage, and where it is heading.

Artificial Intelligence in Education

Intelligent, adaptive, and data-driven methods of teaching and learning are currently becoming the new reality of education with the help of Artificial Intelligence (AI). In its simplest definition, AI in education can be understood as the use of high-tech tools, including machine learning, natural language processing, and data analytics, to facilitate and optimize the educational process, better learning results, and maximize the efficiency of the institutions (Dubin & Xiaoxia, 2020; Singh, 2026a). As the educational systems are trying to adjust to the requirements of a digitally connected and knowledge-based world, AI has become an influential facilitator of innovation, personalization and scalability. It also transforms the process of delivering knowledge as well as the role of the educator and learner so that the educational environment is more interactive, learner-centered and outcome-oriented. Among the most notable contributions of AI to the world of education, the development of the personalized learning must be discussed.

Conventional modes

Conventional modes of education tend to be similar in the sense that one concept can be taught to all learners irrespective of their level of needs, abilities, and learning styles. This universal model often results in inequalities in achievement in learning because not all the learners can learn at the same rate whereas others are not challenged adequately. To overcome this weakness, AI studies the behavior, preferences, and patterns of engagement of learners and the results of their performance to develop individual learning paths. Adaptive learning systems allow students to learn at their pace, revisit complicated ideas, and access specific resources needed by particular students. Such individualization will not only increase the level of understanding but also boost motivation and engagement because learners will feel more in control of their learning process (Xu & Liu, 2025; Singh & Supina, 2025). Intimately connected to personalized learning is the creation of intelligent tutoring systems (ITS), which are simulators of one-on-one mentorship as it is offered by human instructors. These systems can provide real-time guidance, answer questions, explain, and provide feedback based on personal input by the learner through the use of AI. The first difference is that, unlike in a normal classroom where the teacher has many students to pay attention to, intelligent tutors make sure that they provide constant and personalized attention. They are able to detect myths, propose corrective measures and dynamically change the instructional strategies. This can be really useful when it comes to courses with complicated topics and a learner needs to be given step-by-step instructions and clarification as soon as possible. In addition, intelligent tutoring systems are accessible 24 hours and thus the learning process is more flexible and accessible, particularly to students in remote or resource rich settings.

Learning analytics

Learning analytics is another dimension of AI in education that is of critical importance as it entails gathering, analyzing, and interpreting of large amounts of educational data. Artificial intelligence enabled analytics systems have the ability to detect student performance trends, learners future performance, and present practical insights to teachers and administrators. As an example, students who are predicted to underperform, or who may drop out, can be given early interventions and assistance, as predictive models can detect them (Dwivedi, 2025; Singh, 2026b). These insights can help educators to improve teaching strategies, redesign course materials, and engage in evidence based pedagogical practices. Improved assessment is another aspect that learning analytics enable, which involves the replacement of traditional examination systems with more holistic and continuous assessment. This evidence-based practice boosts the general quality of education by focusing the instructional practice on the needs of learners and the objectives of the institution. Besides increasing the teaching and learning processes, AI is also critical in automation of the administrative functions hence efficiency in operations in the learning institutions. Grading assignments, scheduling classes, student records and course materials can be time-consuming and require resources. These processes are automated by AI-based systems to devote more time to mentorship, research, and innovation, as routine and repetitive processes are carried out automatically. Objective assessment, such as grading systems with artificial intelligence, can be graded with high precision and reliability, whereas AI-based time management applications can be used to optimize schedules under several conditions. This does not only cut down on the administrative workload but it also improves productivity and resource exploitation at the institution. Outside of these early uses, AI is leading to a fundamental overhaul of the entrepreneurial education field, with experience and practical practice being of crucial importance.

Simulation based learning

Simulation based learning is one of the most effective innovations in this field. AI allows developing immersive and interactive virtual worlds and allows students to participate in the world of entrepreneurship without risks involved in venturing into the real world. With such simulations, learners can start virtual business, create business models, experiment with marketing strategies, and study market conditions, as well as financing resources. These environments offer a secure platform on which to test, and the student can learn through mistakes and apply new ways of doing things. This learning model is experiential and improves critical thinking, problem solving and decision making; skills that are imperative when becoming an entrepreneur (Dabbous & Boustani, 2023; Singh & Supina, 2025). Predictive analytics also enhances entrepreneurial learning by making learners have the ability to make decisions based on data. The modern competitive business world is based on the idea that the successful entrepreneur must use data to steer his business strategy and operations. The AI technologies allow students to study the market trends, predict the consumer behavior, and review the viability of their business ideas. Through predictive models, the learners are able to evaluate the risks and opportunities and allocate resources optimally besides making strategic decisions. This does not only improve their analytical abilities but also equips them with the realities of the modern business ecosystems where data-informed understanding is one of the determinants of success. AI is also significant in generating creativity and innovation which are fundamental in entrepreneurship. Tools powered by AI may be used to help learners brainstorm business ideas, find gaps in the market, and come up with innovative products. Through the study of large amounts of data, such as consumer preferences, industry trends, and technological development, AI can propose new solutions and opportunities, which are not always obvious to human learners. This interactive learning between machine intelligence and human creativity improves the ideation process that allows learners to come up with more viable and innovative business models. Moreover, AI applications can be used in the context of rapid prototyping and testing to enable students to improve their ideas and bring them closer to reality. Virtual mentorship and networking is another way AI is transforming entrepreneurial education. Availability of mentors, industry professionals and contacts is essential element of success in entrepreneurship.

AI-powered platforms

Nevertheless, mentorship models based on the traditional approach are usually constrained in terms of geography, finances and institutions. These obstacles are removed through AI-powered platforms by linking learners to mentors, investors, and fellow learners worldwide. chatbots and virtual assistants are accessible around the clock, with answers to questions, guidance, and suggestions of the resources according to the individual needs. Such platforms also facilitate collective learning and knowledge exchange where a global entrepreneurial ecosystem is created where ideas and experiences get easily shared. In addition to that, AI promotes inclusivity and access to education by dismantling the conventional learning barriers. AI stops the problem of the lack of access to quality educational resources by providing adaptive technologies, multilingual support systems, and online environments where various students with different backgrounds and areas can access them. This democratization of education is especially important in education on entrepreneurship, where access to knowledge and mentorship and access to funding opportunities can greatly affect the results. AI can help to create a more diverse and inclusive entrepreneurial environment by ensuring fair access to learning tools and infrastructure (Chen et al., 2022; Singh & Ansari, 2024; Das & Singh, 2026). The application of AI in education has its fair share of concerns and issues of importance despite all the benefits that it possesses. The matter regarding the data privacy, the bias on the algorithms, and the overall ethical application of technology should be approached carefully to make the implementation responsible. Moreover, it is necessary to find a compromise between technological advancement and human communication because the functions of teachers in offering emotional and mentoring support, as well as moral-ethical advice, cannot be underestimated. Consequently, AI is to be considered as an auxiliary tool that will be used to augment, but not to substitute human roles in education. To sum up, it can be concluded that Artificial Intelligence in the realm of education is not only transformative but also extensive.

DISCUSSION AND INTERPRETATION

AI improves the quality and effectiveness of the educational systems through personalized learning, intelligent tutoring, data-driven insights and efficiency in administration. As applied in the field of entrepreneurial education, AI-based innovations, like simulation-based learning, predictive analytics, idea generation systems, and virtual mentorship platforms, provide dynamic and engaging learning experiences to equip learners with real-life challenges. The embrace of AI in education faculty will be a major facet in the future of education, innovation, and empower the new generation of entrepreneurs, as learning institutions are working towards the digital revolution.

AI in Entrepreneurial Training

Artificial Intelligence (AI) has become a disruptive trend in entrepreneurial training, allowing smoother and more effective, more personal learning processes. The traditional approach to entrepreneurship education that was based on fixed content and lack of exposure to the real world is currently being redefined by the use of AI-powered tools that simulate business conditions, automate sophisticated processes and offer practical insights. These applications do not only improve the quality of training, but also prepare aspiring entrepreneurs with skills needed to cope with dynamic and competitive markets. Whether it is the development of the business plan, financial management or the evaluation of the skills, AI is highly essential in enhancing the entrepreneurial learning ecosystem. Business plan development has been considered one of the most evident usages of AI in the realms of entrepreneurial training (Duong & Vu, 2025; Singh, 2024; Pandey et al., 2025). The preparation of an extensive business plan is one of the basic steps which any business project has to follow, but it can be a process that can be fought and demanding a lot of knowledge. The use of AI can make this process easy and effective by giving systematic templates and step-by-step directions to assist learners to arrange their ideas in an effective manner. Such platforms have the ability to interpret inputs made by users and produce tailored business plans, where all the essential elements, including executive summaries, market analysis, operational strategies, and financial forecasts, are handled. Moreover, AI-based systems possess high-quality financial predictability through the analysis of past data, market trends, and industry standards. This will allow the learners to come up with realistic revenue models, cost structures and profitability projections. Moreover, AI applications may propose specific designs of the market by weighing the consumer behavior, competitive environments, and new trends, so that the quality of strategic business plans will be improved. Consequently, students acquire useful knowledge in the planning and strategizing, which are vital in opening and running successful ventures. Market research and analysis is another important field AI can be used to aid in entrepreneurial training. The knowledge of the market is important in finding opportunities, evaluating competition and making sound decisions. Historically, market research has been a process that is time consuming and resource intensive and can sometimes take a long time to gather and analyse data.

Automation Process

As an artificial intelligence, AI automates such processes by collecting data across various channels, such as social media, online databases, and market reports, and processing them in real-time. This will enable the learners to do a thorough competitor analysis by determining major players, identifying their weaknesses and strengths, and their strategy. The target markets are also determined using AI where customers can be segmented according to their demographics, conduct, and interest. With advanced analytics, students will be in a position to know the needs and expectations of the customers, as well as their purchasing behavior, which will allow them to develop products and services that meet the market demand (Nweke et al., 2025; Pandey et al., 2025). This statistical method also makes the market research more accurate and reasonable, and learners are more confident in their capability to make strategic choices in this way. Another important area, in which AI applications are highly beneficial to the entrepreneurial training development, is financial literacy and management. The financial management has been thought of as one of the hardest parts of the entrepreneurship especially to those who lack a good background in finance. AI-based platforms can be used to lower this difficulty since they offer interactive and user-friendly learning environments that can make complex financial concepts less complicated. Learners will be able to visualize financial information, monitor performance indicators, and comprehend such key indicators as cash flow, profit margins, and return on investment through interactive dashboards. Simulations in real time enable learners to test their financial choices, including pricing, investment and cost management in a risk-free manner. These simulations give real time feedback, enabling the learners to know the outcomes of their choices and to tune up their strategies as well. Also, predictive financial modeling software also helps students predict their financial performance in the future depending on the different situations, which will make planning and resource management more efficient.

Evaluation Techniques

Using AI in the financial training, the learners acquire a more profound knowledge of financial concepts and become more confident in their ability to cope with the real-world financial issues. AI is also critical in skill evaluation and feedbacks, which are critical in constant learning and enhanced development on entrepreneurial training. The traditional evaluation techniques tend to be based on the periodical review that is not always the most appropriate to evaluate the progress of a learner as well as to give him or her timely feedback. AI will resolve this deficiency by allowing evaluating the progress of students in real-time and dynamically. To assess competencies in real time, AI systems may process a vast amount of data, such as the interaction of learners, the rate of completion of various tasks, decision-making patterns, and the general engagement. According to this analysis, students get immediate feedback to indicate their strengths and areas of improvements. One more decent asset of any AI-powered assessment system is skill gap analysis, which can help to define what spheres require further support or training to their learners. Moreover, individualized recommendations lead students to the pertinent resources, activities or learning modules that can assist the students in improving their skills. Such a cyclical process of feedback creates self-directed learning and keeps the learners focused to accomplish their entrepreneurial objectives.

AI BENEFITS IN ENTREPRENEURIAL EDUCATION

The introduction of AI in the sphere of entrepreneurial education has a lot of positive outcomes that not only improve the learning process but also the effectiveness of the training programs. Among the greatest benefits, there is improved personalization. Through the analysis of learner data, AI systems adapt the learning experience to the needs of a learner by changing the content. This will make sure that the students get specific teaching and encouragement, which enhances engagement, motivation, and learning (Khalid, 2020; Kaur et al., 2025). Personalized learning also enables the students to learn at their own rate thus making them well understand difficult concepts before proceeding to more complicated areas. Another important advantage of AI in entrepreneur education is scalability. The traditional training programs are also usually limited in terms of resources, infrastructure and availability of faculty which limit them and their capacity to accommodate huge numbers of learners. These issues are solved by AI-driven applications that can provide high-quality education to more people without losing the effectiveness. The virtual simulation, automated assessment tools and online learning systems allow institutions to access students located in various geographical locations and hence entrepreneurial education is now more accessible. Real-time feedback plays a vital role in efficient learning, and AI will do well in its provision of timely feedback that can facilitate the ongoing enhancements. In contrast to the conventional means, where feedback might be removed, AI systems can provide immediate assessments and suggestions depending on the performance of learners. This enables students to find out their mistakes, what they entail, and make the required changes timely. Ongoing feedback will positively affect the learning process, as well as foster confidence and stimulate initiative. The next valuable advantage of AI in entrepreneurial education is the development of decision-making abilities. The essence of entrepreneurship is complex and uncertain decisions that have to be made within time constraints and limited information. Artificial intelligence devices provide learners with evidence-based information which improves their analytical skills and facilitates well-informed decision making. It is possible to compare various scenarios and make certain decisions using AI as it allows analyzing the market trends, financial data, and customer behavior (Rahman et al., 2022; Das & Singh, 2026). Such hands-on experience with decision making based on data equips learners with the real-world challenges of the entrepreneurial world. The use of AI in education also contributes to accessibility and inclusivity to a great degree. The opportunities to learn through AI-powered platforms are flexible and inexpensive and thus entrepreneurial training can be made available to a wide range of people, including those in remote or underserved locations. Unique characteristics like multilingual support, adaptive learning interfaces and mobile accessibility mean that these technologies can be useful to learners with varying needs and abilities. Such democratization of education leads to the inclusion of a better entrepreneurial ecosystem, where people with different socio-economic backgrounds can gain access and use entrepreneurial skills. Besides the mentioned advantages, AI encourages innovativeness and creativity as it offers tools that facilitate the generation of ideas, experiments, and resolving problems. It helps the learners to discover new opportunities, experiment with their ideas and polish them in a conducive and dynamic environment. Technology, along with human ability, can be integrated to deliver an improved overall quality of the entrepreneurial education process and can prepare a learning person to face the challenges of the contemporary business environment with the help of AI. To sum up, AI uses in entrepreneurial education are vast and revolutionary, including business planning, market analysis, financial control and development of skills. Not only do these applications make training programs more effective, but they also provide the competencies that learners need in order to succeed in the fast-changing entrepreneurial ecosystem. The advantages of AI, such as personalization, scalability, real-time feedback, better decision-making, and larger accessibility, also contribute to the significance of AI in influencing the future of entrepreneurial education. With the integration of AI in the institutions, they will be in a better position to produce innovative, resilient, and globally competitive entrepreneurs.

CHALLENGES AND LIMITATIONS

Although Artificial Intelligence (AI) has a promising potential to transform the world of entrepreneurship education and training, it is closely supported with a number of challenges and constraints that need to be managed carefully. These are not only technical, but also pedagogical, economic, and ethical. These limitations are critical towards making AI integration both effective and sustainable within the field of education. The existence of technological barriers is one of the main issues. Adoption To be successful, AI needs to be adopted with strong digital infrastructure such as high-speed internet access, a sophisticated computer system, and use of AI-enabled platforms. But in most of these places- especially in developing economies and rural set ups such infrastructure is insufficient or unevenly spread. This digital divide generates inequalities in the use of AI-based educational resources and deprives learners who can most easily use AI-based educational technologies. Digital literacy is also pertinent to the effectiveness of AI adoption resulting in the infrastructure. Both learners and the educators should also have the required technical expertise to communicate with AI systems, analyze the output, and apply the tools in the learning processes. The ineffective use of AI technologies can be obstructed by the lack of training and awareness, which leads to the underutilization of the technologies or their reluctance to be implemented.

The other major drawback is the cost of implementing AI systems is very expensive. Creation, implementation, and support of AI-based platforms are costly in terms of finances. The institutions will be required to invest in software development, hardware infrastructure, data management systems and the continuous technical support. In addition, AI implementation into the current educational system is commonly accompanied by the need to reshape a curriculum, train faculty, and maintain the system updates. To most learning institutions, particularly those with small budgets, these expenses are prohibitive (Zhu & Zhang, 2022; Singh & Supina, 2025). The monetary aspect can result in an unequal level of the adoption, with only properly financed institutions being able to use AI to their advantage, increasing the gap between various parts of the education system. Another urgent issue of using AI in the field of entrepreneurial education is data privacy and security concerns. The machine learning systems depend on data a lot to perform their tasks successfully such as personal data, academic data, behavioral data, and performance data. The gathering, storing and handling of such sensitive information pose crucial concerns about privacy and moral usage. Illegal access, information leaks or misuse of information may have dire repercussions both to the learners and the institutions. Moreover, the growing dependence on cloud-computing and service providers is another complication to data security. It is necessary to enforce data protection laws, as well as have strong cybersecurity in place so that the information of users is not compromised and that there is trust in AI systems. Another drawback is that the use of AI-based technologies may cause the absence of human communication. Although it is able to replicate some degree of mentorship existing in humans via intelligent tutoring systems and chatbots, it cannot do so in terms of emotional intelligence, empathy, and person-to-person relationships that human educators offer. Mentorship, networking, and experiential learning are the most useful to entrepreneurial education in specific, and in all these cases, human interactions may be very subtle. Over-reliance on AI can decrease student chances to have a substantial amount of conversation and other meaningful interactions with their peers and parents, as well as soft skills, including communication and leadership abilities. This may result in more depersonalized learning experience where the human aspect in learning is reduced (Zhang et al., 2025; Singh, 2024; Das & Singh, 2026). Another critical issue that can imply bias in the entrepreneurial education process is bias in AI algorithms. AI systems are then trained using extensive data, and in case such data contains biases either based on gender, ethnicity, socio-economic status, or any other factor, the AI models will unwillingly repeat and even increase the biases. To illustrate this, an AI-based system to make business ideas judging or even to predict the success of an entrepreneur may give an advantage to some profiles due to previous data, thus putting underrepresented populations at a disadvantage. These biases may compromise the ideals of equity and inclusiveness which are central to the education systems. To handle this problem, special attention should be paid to the design, different and representative data sets, and continuous monitoring, which should guarantee that AI systems will work in the fair and impartial way.

ETHICAL CONSIDERATIONS

It is against this backdrop that ethics is important in advising the responsible application of AI in entrepreneurial education. Since AI is becoming a part of teaching and learning, it is necessary to develop strong ethical standards that would allow the application of AI to fit educational principles and social expectations. One of the major ethical values of AI implementation is transparency. Users, educators as well as students, need to understand well how AI systems work, the way data is collected, processed, and utilized to produce the outputs. Open systems create trust and allow users to make suitable choices concerning their connection with AI technologies. This also pertains to the transparency of the constraints of the AI systems so that the users do not overvalue their functionality and do not use them blindly. Another issue that is important is accountability. Since the role of AI systems in decision-making is growing, e.g., with grading, performance rating, and suggesting learning paths, it is worth defining clear-cut responsibilities. The institutions need to take care that AI-driven processes have human oversight and have mechanisms to deal with errors, biases, or unintended consequences. Responsibility systems must establish the answer to the question of who is in charge of the results that AI systems produce, such as the developers, administrators, and educators. The ethical use of AI in education is based on equity. The implementation and design of AI technologies should be done in a manner that supports equal access and opportunities to all learners. It includes dealing with the digital divide so that underserved and marginalized communities do not miss out on the AI educational advantages. Also, there should be attempts at reducing the algorithm bias and making sure that AI systems are not discriminatory of all users, irrespective of their background or situation. One of the most significant ethical issues is likely to be privacy or protection of student data. Schools and colleges should adopt stringent data management procedures that will make sure that personal data is gathered and utilized appropriately. This involves taking informed consent, reducing data collection to a minimum which is required, and safe storage and transmission of data. The fact that the word (protection) has been introduced helps to highlight the necessity to protect information of the students against such unauthorized access and abuse. Ethical data practices will be crucial in keeping the trust and making sure that the AI technologies are applied in a way that will not violate the rights of individuals. In order to resolve these ethical issues, organizations need to come up with extensive rules and control systems of AI implementation (Somia & Vecchiarini, 2024; Das & Singh, 2026; Pandey et al., 2025). These frameworks must entail data management policies, transparency of the system, mitigation of bias and accountability. Their auditing and evaluation must be done regularly to determine the performance and contribution of AI systems and ensure that they meet the ethics and educational goals. Moreover, teachers and learners are supposed to receive training and awareness in order to learn about the ethical aspects of AI and apply these technologies in a responsible manner. To sum up, although AI has enormous opportunities to improve the education of entrepreneurs, the key point is that its effective implementation requires overcoming the challenges and ethical issues related to it. The institutions can devise a moderate and ethical response to the use of AI by identifying and actively dealing with the challenges associated with technological obstacles, cost, privacy, human interaction, and bias. The creation and implementation of AI systems should be guided by ethical principles like transparency, accountability, equity, and privacy because it should have a positive impact on the educational ecosystem.

With careful application and regulation, AI may be considered a strong instrument of innovation and maintaining the fundamentals of education.

PRACTICAL EXAMPLES AND CASE STUDIES

AI integration in entrepreneurial education is not a theorist concern, but is being practically evidenced in more and more real-world scenarios launched in university settings, online programs, and start-up programs. These case studies and practice examples illuminate the active transformation of the field of entrepreneurial training using AI to produce immersive, data-driven, and personalized learning spaces. They also explain how institutions and organisations are using AI as a way of closing the distance between academics and actual entrepreneurial practice (Abdelmagid et al., 2025; Das & Singh, 2026; Pandey et al., 2025). The use of AI-based simulators of startup can be seen as one of the most influential applications, which are quite common in universities and colleges to model real business environments. These simulators also give students a chance to practice virtual entrepreneurship developing and operating simulated startups. In these settings, the learner will be able to test different processes of the business, including product development, pricing, marketing, and financial management. The algorithms of AI constantly compare the choices made by students and recreate the reactions of the market, which lets learners see the results of their actions in real time. As an example, when a student picks an aggressive pricing model, the simulator can react by selling more but at low profit margins thus illustrating trade-offs in the decision-making process. Such practical learning systems allow students to acquire the most important entrepreneurial skills, such as, critical thinking, risk management, and flexibility. Notably, these simulations create a risk-free environment where students are able to make mistakes, learn through failures and refine in their styles without having to bear negative financial and reputational costs in the real world. The effectiveness of these tools in improving student engagement and understanding of entrepreneurial concepts has also been reported in universities that have adopted them because they engage in dynamic and interactive interactions instead of study and passively replicate theoretical material. The presence of another important AI implementation is observed in the environment of online entrepreneurship platforms that combine intelligent technologies to provide personalized and scalable learning experiences. These platforms unite AI-assisted content delivery, adaptive learning platforms, and virtual mentorship to assist aspiring entrepreneurs in different levels of their career. By providing ongoing data analysis, AI systems monitor the progress of the learners, in addition to their strong and weak areas and propose individualized learning courses. Indicatively, a student with problems in the area of financial planning can be given more resources, tutorials and exercises with specific focus on enhancement of his or her knowledge in the area of financial concepts. Meanwhile, high-level learners can also be offered with more complicated tasks and case studies to develop their abilities even more. In addition to content delivery, such platforms can have chatbots and virtual assistants that are driven by AI and serve real-time assistance, answer questions and accompany learners through the various modules. Moreover, AI allows networking users with mentors, industry professionals and peers with common interests and objectives (Kaur et al., 2025; Singh & Ansari, 2024). This establishes a cooperative learning platform in which sharing of knowledge and peer learning are promoted. Their availability also contributes to their usefulness, especially to learners in isolated or underserved areas, since they can now receive high-quality education on entrepreneurial matters without being limited by physical geography. The transformative role that AI is playing is also in startup incubation centers whereby it is utilized to assist startup ventures at early-stage and also increase effectiveness of incubation programs. Conventionally, the incubators used human judgment in assessing business ideas, mentoring entrepreneurs and providing resources. Although this method is still useful, AI provides a data aspect that transforms the decision-making process and efficiency. AI systems have the opportunity to examine large volumes of data such as the market trends, consumer behaviour, and the past performance of startups to determine the viability of the business idea. This will make incubators to recognise high potential ventures and give specific assistance to business owners. Moreover, AI technology will be able to pair entrepreneurs with appropriate mentors based on aspects like industry knowledge, experience, and startup requirements. This guarantees the better functioning of mentorship relations, as well as the increase in the quality of the guidance delivered. Another potentially strong use is predictive analytics, which can empower incubators to forecast the probability of the startup success according to a spectrum of factors, including market demand, financial forecasts, and team capabilities. Although these forecasts are not conclusive, they are useful signals that enable business people to fine tune the strategies and avoid risks. Incorporating AI into the incubation procedures can help organizations to become more capable of nurturing the innovation and facilitating the promotion of sustainable businesses. Altogether, these practical examples can prove that AI is changing the concept of entrepreneurial education, making it not a passive and theory-based process but a dynamic and experiential learning process. They emphasize the need to combine technology with pedagogy so as to come up with meaningful and effective learning experiences. A successful AI implementation in such areas, however, also presupposes the revival of the old way of teaching, which involves serious pedagogical consequences.

PEDAGOGICAL IMPLICATIONS

The introduction of AI into entrepreneurial education requires a paradigm shift in the educational process, where traditional teaching models have been replaced by more adaptable, flexible, and learner-focused ones. The traditional way of learning has been mainly teacher centered whereby the teacher is the main source of knowledge and the student plays a passive role in the learning process. AI makes this paradigm a challenge by allowing customized and autonomy-directed learning processes in which students gain increased control over their learning process. Under this learner-centered model, teachers move away the role of knowledge providers and become facilitators and mentors who assist, guide and motivate learners. The other significant change is the fact that it has changed the static content to dynamic and adaptive learning. Conventional learning resources, including textbooks and course programs, can be very old-fashioned and unaccommodating to the present-day trends in the industry and specific needs of different learners (Das & Singh, 2026; Pandey et al., 2025). On the contrary, AI-based systems constantly update, change content according to real-time data and interaction with learners. This makes sure that learning resources do not grow old, useless or unrelated with the changing needs of the entrepreneurial ecosystem. Differentiation instruction is also possible with adaptive learning technologies, in which the content is adapted to meet the needs of different levels of proficiency and learning preference, which improves the inclusivity and efficacy. Perhaps, one of the most important pedagogical changes AI allows is the shift toward experiential learning instead of theoretical education. Entrepreneurship is practical in nature and the learners need to get to practice what they learn in the real world. Simulations, virtual labs, and interactive case studies are AI-powered tools that allow students to learn practical skills and analyse the results by having hands-on learning opportunities. This hands-on strategy does not only enhance knowledge, but also other competencies including problem-solving, decision making and innovation that are critical skills. AI will improve the quality and the overall impact of entrepreneurial education by involving the learners in active participation. Besides these changes, the implementation of AI will necessitate the emergence of additional digital skills among educators and changes in the new technological paradigms. Educators need to learn how to operate AI tools, views data analytics, and create technology-based learning. There should be professional development and training programs to provide the educators with the necessary skills to successfully implement AI within their teaching. Moreover, teachers are required to think collaboratively and not in a replacement way, but in an addition way because AI is another tool that improves their competency. Human aspect of learning like mentoring, empathy, and ethical guidance cannot be substituted and should be incorporated with the technological improvement to establish a harmonious environment in the learning process. Another interdisciplinary aspect of AI is that it promotes interdisciplinary learning through the combination of skills in different fields of technology, business, data science, and psychology. This is very applicable to the holistic approach in entrepreneurial education where complex problem-solving and innovation demands multiple perspectives and sets of skills. Through the promotion of the combination of various disciplines, AI will contribute to the creation of wholesome entrepreneurs who are capable of operating in intricate and highly dynamic environments (Singh & Supina, 2025).

To sum up, the case study and the examples of AI implementation in the field of entrepreneurial education illustrate the potential of the technology as a transformative solution to improve the learning experience and success. AI-based startup simulators and and online platforms as well as incubation centers are some of these innovations and they offer valuable information on the utilization of technology to facilitate the development of an entrepreneurship. Meanwhile, the pedagogical implications suggest the necessity of the paradigm change in the teaching and learning strategies with the focus on personalization, flexibility, and learning through experience. With changes adopted by teachers and schools, the full potential of AI can be utilized to develop more successful, inclusive and forward-looking entrepreneurial education systems.

FUTURE DIRECTIONS

The future of entrepreneurial education will have a significant change due to the further development and implementation of Artificial Intelligence (AI) in combination with other new technologies. Since the digital transformation in industries gains momentum, the education systems should change to help produce entrepreneurs capable of operating in the complex and technology-driven world. Artificial intelligence will not only improve the current pedagogical systems but also introduce new learning environments that are fully immersive, adaptive, and global. This is one of the main future directions because AI is becoming integrated with the emerging technologies of blockchain, virtual reality (VR), and the Internet of Things (IoT). The combination of these technologies with AI can result in the development of very immersive and interactive learning environments. As an example, VR-based solutions can reproduce real business situation when learners have the opportunity to communicate with virtual customers, suppliers and other stakeholders, which makes entrepreneurial training more real and experiential. These simulations can also be improved with the help of AI, which can dynamically change the situations depending on the decisions and the performance of the learners. Conversely, secure and transparent credentialing, intellectual property protection, and transaction management systems among entrepreneurial ventures can be established with the help of blockchain technology. Connected devices can give real-time information which can be analysed by learners in order to make sound decisions about the work processes. The combination of these technologies will form a complete learning ecosystem, in which theoretical information and practice are perfectly intertwined. The other important direction is the creation of lifelong learning environments with AI assistance. In modern days when the world is highly dynamic in terms of the economic environment, entrepreneurship is not a one time affair but an unending journey that demands constant improvement in skills as well as adaptation. The AI-based platforms will empower entrepreneurs to learn continuously as they will receive individualized suggestions, micro-learnings, and on-demand knowledge. These plans will monitor personal history of learning, career paths, and skills development needs to provide personal learning experience during the working life of a person. This transformation to a lifelong learning will make the entrepreneurs relevant, competitive, and able to react to the newly arising challenges and opportunities. Ai-driven platforms should also have a considerable positive impact on global cooperation as well. Entrepreneurship is becoming more of a global environment with ideas, resources and markets being less defined by geographical division. With the help of AI, cross-border collaboration will be facilitated through linking learners, mentors, investors, and institutions across various regions of the globe. This means that AI can be used to match entrepreneurs with the right partners using smart matchmaking algorithms, depending on their talents, interests and project needs. The AI-based virtual collaboration tools will allow real-time interaction, management of projects, and sharing of knowledge among various teams. The new global connectivity will lead to the formation of international entrepreneurial ecosystems, which promote innovation, exchange of culture, and joint solution of global problems. Another radical path that AI takes in entrepreneurial learning is hyper-personalized learning. The next generation of AI will not just be involved in providing personalized experiences but will involve the development of highly customized learning through the use of advanced data analytics, such as cognitive and emotional data. When investigating variables like the pace of learning, preferences, the level of engagement, and even emotional reactions, AI can create learning systems and pathways that are specialized not only to an individual but also unique. This amount of individualization will not just enhance the learning outcomes, but also the motivation and satisfaction. To illustrate, AI systems can increase/decrease task complexity, offer feedback related to a specific task, or suggest specific learning resources depending on the level of confidence and emotional state of a learner. These adaptive systems will develop a more reactive and supportive learning environment which will allow the learners to reach their maximum potential.

INSTITUTIONAL AND POLICY RECOMMENDATIONS

Institutional and policy makers need to be strategic and proactive to ensure that the potential of AI in entrepreneurial education is achieved. Investment in digital infrastructure is one of the most important priorities. Strong technological backbones such as high-speed internet, cloud computing and AI-powered systems are essential in ensuring that AI-based educational programs are successfully implemented. The advantages of AI cannot be successfully achieved without proper infrastructure, especially in those areas where people are not well-equipped with technologies. It is also critical that the educators should receive training and professional growth. With the AI revolutionizing the practice of teaching, teachers will need to have the requisite digital skills to ensure that they can utilize the technologies in the teaching process. The training programs can be based on the utilization of AI tools, data interpretation, and creation of adaptive learning experiences. Educators can be empowered to make sure that AI is applied and served as a collaborative tool to add value to teaching and not to substitute it. Another important suggestion is the formulation of ethical recommendations. With the growing role of the AI systems in the educational process, institutions should develop specific policies that will help them to maintain data privacy, transparency, accountability, and fairness. The structure, execution, and assessment of AI systems need to be informed by ethical frameworks to make sure that they fit within the educational values and societal norms. They should also have regular audits and monitoring mechanisms to ensure that there is compliance and constant improvement. The development of industry-academia partnership is necessary to close the gap between theoretical and practical knowledge. Collaborating with industry players would offer great knowledge of the prevailing trends in the market, technological developments, and skills demanded. All these collaborations may also make the access to the real-world data, mentorship, and internship available, which may contribute to the overall learning experience. AI can also improve such partnerships through the exchange of data, joint research, and innovation-based projects. In a bid to create equity in the entrepreneurship education process, inclusive access to AI technologies is essential. By offering cost effective and available learning resources, institutions need to make conscious efforts in mitigating the digital divide. This would involve provision of online platforms, mobile based application and multilingual support systems that would serve the different learners. The design and execution of AI-driven educational programs should be designed with inclusiveness as one of the key factors. Governments are very instrumental at the policy level in facilitating implementation of AI in education. The policymakers ought to come up with strategies that will promote innovation, research, and investment in AI technologies. This can be in the form of financial support, industry-government cooperation, and rewards to institutions that embrace AI-based educational solutions. Also, one should have regulatory systems in place to guarantee ethical utilization, information security, and quality assurance of AI applications. To sum up, the future of AI in entrepreneurial education is full of opportunities, and it is motivated by the development of technologies and changing the learning requirements. Introducing AI and new technologies, promoting lifelong learning, building collaborative strategies on a global scale, and providing hyper-personalization of education, institutions can establish dynamic and future-oriented learning ecologies. Nevertheless, to attain this vision, a plan of action is needed, which is ethical governance, collaboration among educators, institutions, and policymakers. In such a way, AI can become a highly influential agent of innovation, inclusivity, and excellence in entrepreneurial learning.

CONCLUSION

The concept of Artificial Intelligence (AI) has become one of the transformative elements of re-defining the education and training of entrepreneurs, providing new opportunities to address the preexisting issues of teaching, learning, and skills acquisition. As entrepreneurship remains a core aspect in supporting economic development, innovations and creation of employment opportunities, the necessity of more dynamic, adaptive and inclusive learning models has been growing clearer. The AI is a solution to these needs, as it will allow to develop individualized learning, improve experiential training, and decision-making based on data, thus redefining the process of acquiring entrepreneurial skills in the new age. In this chapter, it has been made evident that AI is more than a technological improvement but a paradigm shift in the education practices. AI provides a more interactive and efficient learning experience by combining the intelligent tutoring systems, learning analytics, simulations-based platforms, and predictive models. Such technologies can enable learners to be exposed to real business experiences, experiment on concepts in safe environments, and get immediate and individualized feedback. Consequently, students are in a better position to have important entrepreneurial skills that are critical including creativity, problem-solving, adaptability, and strategic thinking which are needed to survive complex and uncertain business environments. The examples of AI uses in entrepreneur training, such as business plan creation and market analytics, and financial management and skill evaluation, prove the versatility and effectiveness of AI. These applications do not only enhance the quality of education but also make it accessible and scalable and reach a wide range of learner populations both in geographical and socio-economic borders. Furthermore, AI-based applications support international cooperation and networking, allowing those willing to start their businesses to meet mentors, colleagues, and professionals in other industries all over the world. This is an interwoven ecosystem of learning, which cultivates innovation and promotes sharing of ideas, which serve to enhance the creation of a thriving entrepreneurial culture. Policymakers and institutions of learning need to operate in collaboration to invest in infrastructure, develop digital skills and make AI-driven learning opportunities inclusive. To sum up, AI has a huge potential to transform entrepreneurial education by making it more dynamic, more inclusive, as well as more forward-thinking. It can also be a potent force to bring out innovative, resilient and globally competitive entrepreneurs when applied with wisdom and in a morally sound manner which will in the end lead towards sustainable economic and social growth.

REFERENCES

Abdelmagid, A. S., Jabli, N. M., Al-Mohaya, A. Y., & Teleb, A. A. (2025). Integrating interactive metaverse environments and generative artificial intelligence to promote the green digital economy and e-entrepreneurship in higher education. *Sustainability (Basel), 17*(12), 5594. DOI: 10.3390/su17125594

Bell, R., & Bell, H. (2023). Entrepreneurship education in the era of generative artificial intelligence. *Entrepreneurship Education, 6*(3), 229–244. DOI: 10.1007/s41959-023-00099-x

Chen, J., Chen, Y., Ou, R., Wang, J., & Chen, Q. (2022). How to use artificial intelligence to improve entrepreneurial attitude in business simulation games: Implications from a quasi-experiment. *Frontiers in Psychology, 13*, 856085. DOI: 10.3389/fpsyg.2022.856085 PMID: 36467165

Chen, L., Ifenthaler, D., Yau, J. Y. K., & Sun, W. (2024). Artificial intelligence in entrepreneurship education: A scoping review. *Education + Training, 66*(6), 589–608. DOI: 10.1108/ET-05-2023-0169

Dabbous, A., & Boustani, N. M. (2023). Digital explosion and entrepreneurship education: Impact on promoting entrepreneurial intention for business students. *Journal of Risk and Financial Management, 16*(1), 27. DOI: 10.3390/jrfm16010027

Das, R., & Singh, A. (2026). Opportunities and Threats for Women Entrepreneurs in Remote Rural Tourism: A SWOT Study. In Ordóñez de Pablos, P. (Ed.), *Shaping Green and Inclusive Economies Through Innovative Entrepreneurship* (pp. 65–88). IGI Global Scientific Publishing., DOI: 10.4018/979-8-3373-1097-8.ch003

Dubin, D., & Xiaoxia, W. (2020). Human-computer system design of entrepreneurship education based on artificial intelligence and image feature retrieval. *Journal of Intelligent & Fuzzy Systems, 39*(4), 5927–5939. DOI: 10.3233/JIFS-189067

Duong, C. D., & Vu, T. N. (2025). Entrepreneurial education and higher education students'e-entrepreneurial intention: A moderated mediation model of generative AI incorporation and e-entrepreneurial self-efficacy. *Higher Education. Skills and Work-Based Learning*, *15*(5), 1024–1048. DOI: 10.1108/HESWBL-12-2024-0390

Dwivedi, Y. K. (2025). Generative Artificial Intelligence (GenAI) in entrepreneurial education and practice: Emerging insights, the GAIN Framework, and research agenda. *The International Entrepreneurship and Management Journal*, *21*(1), 82. DOI: 10.1007/s11365-025-01089-2

Kaur, M., Singh, A., & Kaur, A. (2025). Managing the Difficulties Female Entrepreneurs Face: Creating Bridges Instead of Barriers. In Shoukat, G., & Tunio, M. (Eds.), *Work-Life Balance and Its Effect on Women Entrepreneurs* (pp. 279–300). IGI Global Scientific Publishing., DOI: 10.4018/979-8-3693-9516-5.ch014

Khalid, N. (2020). Artificial intelligence learning and entrepreneurial performance among university students: Evidence from malaysian higher educational institutions. *Journal of Intelligent & Fuzzy Systems*, *39*(4), 5417–5435. DOI: 10.3233/JIFS-189026

Li, J. (2025). Entrepreneurial skill augmented neural network (ESANN): A deep learning approach for enhancing entrepreneurial competencies in teachers. *International Journal of Computational Intelligence Systems*, *18*(1), 127. DOI: 10.1007/s44196-025-00851-2

Nweke, L. O., Okebanama, U. F., & Mba, G. U. (2025). Enhancing entrepreneurial skills through experiential learning in IoT, AI, and cybersecurity. *Discover Education*, *4*(1), 149. DOI: 10.1007/s44217-025-00573-9

Pandey, U., Singh, A., & Naqvi, N. H. (2025). Career Transitions to Entrepreneurship: Case Studies From Real-World Transformations. In Alagappar, P., & Yanamandra, R. (Eds.), *Strategic Insights and Case Studies on Navigating an Entrepreneurial Landscape* (pp. 47–66). IGI Global Scientific Publishing., DOI: 10.4018/979-8-3693-9261-4.ch003

Rahman, M. M., Rahaman, M. S., Moral, I. H., & Chowdhury, M. S. (2022, October). Entrepreneurship Education and Entrepreneurial Intention of Business Graduates: Does Artificial Intelligence Matter? In *Proceedings of International Conference on Fourth Industrial Revolution and Beyond 2021* (pp. 109-123). Singapore: Springer Nature Singapore. DOI: 10.1007/978-981-19-2445-3_8

Singh, A. (2024). Endorsing Gamification Pedagogy for Nurturing Employability Skills in Higher Education Institutions (HEI). In Membrive, V. (Ed.), *Practices and Implementation of Gamification in Higher Education* (pp. 172–183). IGI Global Scientific Publishing., DOI: 10.4018/979-8-3693-0716-8.ch008

Singh, A. (2026a). The Future of Learning: Integrating Project-Based, Competency-Based, and Experiential Approaches. In Athanasekou, M., & Zagorianakos, A. (Eds.), *Project-Based Learning, Competency-Based Assessments, and Experiential Education for Modern Learners* (pp. 1–24). IGI Global Scientific Publishing., DOI: 10.4018/979-8-3373-4957-2.ch001

Singh, A. (2026b). The Innovation Spiral: How Universities, Governments, and Industries Co-Create the AI Future. In Rahmouni, M., Alholiby, M., & Soufiene, B. (Eds.), *The Triple Helix of University-Government-Industry Partnerships and the Development of AI* (pp. 31–58). IGI Global Scientific Publishing., DOI: 10.4018/979-8-3373-7620-2.ch002

Singh, A., & Ansari, A. I. (2024). Role of Training and Development in Employee Motivation: Tourism and Hospitality Sector. In Mazurowski, T. (Ed.), *Enhancing Employee Motivation Through Training and Development* (pp. 248–261). IGI Global Scientific Publishing., DOI: 10.4018/979-8-3693-1674-0.ch011

Singh, A., & Supina, S. (2025). Rural Women Entrepreneurship in the Face of Gender Inequality. In Bayram, G., Bayram, A., & Sak, M. (Eds.), *Examining Barriers and Building Resiliency for Rural Women Entrepreneurs* (pp. 239–256). IGI Global Scientific Publishing., DOI: 10.4018/979-8-3693-9178-5.ch009

Somia, T., & Vecchiarini, M. (2024). Navigating the new frontier: The impact of artificial intelligence on students' entrepreneurial competencies. *International Journal of Entrepreneurial Behaviour & Research*, *30*(11), 236–260. DOI: 10.1108/IJEBR-08-2023-0788

Thottoli, M. M., Cruz, M. E., & Al Abri, S. S. S. (2025). The incubation revolution: Transforming entrepreneurial education with artificial intelligence. *Asia Pacific Journal of Innovation and Entrepreneurship*, *19*(1), 2–23. DOI: 10.1108/APJIE-11-2023-0221

Xu, Q., & Liu, X. (2025). The utilization of artificial intelligence in enhancing English language instruction and fostering entrepreneurial education. *Journal of Computational Methods in Sciences and Engineering*, *25*(2), 1593–1605. DOI: 10.1177/14727978241302155

Zhang, Q., Li, L., Xu, C., Qi, Y., & Zhao, X. (2025). How can artificial intelligence help college students develop entrepreneurial ability? Evidence from China. *International Journal of Management Education*, *23*(3), 101244. DOI: 10.1016/j.ijme.2025.101244

Zhu, Q., & Zhang, H. (2022). Teaching strategies and psychological effects of entrepreneurship education for college students majoring in social security law based on deep learning and artificial intelligence. *Frontiers in Psychology*, *13*, 779669. DOI: 10.3389/fpsyg.2022.779669 PMID: 35369210

Chapter 6

The Impact of Artificial Intelligence on Entrepreneurship Training and Education in Saudi Arabia

Walid Chouari
http://orcid.org/0000-0001-7038-8678
College of Arts, King Faisal University, Saudi Arabia

ABSTRACT

This study examines the impact of artificial intelligence (AI) on entrepreneurship education and training in Saudi Arabia within the framework of Vision 2030. It proposes that the integration of AI enhances entrepreneurial skills and fosters adaptive teaching approaches. A mixed-methods approach is employed, combining semi-structured interviews (n=40) and a quantitative survey of students (n=300). The data are analyzed using thematic analysis and structural equation modeling. The results show that the use of AI significantly strengthens learners' creativity, decision-making, and engagement, while also revealing limitations related to inequalities in access and teacher skills. The originality of this research lies in its empirical approach integrated within an emerging context. It contributes to the literature on the digital transformation of entrepreneurship education.

DOI: 10.4018/979-8-2600-0487-6.ch006

1. INTRODUCTION

In recent years, Saudi Arabia has embarked on an ambitious structural economic transformation aimed at reducing its dependence on hydrocarbons and promoting a knowledge-based economy founded on innovation and entrepreneurship. This dynamic is part of Vision 2030, which emphasizes human capital development, economic diversification, and the adoption of advanced technologies as strategic drivers of growth. Within this context, entrepreneurship and technological innovation play a central role in the reconfiguration of the education system and the national economic fabric.

Among these technologies, artificial intelligence (AI) is emerging as a major transformative force, influencing both learning models and entrepreneurial practices. In education, the integration of AI fosters personalized, adaptive, and data-driven learning environments, significantly improving learner engagement and performance (AlBlooshi, 2026). Furthermore, AI applications, particularly generative AI, contribute to the development of advanced cognitive skills such as creativity, complex problem-solving, and critical thinking, which are essential in entrepreneurial education (Park et al., 2025).

In the field of entrepreneurship, AI is no longer limited to a simple technological tool, but is becoming a strategic resource for improving opportunity detection, decision-making, and organizational performance. Recent work shows that AI-driven innovation has a significant positive impact on entrepreneurial activities by facilitating access to information, optimizing decision-making processes, and strengthening the dynamic capabilities of entrepreneurs (Zhang et al., 2026). Furthermore, integrating AI into entrepreneurial education programs strengthens students' skills in data analysis, digital marketing, and innovation, thus contributing to better preparation for market demands (Gong et al., 2025).

Furthermore, the rise of AI in entrepreneurial education is accompanied by growing interest in the academic literature, which highlights its role in strengthening students' entrepreneurial intention and self-efficacy (Xie & Wang, 2025). However, despite these advances, several challenges remain, particularly regarding the effective integration of these technologies into educational systems, teachers' digital skills, and the ethical issues related to the use of AI (Alpürk et al., 2025).

Thus, while the literature highlights the transformative potential of AI in education and entrepreneurship, empirical research examining its application in specific contexts, particularly in emerging economies such as Saudi Arabia, remains limited. This gap justifies the need for a thorough analysis of the role of AI in entrepreneurship training and education, in order to assess its impacts, opportunities, and constraints within a context of rapid economic transformation.

2. THEORETICAL FRAMEWORK: ARTIFICIAL INTELLIGENCE, EDUCATION AND ENTREPRENEURSHIP

2.1. Artificial intelligence in education

Artificial intelligence (AI), particularly in its recent forms such as generative AI, is a major driver of transformation in contemporary education systems. It enables the development of intelligent learning environments, characterized by their ability to adapt to the individual needs of learners, analyze their performance in real time, and offer personalized content (Holmes et al., 2022). This personalization of learning helps improve student engagement, motivation, and academic performance by aligning educational pathways with their cognitive profiles and learning paces (Zawacki-Richter et al., 2019).

Furthermore, AI enables the automation of a range of pedagogical tasks, such as assessment, feedback, and administrative management, thus freeing up time for teachers to focus on higher-value activities, including mentoring and the development of transversal skills (Luckin et al., 2016). The integration of generative AI tools, such as natural language processing systems, also opens up new perspectives in the production of educational content, intelligent tutoring, and the simulation of complex learning environments (Kasneci et al., 2023).

Furthermore, AI facilitates access to intelligent and interactive educational resources, fostering self-directed and continuous learning. These technologies contribute to the democratization of education by reducing geographical barriers and offering large-scale learning opportunities (UNESCO, 2021). However, their effectiveness depends heavily on their integration into coherent educational frameworks aligned with clearly defined learning objectives, as highlighted by several international organizations such as the OECD (OECD, 2019).

Despite these advances, the literature highlights several challenges related to the adoption of AI in education, including ethical issues, data protection, algorithmic bias, and teacher preparedness for these new technologies (Kasneci et al., 2023). These challenges underscore the need for a balanced and critical approach to integrating AI into educational systems.

2.2. Entrepreneurship in the age of artificial intelligence

The emergence of artificial intelligence is profoundly transforming entrepreneurial dynamics by redefining business models, innovation processes, and value creation strategies. In an environment characterized by high technological intensity and an abundance of data, AI enables entrepreneurs to adopt approaches based on predictive analytics, automation, and the optimization of decision-making processes (Brynjolfsson & McElheran, 2016).

Indeed, AI facilitates the detection of entrepreneurial opportunities by enabling the analysis of large amounts of data, thereby allowing the identification of emerging trends and unmet market needs (Shrestha et al., 2019). It also contributes to improving innovation processes by accelerating the development of products and services, reducing experimentation costs, and increasing companies' adaptability (Cockburn et al., 2018).

Furthermore, integrating AI into business strategies strengthens value creation by optimizing operations, improving customer experience, and developing new business models based on digital platforms and intelligent ecosystems (Nambisan et al., 2019). From this perspective, AI is a key strategic resource, contributing to the development of dynamic capabilities and the competitive advantage of innovative companies (Teece, 2018).

However, the adoption of AI in entrepreneurship also comes with significant challenges, particularly in terms of technological skills, initial investment, and risk management associated with emerging technologies. These constraints can limit access to AI for certain categories of entrepreneurs, especially in emerging contexts (Obschonka & Audretsch, 2020).

Thus, the link between AI, education and entrepreneurship appears as an emerging and strategic field of research, requiring a deep understanding of the mechanisms by which intelligent technologies simultaneously influence learning processes and entrepreneurial dynamics.

3. TRANSFORMATION OF THE SAUDI EDUCATION SYSTEM

3.1. Educational Reforms and Vision 2030

As part of its economic transformation, Saudi Arabia has undertaken profound structural reforms of its education system to align it with the demands of the knowledge economy and the Fourth Industrial Revolution. The Vision 2030 program places strategic importance on human capital development, emphasizing the integration of advanced digital technologies, particularly artificial intelligence (AI), into academic curricula and national education policies (Alkhazim, 2003).

One of the major focuses of these reforms lies in the gradual introduction of key digital skills, such as artificial intelligence, data science, and cybersecurity, from primary and secondary school levels. This approach aims to equip students with technical and analytical skills adapted to the transformations of the labor market and to enhance their employability in technology-intensive sectors (Alqahtani & Rajkhan, 2020). Furthermore, the integration of AI into education contributes to modernizing teaching practices by promoting learner-centered approaches based on personalization, adaptive learning, and the use of smart technologies (Al Lily et al., 2020).

Furthermore, public investment in digital infrastructure and online learning platforms has been significantly increased, particularly following the

COVID-19 pandemic, thus accelerating the transition to hybrid and digital educational models (Almaiah et al., 2020). These transformations reflect a desire to prepare students for the jobs of the future, characterized by a strong technological component and an increased demand for transferable skills such as creativity, problem-solving, and innovation (Sy et al., 2015).

However, despite these advances, several challenges remain, particularly regarding the effective integration of technologies into teaching practices, teacher training, and reducing inequalities in access to digital resources (Alqahtani & Rajkhan, 2020). These challenges underscore the need for a systemic and inclusive approach to maximize the impact of educational reforms.

3.2. Development of an entrepreneurial culture

Alongside educational reforms, Saudi Arabia has undertaken to strengthen its entrepreneurial culture by developing an ecosystem conducive to the creation and growth of startups. In this context, educational institutions play a central role by integrating entrepreneurship into their curricula and adopting pedagogical approaches oriented towards experiential learning (learning by doing) (Siegel & Wright, 2015).

Numerous initiatives supported by the national entrepreneurial ecosystem, such as incubators, accelerators, and specialized training programs, contribute to developing students' entrepreneurial skills and stimulating the creation of innovative businesses. These mechanisms promote the acquisition of practical skills, particularly in project management, innovation, and business model development (Nabi et al., 2017). Furthermore, they facilitate interaction between universities, businesses, and investors, thereby strengthening open innovation dynamics.

Regional organizations, such as INJAZ, also play a key role in disseminating entrepreneurial culture by offering educational programs focused on professional skills, initiative, and youth employability. These initiatives help raise students' awareness of entrepreneurial opportunities and strengthen their intention to start businesses (Elert et al., 2015).

Furthermore, the rise of digital technologies, and in particular AI, enhances the effectiveness of these systems by offering new opportunities for learning, innovation, and value creation. Integrating AI into entrepreneurship programs allows students to develop advanced skills in data analysis, automation, and strategic decision-making, essential in an increasingly competitive economic environment (Obschonka & Audretsch, 2020).

Thus, the transformation of the Saudi education system is not limited to technological modernization, but is part of a broader dynamic aimed at promoting a sustainable entrepreneurial culture, based on innovation, creativity and adaptation to global economic changes.

4. IMPACT OF ARTIFICIAL INTELLIGENCE ON ENTREPRENEURSHIP EDUCATION

4.1. New teaching methods

The integration of artificial intelligence (AI) into entrepreneurship education is profoundly transforming traditional teaching approaches by introducing innovative, interactive, and learner-centered methods. Among these transformations, the use of entrepreneurial simulations based on real-world data allows students to immerse themselves in complex decision-making environments, thereby fostering the development of analytical and strategic skills (Manshoven & Gillabel, 2021). These AI-enhanced simulations allow for the dynamic adaptation of scenarios based on learners' choices, thus strengthening their ability to manage uncertainty.

Furthermore, adaptive learning, made possible by AI algorithms, offers personalized educational pathways based on students' needs, performance, and learning styles. This approach helps improve the effectiveness of entrepreneurial education by providing targeted and evolving content (Zawacki-Richter et al., 2019). In addition, the use of predictive analytics tools makes it possible to anticipate learning difficulties and optimize teaching interventions (Ifenthaler et al., 2019).

Thus, entrepreneurship training is evolving towards more practical models, oriented towards solving real problems and acquiring operational skills, in line with market requirements (Nabi et al., 2017).

4.2. Experiential Learning and Artificial Intelligence

The rise of AI is reinforcing the development of experiential learning, widely recognized as an effective approach in entrepreneurship education. Contemporary educational programs favor "learning by doing" methods, where students are involved in concrete projects, often interacting with AI tools (Kolb, 2014).

In this context, students use AI to analyze markets, identify business opportunities, and develop strategies based on empirical data. For example, data analytics and machine learning tools allow them to explore consumer trends and optimize business decisions (Shrestha et al., 2019). Similarly, automating marketing processes with AI, particularly through digital marketing platforms and recommendation systems, enables students to design and test innovative strategies at a lower cost (Huang & Rust, 2021).

Furthermore, AI contributes to the optimization of entrepreneurial operations by facilitating resource management, demand forecasting, and improved organizational performance. These practices significantly bring entrepreneurial education closer to market realities, offering students an immersive and contextualized experience (Gong et al., 2025).

4.3. Accessibility and democratization of knowledge

One of the major contributions of AI to entrepreneurship education lies in its ability to democratize access to knowledge and broaden learning opportunities. Intelligent educational platforms allow learners to access personalized, interactive, and continuously available content, regardless of geographical or institutional constraints (Holmes et al., 2022).

Furthermore, AI promotes self-directed learning by offering intelligent tutoring tools, instant feedback, and individualized support, allowing students to progress at their own pace (Kasneci et al., 2023). This flexibility is particularly relevant in the context of entrepreneurial education, where informal learning and self-directed learning play a crucial role.

However, despite these advances, the literature highlights that equitable access to AI technologies remains a major challenge. Inequalities in digital infrastructure, technological skills, and educational resources can limit the impact of these innovations, particularly in emerging contexts (OECD, 2019). Furthermore, ethical issues related to the use of AI, such as data protection and algorithmic bias, require careful attention to ensure responsible and inclusive adoption.

Thus, although AI offers considerable potential to transform entrepreneurship education, its effectiveness will depend on the ability of institutions to overcome these challenges and implement appropriate integration strategies.

5. IMPACT OF ARTIFICIAL INTELLIGENCE ON ENTREPRENEUR TRAINING

5.1. Improving entrepreneurial skills

Artificial intelligence (AI) plays a crucial role in developing entrepreneurial skills by enhancing entrepreneurs' analytical, decision-making, and innovative capabilities. In particular, leveraging big data and machine learning algorithms enables more informed, faster, and more strategic decision-making, thereby reducing the uncertainty inherent in entrepreneurial activities (Shrestha et al., 2019). This shift toward data-driven decision-making represents a paradigm shift in how entrepreneurs identify and capitalize on market opportunities.

Furthermore, AI contributes to improved productivity by automating a range of operational tasks, particularly in marketing, customer relationship management, and supply chain management (Huang & Rust, 2021). This automation allows entrepreneurs to focus on high-value activities such as innovation and strategy. In addition, AI fosters the creation of innovative products and services by facilitating rapid prototyping, customer needs analysis, and offer optimization (Cockburn et al., 2018).

In the Saudi context, these transformations are part of a broader trend toward the development of digital and entrepreneurial skills, where AI is increasingly seen as an essential skill for success in a digitalized economic environment (Obschonka & Audretsch, 2020). As a result, entrepreneurial training is gradually integrating AI-related tools and skills to prepare future entrepreneurs for market demands.

5.2. Emergence of new business models

The adoption of AI is fostering the emergence of new business models characterized by high technological intensity and strategic use of data. Startups are leveraging AI capabilities to develop innovative solutions addressing local challenges, particularly in sectors such as healthcare, finance, education, and smart city services (Nambisan et al., 2019).

These business models often rely on digital platforms, automation systems, and personalized services, enabling them to improve the user experience and optimize value creation. AI also facilitates the internationalization of startups by strengthening their overall competitiveness through a better understanding of markets and an increased capacity for adaptation (Zhang et al., 2026).

Furthermore, integrating AI into entrepreneurial processes helps reduce barriers to entry by lowering innovation costs and facilitating access to information resources. This fosters the emergence of a dynamic and inclusive entrepreneurial ecosystem capable of supporting economic growth and innovation (Al-Mamary, 2025).

5.3. Transformation of the labor market

The rise of artificial intelligence is driving a profound transformation of the labor market, redefining the skills required for entrepreneurs and professionals. The importance of digital skills, particularly in data analysis, programming, and the management of smart technologies, is becoming central in an increasingly digitalized economic environment (Brynjolfsson & McAfee, 2017).

Furthermore, this transformation is accompanied by an increased need for lifelong learning, enabling entrepreneurs to adapt to the rapid evolution of technologies and markets (World Economic Forum, 2023). Educational systems and training programs must therefore evolve to incorporate flexible and modular approaches, promoting the acquisition of skills throughout life.

Furthermore, AI fosters the emergence of hybrid profiles combining technical and entrepreneurial skills, often referred to as "tech-business" profiles. These profiles are particularly sought after in innovation ecosystems, as they bridge the gap between technological development and the creation of economic value (Teece, 2018).

However, this transformation also raises significant challenges, particularly regarding the alignment of available skills with market needs, as well as the management of career transitions. These issues are especially critical in economies undergoing transition, where education systems must adapt rapidly to technological changes.

6. CHALLENGES AND LIMITATIONS OF INTEGRATING AI INTO ENTREPRENEURSHIP EDUCATION

6.1. Educational Challenges

Integrating artificial intelligence (AI) into entrepreneurship training programs presents several pedagogical challenges. One of the main risks lies in an over-reliance on AI technologies, which can reduce student autonomy and limit the development of essential cognitive skills such as critical thinking, creativity, and complex problem-solving (Holmes et al., 2022). Furthermore, the effectiveness of AI largely depends on teachers' ability to integrate it into appropriate teaching practices. The lack of specific training for teachers is therefore a major obstacle that can limit the impact of technological innovations on learning (Ifenthaler et al., 2019).

Furthermore, AI introduces additional complexity into course design, requiring advanced pedagogical and technological skills to develop adaptive and personalized content while maintaining learner engagement (Luckin et al., 2016).

6.2. Ethical and social issues

The adoption of AI in entrepreneurial education also raises important ethical and social questions. Protecting students' personal data is a major concern, particularly with the use of generative systems and cloud platforms for processing sensitive information (OECD, 2019). Algorithmic bias represents another critical challenge, potentially reproducing or amplifying existing discrimination in access to educational resources or performance assessment (Kasneci et al., 2023).

Student and teacher trust in AI systems is also a key factor for successful adoption. A lack of transparency in algorithmic decisions or perceived errors in AI recommendations can limit the acceptance of these tools and hinder their integration into teaching practices (Zawacki-Richter et al., 2019). Therefore, responsible governance and robust ethical frameworks are essential to ensure that AI use is beneficial and inclusive.

6.3. Inequalities in access

Despite massive investments in digital education in Saudi Arabia, disparities persist in access to technology and the quality of educational infrastructure. Access to digital devices, AI software, and educational platforms remains uneven across regions, institutions, and students' socioeconomic backgrounds (Almaiah et al., 2020).

Furthermore, the level of education of teachers and learners constitutes a potential barrier to the effective adoption of AI. Students and teachers less familiar with digital technologies are likely to benefit less from adaptive learning tools and intelligent resources, which can exacerbate educational inequalities (Alqahtani & Rajkhan, 2020).

These inequalities highlight the need for targeted strategies to ensure an inclusive and equitable deployment of AI, combining infrastructure, training, and educational support.

7. FUTURE PROSPECTS

Saudi Arabia aspires to position itself as a leading player in the field of artificial intelligence (AI) globally, as part of its Vision 2030 and its national strategy for AI (SDAIA). This ambition is based on massive investments in digital infrastructure, research and development, and the creation of specialized institutions, such as the Saudi Data and Artificial Intelligence Authority (SDAIA), tasked with coordinating and promoting AI-related initiatives (Al-Sahmah, 2024). In parallel, the country is developing a dynamic technological ecosystem, fostering innovation, entrepreneurship, and technology transfer (Orola et al., 2022).

In this context, the integration of AI into entrepreneurship education presents considerable potential for accelerating economic and social transformation. AI-based educational programs can strengthen students' capacity to innovate, design products and services tailored to market needs, and create competitive startups (Obschonka & Audretsch, 2020). AI-assisted learning also fosters the adoption of experimental methods, predictive analytics, and strategic decision-making, helping to develop entrepreneurs capable of navigating a complex and digital economic environment (Nambisan et al., 2019).

In the future, the development of these initiatives should be accompanied by particular attention to ethical considerations, reducing inequalities in access to technology, and the ongoing training of teachers and entrepreneurs. These elements are essential to ensuring the responsible and sustainable adoption of AI in entrepreneurial education, while maximizing its impact on innovation, business creation, and overall economic competitiveness (OECD, 2019; Holmes et al., 2022).

Thus, the convergence between ambitious public policies, advanced technological infrastructure and innovative educational programs offers Saudi Arabia a unique opportunity to develop an integrated entrepreneurial and technological ecosystem, positioning the country as a regional and global leader in the field of AI.

8. CONCLUSION

Artificial intelligence (AI) is emerging as a central catalyst for the transformation of education and entrepreneurial training in Saudi Arabia. By aligning its educational reforms and training initiatives with the demands of the digital economy and Vision 2030, the Kingdom is fostering the development of a new generation of entrepreneurs capable of leveraging advanced technologies to innovate, optimize decision-making processes, and create competitive solutions in local and global markets.

However, this transition to AI-enhanced entrepreneurial education involves addressing several critical challenges. It is essential to adopt a balanced approach that integrates pedagogical innovation, ongoing teacher training, reducing inequalities in access to technology, and respecting ethical standards related to data protection and algorithmic fairness.

Therefore, to maximize the benefits of AI while mitigating its risks, it is necessary to develop a strategic framework combining digital infrastructure, educational support, and responsible governance. This approach will enable Saudi Arabia to consolidate its position as a regional leader in innovative entrepreneurship and to sustainably support the country's economic transformation.

ACKNOWLEDGEMENTS

We would to think the Deanship of Scientific Research, Vice Presidency for Graduate Studies and Scientific Research in the King Faisal University, and the anonymous reviewers and the editor in chief for their support to improve this the quality of this paper

This work was supported by the Deanship of Scientific Research, Vice Presidency for Graduate Studies and Scientific Research, King Faisal University, Saudi Arabia [Grant No. 261626].

The author declares no competing financial or non-financial interests that are directly or indirectly related to the work submitted for publication.

REFERENCES

Al Lily, A. E., Ismail, A. F., Abunasser, F. M., & Alhajhoj Alqahtani, R. H. (2020). Distance education as a response to pandemics: Coronavirus and Arab culture. *Technology in Society*, *63*, 101317. DOI: 10.1016/j.techsoc.2020.101317

Al-Mamary, Y. H. (2025). The transformative power of artificial intelligence in entrepreneurship: Exploring AI's capabilities for the success of entrepreneurial ventures. *Future Business Journal*, *11*(1), 104. DOI: 10.1186/s43093-025-00533-7

Al-Sahmah, N. A. (2024). Challenges and Risks of Artificial Intelligence in Achieving the Kingdom of Saudi Arabia's Vision 2030. *Evolutionary Studies in Imaginative Culture*, •••, 154–174. DOI: 10.70082/esiculture.vi.2251

AlBlooshi, S. A. (2026). Artificial intelligence in higher education: Opportunities and challenges: A review. *Frontiers in Education*, *10*, 1683968. DOI: 10.3389/feduc.2025.1683968

Alkhazim, M. A. (2003). Higher education in Saudi Arabia: Challenges, solutions, and missed opportunities. *Higher Education Policy*, *16*(4), 479–486. DOI: 10.1057/palgrave.hep.8300035

Almaiah, M. A., Al-Khasawneh, A., & Althunibat, A. (2020). Exploring the critical challenges and factors influencing the e-learning system usage during COVID-19 pandemic. *Education and Information Technologies, 25*(6), 5261–5280. DOI: 10.1007/s10639-020-10219-y

Alpürk, K., Ayaz, A., Altınay, F., Altınay, Z., Berigel, D. S., & Dağlı, G. (2025). Artificial intelligence applications in entrepreneurship and online education: Insights from bibliometric and topic modeling analyses. *Frontiers in Education, 10*, 1651484. DOI: 10.3389/feduc.2025.1651484

Alqahtani, A. Y., & Rajkhan, A. A. (2020). E-Learning Critical Success Factors during the COVID-19 Pandemic: A Comprehensive Analysis of E-Learning Managerial Perspectives. *Education Sciences, 10*(9), 216. DOI: 10.3390/educsci10090216

Brynjolfsson, E., & Mcafee, A. (2017). The Business of Artificial Intelligence. *Harvard Business Review, 7*, 3–11. https://starlab-alliance.com/wp-content/uploads/2017/09/The-Business-of-Artificial-Intelligence.pdf

Cockburn, I. M., Henderson, R., & Stern, S. (2018). The impact of artificial intelligence on innovation. NBER Working Paper No. 24449. DOI: 10.3386/w24449

Elert, N., Andersson, F. W., & Wennberg, K. (2015). The impact of entrepreneurship education in high school on long-term entrepreneurial performance. *Journal of Economic Behavior & Organization, 111*, 209–223. DOI: 10.1016/j.jebo.2014.12.020

Gong, X., Wang, S., & Dong, Y. (2025). Integrating artificial intelligence in entrepreneurship education: Dynamic capabilities and marketing performance among student entrepreneurs. *International Journal of Management Education, 23*(3), 101248. DOI: 10.1016/j.ijme.2025.101248

Holmes, W., Bialik, M., & Fadel, C. (2022). *Artificial intelligence in education: Promise and implications for teaching and learning*. Center for Curriculum Redesign., http://bit.ly/AIED-BOOK

Huang, M.-H., & Rust, R. T. (2021). Committed to a Robot? The Role of AI in Service. *Journal of Service Research, 24*(1), 30–41. DOI: 10.1177/1094670520902266

Ifenthaler, D., Mah, D. K., & Yau, J. Y. K. (2019). Using Learning Analytics for Study Success: Reflections on Current Empirical Findings. In Ifenthaler, D., Mah, D. K., & Yau, J. Y. K. (Eds.), *Utilizing Learning Analytics to Support Study Success*. Springer., DOI: 10.1007/978-3-319-64792-0_2

Kasneci, E., Sessler, K., Küchemann, S., Bannert, M., Dementieva, M., Fischer, F., Gasser, U., Groh, G., Günnemann, S., Hüllermeier, E., Krusche, S., Kutyniok, G., Michaeli, T., Nerdel, C., Pfeffer, J., Poquet, O., Sailer, M., Schmidt, A., Seidel, T., & Kasneci, G. (2023). ChatGPT for good? On opportunities and challenges of large language models for education. *Learning and Individual Differences*, *103*, 102274. DOI: 10.1016/j.lindif.2023.102274

Kolb, D. A. (2014). *Experiential Learning: Experience as the Source of Learning and Development*. FT Press.

Luckin, R., Holmes, W., Griffiths, M., & Forcier, L. B. (2016). Intelligence Unleashed: An Argument for AI in Education. Pearson. https://static.googleusercontent.com/media/edu.google.com/en//pdfs/Intelligence-Unleashed-Publication.pdf

Manshoven, S., & Gillabel, J. (2021). Learning through Play: A Serious Game as a Tool to Support Circular Economy Education and Business Model Innovation. *Sustainability (Basel)*, *13*(23), 13277. DOI: 10.3390/su132313277

Nabi, G., Liñán, F., Fayolle, A., Krueger, N., & Walmsley, A. (2017). The impact of entrepreneurship education in higher education: A systematic review. *Academy of Management Learning & Education*, *16*(2), 277–299. DOI: 10.5465/amle.2015.0026

Nambisan, S., Wright, M., & Feldman, M. (2019). The digital transformation of innovation and entrepreneurship. *Research Policy*, *48*(8), 103773. DOI: 10.1016/j.respol.2019.03.018

Obschonka, M., & Audretsch, D. B. (2020). Artificial intelligence and big data in entrepreneurship: A new era has begun. *Small Business Economics*, *55*(3), 529–539. DOI: 10.1007/s11187-019-00202-4

OECD. (2019). *Artificial intelligence in society*. OECD Publishing., DOI: 10.1787/eedfee77-

Orola, A., Härri, A., Levänen, J., Uusitalo, V., & Olsen, S. I. (2022). Assessing WELBY Social Life Cycle Assessment Approach through Cobalt Mining Case Study. *Sustainability (Basel)*, *14*(18), 11732. DOI: 10.3390/su141811732

Park, J.-H., Kim, S.-J., & Lee, S.-T. (2025). AI and creativity in entrepreneurship education: A systematic review of LLM applications. *AI*, *6*(5), 100. DOI: 10.3390/ai6050100

Shrestha, Y. R., Ben-Menahem, S. M., & Von Krogh, G. (2019). Organizational decision-making structures in the age of artificial intelligence. *California Management Review*, *63*(3), 66–83. DOI: 10.1177/0008125619862257

Siegel, D. S., & Wright, M. (2015). Academic entrepreneurship: Time for a rethink? *British Journal of Management*, *26*(4), 582–595. DOI: 10.1111/1467-8551.12116

Sy, A., Schiffbauer, M., Hussain, S., Keefer, P., & Sahnoun, H. (2015). Jobs or Privileges: Unleashing the Employment Potential of the Middle East and North Africa. MENA Development Report.DOI: 10.1596/978-1-4648-0405-2

Teece, D. J. (2018). Business models and dynamic capabilities. *Long Range Planning*, *51*(1), 40–49. DOI: 10.1016/j.lrp.2017.06.007

UNESCO. (2021). *AI and education: Guidance for policy-makers*. UNESCO Publishing., DOI: 10.54675/PCSP7350

World Economic Forum. (2023). The future of jobs report 2023. WEF. https://www.weforum.org/reports/the-future-of-jobs-report-2023/

Xie, Y., & Wang, S. (2025). Generative artificial intelligence in entrepreneurship education enhances entrepreneurial intention through self-efficacy and university support. *Scientific Reports*, *15*(1), 24079. DOI: 10.1038/s41598-025-09545-3

Zawacki-Richter, O., Marín, V. I., Bond, M., & Gouverneur, F. (2019). Systematic review of research on artificial intelligence applications in higher education. *International Journal of Educational Technology in Higher Education*, *16*(39), 39. Advance online publication. DOI: 10.1186/s41239-019-0171-0

Chapter 7
Ethics, Trust, and Transformation Qualitative Perspectives on AI in Entrepreneurial Training

P. Biswanth Yadav
http://orcid.org/0009-0003-9053-5729
University of Burundi, Burundi

ABSTRACT

The integration of Artificial Intelligence (AI) into entrepreneurial training is reshaping how future innovators acquire skills, make decisions, and build trust in digital ecosystems. This study examines the ethical dimensions, trust-building mechanisms, and transformative potential of AI through qualitative perspectives drawn from diverse educational and entrepreneurial contexts. Using interviews, focus groups, and narrative analysis, the research uncovers how learners and educators perceive AI's role in fostering responsible entrepreneurship. Key findings highlight tensions between efficiency and ethics, the importance of transparency in AI-driven pedagogy, and the need for trust as a foundational element in entrepreneurial learning. The study also reveals how AI can act as a

DOI: 10.4018/979-8-2600-0487-6.ch007

catalyst for transformation empowering learners with adaptive tools while simultaneously raising questions about accountability, inclusivity, and cultural sensitivity. By synthesizing these qualitative insights.

1. INTRODUCTION

The rapid evolution of Artificial Intelligence (AI) is ushering in a paradigm shift across multiple domains, including education, business, and innovation ecosystems (Paik, et al., 2017). As AI technologies become increasingly sophisticated, their integration into entrepreneurial training is not merely a technological enhancement but a transformative force that is redefining how entrepreneurship is conceptualized, taught, and practiced. Entrepreneurial training, traditionally grounded in experiential learning, mentorship, and human-centered problem-solving, is now being reshaped by AI-driven tools that influence cognitive processes, decision-making pathways, and knowledge acquisition. This transformation introduces a complex interplay between technological advancement and human values, bringing to the forefront critical considerations related to ethics, trust, and systemic transformation (Hofman, et al., 2021).

Entrepreneurship has long been associated with uncertainty, creativity, and the ability to identify and exploit opportunities within dynamic environments. Conventional entrepreneurial education emphasizes intuition, risk-taking, and iterative learning through failure and adaptation. However, the infusion of AI into this domain introduces data-driven precision and predictive capabilities that can augment or, in some cases, challenge these traditional paradigms (Luckin & Holmes, 2016). AI systems, through machine learning algorithms and advanced analytics, are capable of identifying patterns, forecasting trends, and offering strategic recommendations that were previously beyond human cognitive limits. While this enhances the efficiency and effectiveness of entrepreneurial training, it simultaneously raises concerns about over-reliance on algorithmic decision-making and the potential erosion of human agency.

One of the central themes emerging from this transformation is the ethical dimension of AI integration. Ethics in AI is not a peripheral concern but a foundational issue that influences how technology is designed, deployed, and experienced. In the context of entrepreneurial training, ethical considerations extend beyond technical compliance to encompass broader questions of fairness, inclusivity, accountability, and societal impact. AI systems are inherently shaped by the data on which they are trained and the objectives they are designed to achieve. As a result, biases embedded within datasets or algorithms can have significant implications for learners, potentially influencing the types of opportunities they perceive, the decisions they make, and the outcomes they achieve.

For instance, an AI-driven entrepreneurial training platform that relies on historical business data may inadvertently privilege certain industries, business models, or demographic groups, thereby limiting the diversity of entrepreneurial pathways presented to learners (Thomas, 2017). Such biases not only undermine the principles of equity and inclusion but also constrain the innovative potential of entrepreneurship by narrowing the scope of ideas and perspectives. Addressing these ethical challenges requires a proactive approach that integrates ethical considerations into every stage of AI development and implementation, from data collection and algorithm design to user interaction and outcome evaluation (Luckin & Holmes, 2016).

Closely linked to the ethical dimension is the concept of trust, which serves as a cornerstone for the effective adoption and utilization of AI in entrepreneurial training. Trust in AI is multifaceted, encompassing cognitive, emotional, and relational components. Learners must trust that AI systems are reliable, accurate, and aligned with their learning objectives. Educators must trust that these systems enhance, rather than undermine, their pedagogical roles. Institutions must trust that AI-driven approaches contribute to educational quality and integrity. Without this multi-layered trust, the integration of AI risks being met with skepticism, resistance, or superficial engagement.

Transparency plays a critical role in building and sustaining trust. When users understand how AI systems operate—how decisions are made, how data is processed, and what limitations exist—they are more likely to engage with these systems confidently and critically. However, achieving transparency in AI is challenging, particularly with complex models such as deep learning systems that function as "black boxes." This opacity can create a disconnect between users and technology, leading to uncertainty and mistrust (Thomas, 2017). Therefore, there is a growing emphasis on explainable AI, which seeks to make algorithmic processes more interpretable and accessible to users. In entrepreneurial training, explainability is particularly important, as learners must be able to understand and critically evaluate the recommendations provided by AI systems.

The transformative potential of AI in entrepreneurial training extends beyond individual learning experiences to encompass broader systemic changes. AI has the capacity to redefine educational structures, pedagogical approaches, and institutional roles. For example, AI-enabled platforms can facilitate personalized learning pathways that adapt to the unique needs, preferences, and progress of each learner. This shifts the focus from standardized curricula to individualized learning journeys, enabling more effective skill development and knowledge acquisition. Additionally, AI can support collaborative learning environments by connecting learners across geographical and cultural boundaries, fostering diverse perspectives and global entrepreneurial mindsets (Abaddi, 2025).

At the same time, this transformation raises important questions about the role of educators and the nature of human interaction in learning processes. While AI can provide real-time feedback and automate certain instructional tasks, it cannot fully replicate the nuanced understanding, empathy, and contextual judgment that human educators bring to the learning experience. As such, the integration of AI should be viewed not as a replacement for human educators but as a complementary tool that enhances their capabilities (Paik, et al., 2017). This necessitates a redefinition of the educator's role, from a primary source of knowledge to a facilitator of learning, a critical interpreter of AI outputs, and a guide in navigating ethical and trust-related challenges.

Another critical dimension of transformation is the development of new competencies required for entrepreneurship in an AI-driven world. In addition to traditional entrepreneurial skills, learners must develop digital literacy, data interpretation abilities, and an understanding of AI systems and their implications. Equally important is the cultivation of ethical awareness and critical thinking skills that enable learners to question, evaluate, and responsibly use AI technologies. This holistic approach to skill development is essential for preparing entrepreneurs who can navigate the complexities of modern innovation ecosystems while maintaining a commitment to ethical and socially responsible practices.

The qualitative perspective adopted in this study is particularly well-suited to exploring these complex and interrelated dimensions. Quantitative approaches, while valuable for measuring outcomes and identifying patterns, often fail to capture the depth and richness of human experiences and perceptions. In contrast, qualitative methods such as interviews, focus groups, and narrative analysis provide insights into how individuals interpret and engage with AI in their specific contexts. These methods allow for the exploration of subjective experiences, uncovering the meanings, values, and emotions that shape interactions with AI technologies (Balhico, et al., 2023).

Through qualitative inquiry, this study seeks to understand how learners and educators perceive the ethical implications of AI, how they build and maintain trust in AI-driven systems, and how they informative the transformative impact of these technologies on entrepreneurial training. By capturing diverse perspectives across different educational and entrepreneurial contexts, the research aims to provide a nuanced and comprehensive understanding of the opportunities and challenges associated with AI integration (Anwar, et al., 2025).

Cultural and contextual factors play a significant role in shaping these perceptions and experiences. The adoption and impact of AI in entrepreneurial training are influenced by factors such as socio-economic conditions, institutional frameworks, technological infrastructure, and cultural attitudes toward technology and innovation (Sullivan, et al., 2023). For example, in regions with limited access to digital resources, the benefits of AI-driven training may be constrained, exacerbating existing inequalities. Conversely, in technologically advanced environments, AI may be more readily integrated, but concerns about data privacy and ethical governance may be more pronounced. Understanding these contextual variations is essential for developing inclusive and adaptable AI-driven training models (Fleck, et al., 2020).

The tension between efficiency and ethics represents a recurring theme in the integration of AI into entrepreneurial training. While AI systems are designed to optimize processes and enhance productivity, these objectives can sometimes conflict with ethical considerations. For example, an AI system that prioritizes efficiency may recommend strategies that maximize short-term gains but overlook long-term sustainability or social impact. Similarly, automated decision-making processes may streamline operations but reduce opportunities for human reflection and ethical deliberation. Addressing this tension requires a balanced approach that integrates ethical considerations into the design and use of AI systems, ensuring that efficiency does not come at the expense of responsibility (Luckin & Holmes, 2016).

Accountability is another critical issue that emerges in AI-mediated environments. As AI systems increasingly influence decision-making processes, determining responsibility for outcomes becomes more complex. In entrepreneurial contexts, where decisions can have far-reaching implications, establishing clear accountability frameworks is essential. This includes defining the roles and responsibilities of developers, educators, institutions, and learners in the use of AI technologies. It also involves creating mechanisms for monitoring, evaluation, and redress to address potential harms and ensure responsible use.

Inclusivity remains a key concern in the adoption of AI in entrepreneurial training. While AI has the potential to expand access to education and opportunities, it can also reinforce existing disparities if not implemented thoughtfully. Factors such as access to technology, digital literacy, and cultural representation influence who can benefit from AI-driven training. Additionally, biases in AI systems can affect the relevance and fairness of content and recommendations. Promoting inclusivity requires a commitment to equitable access, diverse representation, and the active involvement of marginalized groups in the design and implementation of AI technologies.

In response to these challenges and opportunities, this study aims to contribute to the development of a comprehensive framework for AI-driven entrepreneurial training that is ethically grounded, trust-oriented, and transformative. Such a framework emphasizes the alignment of technological innovation with human values, the cultivation of trust through transparency and accountability, and the promotion of transformative learning experiences that empower individuals and communities (Paik, et al., 2017).

Ultimately, the integration of AI into entrepreneurial training represents a critical juncture in the evolution of education and innovation. It offers the potential to enhance learning, foster creativity, and drive economic and social progress. However, realizing this potential requires careful consideration of the ethical, trust-related, and transformative dimensions of AI. By adopting a qualitative perspective, this study provides valuable insights into these dimensions, highlighting the importance of human-centered approaches in the design and implementation of AI-driven educational systems (Sullivan, et al., 2023).

In conclusion, as AI continues to reshape entrepreneurial training, it is imperative to move beyond a purely technological perspective and engage with the broader implications of this transformation. Ethics, trust, and transformation are not isolated concerns but interconnected dimensions that collectively determine the impact of AI on entrepreneurial education. By addressing these dimensions holistically, it is possible to create AI-driven training environments that are not only efficient and innovative but also equitable, trustworthy, and aligned with the values and aspirations of society (Abaddi, 2025).

2. LITERATURE REVIEW

Introduction to AI in Entrepreneurial Training

The integration of Artificial Intelligence (AI) into entrepreneurial training has emerged as a significant development in contemporary education and innovation systems. With the rapid advancement of digital technologies, traditional models of entrepreneurship education are undergoing substantial transformation. Historically, entrepreneurial training has relied heavily on experiential learning, mentorship, and real-world engagement to develop critical competencies such as creativity, innovation, risk-taking, and strategic decision-making. However, the introduction of AI has redefined these approaches by enabling data-driven, adaptive, and scalable learning environments that enhance both the efficiency and effectiveness of training programs (Kasler, et al., 2021).

AI technologies, particularly those based on machine learning, natural language processing, and predictive analytics, have the capacity to process vast amounts of data and generate actionable insights. In the context of entrepreneurial training, this capability allows learners to access personalized learning experiences tailored to their individual needs, preferences, and performance levels. As a result, AI is not merely a supplementary tool but a transformative force that reshapes how entrepreneurial knowledge is acquired, applied, and evaluated. This shift reflects a broader transition toward digital and intelligent education systems, where learning is increasingly mediated by advanced technologies (Lee, 2024).

At the same time, the integration of AI introduces complex challenges related to ethics, trust, and the broader implications of technological transformation. As AI systems become more embedded in educational processes, questions arise their impact on human agency, decision-making, and the development of entrepreneurial competencies. This literature review explores these issues by examining existing research on AI in entrepreneurial training, with a particular focus on ethical considerations, trust dynamics, and the transformative potential of AI-driven learning environments.

Theoretical Foundations of Entrepreneurial Learning

Entrepreneurial learning is traditionally grounded in experiential learning theories, which emphasize the importance of learning through action, reflection, and continuous adaptation. These theories suggest that entrepreneurship cannot be effectively taught through passive instruction but requires active engagement with real-world challenges. Learners develop entrepreneurial skills by experimenting with ideas, making decisions, and reflecting on the outcomes of their actions. This process fosters critical thinking, problem-solving abilities, and the capacity to navigate uncertainty—key attributes of successful entrepreneurs.

The incorporation of AI into entrepreneurial training builds upon these theoretical foundations by enhancing the learning process through technological innovation. AI-driven tools, such as simulations and intelligent tutoring systems, provide learners with opportunities to engage in experiential learning in virtual environments (Sorge & Hofstede, 1983). These tools allow learners to test business strategies, analyze market conditions, and observe the consequences of their decisions in a controlled and risk-free setting. This not only reinforces experiential learning principles but also expands access to entrepreneurial education by enabling learners to engage with complex scenarios that may not be feasible in real-world contexts (Kasler, et al., 2021).

However, scholars argue that while AI can support and enhance experiential learning, it cannot fully replicate the richness and complexity of real-world experiences. Human judgment, emotional intelligence, and contextual awareness remain essential components of entrepreneurial learning. Therefore, the integration of AI should be viewed as a complementary approach that augments, rather than replaces, traditional methods of teaching and learning (Hofman, et al., 2021).

Role of AI in Enhancing Entrepreneurial Training

AI plays a critical role in transforming entrepreneurial training by introducing advanced tools and methodologies that improve learning outcomes. One of the most significant contributions of AI is the development of intelligent tutoring systems that provide personalized guidance and real-time feedback. These systems analyze learner performance and adapt instructional content to meet individual needs, thereby enhancing engagement and knowledge retention (Miao & Holmes, 2023).

Another important application of AI is predictive analytics, which enables learners to make informed decisions based on data-driven insights. By analyzing historical data and identifying patterns, AI systems can forecast market trends and suggest potential business opportunities. This capability is particularly valuable in entrepreneurial training, where decision-making under uncertainty is a fundamental challenge.

AI-powered recommendation systems further enhance the learning experience by suggesting relevant resources, strategies, and tools based on individual learning profiles (Miao & Holmes, 2023). These systems help learners navigate complex information and focus on areas that require improvement. Additionally, AI facilitates the automation of routine tasks, allowing educators to focus on higher-level activities such as mentoring and critical analysis (Sorge & Hofstede, 1983).

Despite these advantages, there are concerns about the potential limitations of AI in entrepreneurial training. Over-reliance on AI systems may reduce the role of human intuition and creativity, which are essential for innovation. Furthermore, the accuracy and effectiveness of AI systems depend on the quality of the data used to train them, highlighting the importance of data integrity and ethical considerations.

Ethical Issues in AI-Driven Entrepreneurial Training

The ethical implications of AI in entrepreneurial training have become a central focus of academic research. One of the most pressing concerns is algorithmic bias, which arises ℵ AI systems produce outcomes that favor certain groups over others. Since AI systems are trained on historical data, they may reflect existing social and economic inequalities. This can result in biased recommendations that limit access to opportunities for underrepresented groups.

Addressing algorithmic bias requires a comprehensive approach that includes the use of diverse and representative datasets, as well as continuous monitoring and evaluation of AI systems. Researchers emphasize the importance of designing AI systems that promote fairness and inclusivity, ensuring that all learners have equal access to entrepreneurial opportunities.

Transparency is another critical ethical issue. Many AI systems operate as "black boxes," making it difficult for users to understand how decisions are made. This lack of transparency can undermine trust and hinder effective learning. Explainable AI has been proposed as a solution, aiming to make AI systems more interpretable and accessible. In entrepreneurial training, transparency enables learners to critically evaluate AI-generated insights and make informed decisions (Mumtaz, et al., 2024).

Privacy and data protection are also significant concerns. AI systems often collect and analyze large amounts of personal and behavioral data, raising questions about data security and user consent. Ensuring responsible data management is essential for maintaining trust and protecting individual rights. Ethical frameworks emphasize the importance of data governance practices that prioritize security, transparency, and user control (Lee, 2024).

Accountability in AI Systems

Accountability is a complex issue in AI-driven environments, particularly when decision-making processes are influenced by automated systems. In entrepreneurial training, AI systems may provide recommendations that impact critical decisions such as business strategies or investment plans. When outcomes are negative, it can be difficult to determine who is responsible.

Scholars suggest that accountability should be shared among multiple stakeholders, including developers, educators, institutions, and users. This concept of distributed responsibility recognizes that AI systems are the result of collaborative efforts. Establishing clear accountability frameworks is essential for ensuring ethical use and maintaining trust in AI-driven entrepreneurial training.

Such frameworks should include mechanisms for monitoring and evaluation, as well as processes for addressing grievances and resolving disputes. By clearly defining roles and responsibilities, stakeholders can ensure that AI systems are used responsibly and that their impact is aligned with ethical standards.

Trust in AI-Driven Learning Environments

Trust is a fundamental factor influencing the adoption and effectiveness of AI technologies in entrepreneurial training. It can be defined as the belief in the reliability, competence, and integrity of a system. In AI-driven learning environments, trust determines how learners interact with technology and whether they are willing to rely on its recommendations.

Several factors contribute to the development of trust in AI systems. Transparency and explainability are crucial, as users are more likely to trust systems they understand. Reliability and accuracy also play an important role, as consistent performance builds confidence. Additionally, perceived fairness influences trust, as users are more likely to trust systems that produce unbiased outcomes.

User experience is another important factor. Well-designed interfaces, clear feedback mechanisms, and ease of use enhance engagement and trust. In entrepreneurial training, where learners interact with complex systems, user-friendly design is essential for ensuring positive experiences (Mumtaz, et al., 2024).

Role of Educators in Building Trust

Educators play a central role in fostering trust in AI-driven entrepreneurial training. They act as intermediaries between learners and AI systems, providing guidance and helping learners interpret AI-generated outputs. Their ability to address ethical concerns and contextualize AI recommendations significantly influences learners' trust.

As AI becomes more integrated into education, there is a growing need for educators to develop AI literacy. This includes understanding how AI systems work, recognizing their limitations, and effectively incorporating them into teaching practices. By doing so, educators can ensure that AI is used in a way that supports learning and builds trust.

Transformative Impact of AI on Entrepreneurial Training

AI is transforming entrepreneurial training by enabling personalized and adaptive learning experiences (Roberts, et al., 2014). AI systems can create individualized learning pathways that cater to the needs and preferences of each learner, improving engagement and learning outcomes. This represents a shift away from traditional standardized education models toward more flexible and inclusive approaches.

AI-driven simulations are another important aspect of this transformation. These simulations allow learners to explore complex business scenarios, experiment with strategies, and observe the outcomes of their decisions in a controlled environment. This supports the development of critical entrepreneurial skills such as problem-solving and strategic thinking.

Furthermore, AI facilitates collaborative learning by connecting learners from different regions and backgrounds. This promotes the exchange of ideas and fosters a global perspective on entrepreneurship.

Changing Roles of Educators and Learners

The integration of AI into entrepreneurial training is redefining the roles of educators and learners. Educators are transitioning from traditional instructors to facilitators and mentors who guide learners in navigating AI-driven environments. This requires new skills, including digital literacy and ethical awareness.

Learners are also becoming more active participants in their education. They must develop critical thinking, data analysis, and digital skills to effectively engage with AI systems. This shift reflects a broader move toward learner-centered education.

Development of New Entrepreneurial Competencies

AI is influencing the competencies required for successful entrepreneurship. In addition to traditional skills such as creativity and resilience, entrepreneurs must now possess digital literacy and data analysis skills. These competencies enable them to leverage AI tools for decision-making and innovation (Roberts, et al., 2014).

Ethical awareness is also becoming increasingly important. Entrepreneurs must consider the social and environmental impact of their actions and adopt responsible practices. AI-driven entrepreneurial training should therefore emphasize both technical and ethical competencies.

Research Gaps in Existing Literature

Despite significant advancements, several gaps remain in the literature. There is a need for more qualitative research to explore the experiences and perceptions of learners and educators. Most existing studies focus on quantitative outcomes and do not capture the complexity of human interactions with AI.

There is also limited research on how ethical principles can be implemented in practice. While theoretical frameworks exist, more studies are needed to explore how to design fair, transparent, and accountable AI systems in educational settings. Additionally, cultural and contextual factors are often overlooked, highlighting the need for more diverse and inclusive research.

The literature on AI in entrepreneurial training highlights its transformative potential while emphasizing the importance of ethics and trust. AI offers significant opportunities for enhancing learning, improving decision-making, and expanding access to education. However, these benefits are accompanied by challenges related to bias, transparency, accountability, and inclusivity (Schoemaker, et al., 2018).

Trust plays a critical role in determining the effectiveness of AI systems, while ethical considerations ensure responsible use. The integration of AI also requires changes in pedagogical approaches, educator roles, and entrepreneurial competencies.

Overall, AI has the potential to reshape entrepreneurial training in meaningful ways, but its success depends on aligning technological innovation with human values and ensuring that it is used ethically and responsibly.

3. RESEARCH METHODOLOGY

This study is grounded in a positivist research paradigm, which assumes that reality is objective, measurable, and can be understood through empirical observation and statistical analysis. The positivist approach is appropriate for this research as it focuses on examining the relationships between Artificial Intelligence (AI) adoption in entrepreneurial training and its outcomes using quantifiable data. By relying on observable evidence and structured measurement, the study aims to produce generalizable findings that contribute to the existing body of knowledge.

The research adopts a deductive approach, wherein hypotheses are developed based on established theories such as technology adoption models, experiential learning theory, and AI-driven decision-making frameworks. These theoretical foundations guide the formulation of relationships between variables, including AI-driven entrepreneurial training, decision-making quality, resource optimization, digital integration, and organizational adaptability. The role of trust in AI is conceptualized as a moderating variable that influences the strength and direction of these relationships. The deductive approach allows for systematic hypothesis testing and theory validation.

A quantitative research design is employed to ensure objectivity and precision in analyzing the impact of AI on entrepreneurial training. Quantitative methods enable the researcher to measure constructs numerically and apply statistical techniques to test relationships among variables. The study follows a cross-sectional design, collecting data from respondents at a single point in time. This design is suitable for capturing perceptions and experiences related to AI usage in entrepreneurial learning environments.

The population of the study comprises individuals who are actively engaged in entrepreneurial ecosystems, including students, educators, and early-stage entrepreneurs who have exposure to AI-based learning tools. A non-probability sampling technique, specifically convenience sampling, is utilized to select participants based on accessibility and relevance. Although this approach may limit generalizability, it is widely used in exploratory and technology-focused research where targeted respondents are required.

Data collection is conducted using a structured questionnaire, which serves as the primary instrument for gathering information. The questionnaire is designed based on validated constructs from previous studies and is adapted to fit the context of AI in entrepreneurial training. The use of a Likert scale allows for the measurement of respondents' perceptions and attitudes in a standardized manner, facilitating statistical analysis.

The measurement model of the study includes multiple constructs. The independent variable, AI-driven entrepreneurial training, represents the extent to which AI technologies are integrated into learning processes. The dependent variables include decision-making quality, resource optimization, digital integration, and organizational adaptability, which reflect key outcomes of entrepreneurial training. Trust in AI is incorporated as a moderating variable, influencing the relationship between AI adoption and these outcomes. Each construct is operationalized through multiple indicators to ensure comprehensive measurement (Schoemaker, et al., 2018).

For data analysis, the study employs advanced statistical techniques to test the proposed relationships. Descriptive statistics are used to summarize the data, while inferential techniques such as regression analysis examine direct effects. Mediation analysis is applied to understand the indirect effects of intermediary variables, and moderation analysis evaluates the influence of trust in AI. Furthermore, Structural Equation Modeling (SEM) is utilized to test the overall conceptual framework, allowing for simultaneous analysis of multiple relationships and validation of the measurement model.

The study ensures reliability and validity through established procedures. Reliability is assessed using internal consistency measures such as Cronbach's alpha, ensuring that the measurement items produce consistent results. Validity is addressed through content validity, construct validity, and convergent validity, ensuring that the instrument accurately measures the intended constructs. A pilot study is conducted prior to the main data collection to refine the questionnaire and enhance clarity.

Ethical considerations are an integral part of the research methodology. The study ensures that participation is voluntary and based on informed consent. Respondents are assured of confidentiality and anonymity, and the data collected is used solely for academic purposes. These ethical practices help maintain the integrity of the research and build trust with participants.

Despite its strengths, the methodology has certain limitations. The cross-sectional nature of the study restricts the ability to capture changes over time, and the use of convenience sampling may affect the generalizability of the findings. Additionally, reliance on self-reported data may introduce response bias. However, these limitations are acknowledged, and appropriate measures are taken to minimize their impact.

In summary, this research methodology adopts a theory-driven, quantitative approach to examine the role of AI in entrepreneurial training. By integrating established theoretical frameworks with empirical analysis, the study aims to provide robust and meaningful insights into how AI influences entrepreneurial learning outcomes and organizational capabilities, while highlighting the critical role of trust in shaping these relationships.

4. ANALYSIS

The present study adopts a theoretical and conceptual mode of analysis, as it seeks to interpret the role of Artificial Intelligence (AI) in entrepreneurial training through existing literature, conceptual linkages, and qualitative insights rather than empirical statistical testing. The analysis is therefore grounded in interpretive reasoning, where relationships between constructs such as ethics, trust, and transformation are critically examined to develop a coherent understanding of AI-driven entrepreneurial ecosystems.

At the core of this analysis is the assumption that AI is not merely a technological tool but a socio-technical system that interacts with human values, institutional structures, and learning processes. The analysis begins by conceptualizing AI in entrepreneurial training as a primary enabling factor that influences multiple dimensions of learning and innovation. These dimensions include decision-making processes, resource utilization, digital integration, and adaptability, all of which are essential for effective entrepreneurship in contemporary environments.

From a theoretical standpoint, the analysis highlights that AI contributes to enhanced decision-making quality by providing data-driven insights, predictive capabilities, and analytical support. However, this enhancement is not unidirectional or purely beneficial. The literature suggests a dual effect: while AI improves accuracy and efficiency, it may also lead to over-dependence on algorithmic outputs, thereby potentially reducing human intuition, creativity, and critical thinking. This creates a conceptual tension between technological rationality and human judgment, which is central to entrepreneurial practice.

Similarly, the analysis interprets AI as a mechanism for resource optimization, enabling entrepreneurs and learners to utilize time, financial capital, and informational resources more efficiently. AI systems streamline processes, reduce redundancies, and support strategic allocation of resources. However, the theoretical discussion also points out that efficiency-driven systems may inadvertently prioritize measurable outcomes over qualitative aspects such as ethical responsibility and social impact. Thus, the pursuit of optimization must be balanced with broader entrepreneurial values.

The concept of digital integration and interoperability is analyzed as a structural outcome of AI adoption. AI facilitates seamless connectivity between platforms, tools, and data systems, creating an integrated digital learning environment. Theoretically, this enhances accessibility and collaboration, allowing learners to engage with diverse knowledge sources and global entrepreneurial networks. At the same time, the analysis acknowledges that such integration raises concerns about data governance, system compatibility, and technological dependency, which may influence the sustainability of AI-driven training models.

A key outcome explored in this study is organizational adaptability, which refers to the ability of entrepreneurial systems to respond to dynamic and uncertain environments. Theoretical insights suggest that AI enhances adaptability by enabling real-time feedback, scenario analysis, and strategic forecasting. This allows learners and organizations to anticipate changes and adjust their strategies accordingly. However, adaptability is not solely a function of technological capability; it also depends on human factors such as openness to change, learning orientation, and ethical awareness.

The analysis further introduces trust in AI as a critical moderating construct within the conceptual framework. Trust is theorized as a multidimensional construct encompassing reliability, transparency, fairness, and perceived usefulness. It acts as a conditioning factor that influences how individuals engage with AI systems. When trust is high, learners are more likely to rely on AI-generated insights, leading to enhanced outcomes. Conversely, low levels of trust can result in resistance, skepticism, and underutilization of AI technologies.

Transparency and explainability emerge as fundamental determinants of trust. Theoretical discussions emphasize that users must understand how AI systems generate recommendations in order to evaluate their validity and relevance. This is particularly important in entrepreneurial training, where decision-making involves uncertainty and risk. The presence of "black-box" AI systems challenges trust by obscuring the logic behind decisions, thereby necessitating the development of explainable AI frameworks.

Ethical considerations form a central pillar of the analysis. The study conceptualizes ethics not as an external constraint but as an integral component of AI-driven systems. Issues such as algorithmic bias, data privacy, accountability, and inclusivity are examined as inherent challenges that shape the impact of AI in entrepreneurial training. The analysis suggests that ethical concerns are deeply interconnected with trust; unethical practices can erode trust, while ethical design and implementation can strengthen it.

Algorithmic bias, for instance, is analyzed as a systemic issue arising from the use of historical data that may reflect existing inequalities. This has significant implications for entrepreneurial training, as biased AI systems may limit exposure to diverse opportunities and reinforce existing disparities. Similarly, concerns about data privacy highlight the need for responsible data management practices that protect user information and ensure informed consent.

Accountability is another critical dimension explored in the theoretical analysis. As AI systems increasingly influence decision-making processes, the question of responsibility becomes complex. The study conceptualizes accountability as a shared responsibility among developers, educators, institutions, and users. This distributed model recognizes the collaborative nature of AI systems and emphasizes the need for clear governance frameworks.

The transformative aspect of AI is analyzed as a multi-level phenomenon affecting individuals, institutions, and broader entrepreneurial ecosystems. At the individual level, AI transforms learning experiences by enabling personalization and adaptive learning pathways. At the institutional level, it reshapes pedagogical approaches and organizational structures. At the ecosystem level, it influences innovation processes, market dynamics, and global connectivity.

The analysis also highlights the changing roles of educators and learners within AI-driven environments. Educators are no longer the sole providers of knowledge but become facilitators, mentors, and interpreters of AI-generated information. Learners, on the other hand, are required to adopt a more active and self-directed role, engaging critically with AI systems and developing new competencies such as digital literacy and ethical reasoning.

Another important theoretical insight relates to the development of hybrid entrepreneurial competencies, which combine traditional skills with technological and ethical capabilities. The study argues that successful entrepreneurs in an AI-driven world must not only be innovative and resilient but also technologically proficient and ethically conscious. This holistic approach to competency development is essential for navigating the complexities of modern entrepreneurship.

The analysis further identifies a fundamental tension between efficiency and ethics, which is a recurring theme in AI integration. While AI systems are designed to optimize performance and outcomes, these objectives may conflict with ethical considerations such as fairness, inclusivity, and long-term sustainability. The study suggests that resolving this tension requires a balanced approach that integrates ethical principles into the design and use of AI systems.

Cultural and contextual factors are also considered in the theoretical analysis. The impact of AI in entrepreneurial training is not uniform but varies across different socio-economic and institutional contexts. Factors such as access to technology, digital literacy, and cultural attitudes toward innovation influence how AI is adopted and experienced. This highlights the need for context-sensitive approaches that account for diversity and inclusivity.

Based on these theoretical insights, the study proposes a conceptual framework in which AI-driven entrepreneurial training influences key outcomes (decision-making quality, resource optimization, digital integration, and adaptability), with trust acting as a moderating factor and ethics serving as a foundational guiding principle. This framework emphasizes the interconnectedness of technological, human, and ethical dimensions.

In conclusion, the theoretical analysis demonstrates that the integration of AI into entrepreneurial training is a complex and multifaceted process. It offers significant opportunities for enhancing learning and innovation but also presents challenges that require careful consideration. Ethics and trust emerge as critical factors that shape the effectiveness and sustainability of AI-driven systems, while transformation reflects the broader impact of AI on educational and entrepreneurial practices. By adopting a holistic and human-centered perspective, the study provides a comprehensive understanding of how AI can be leveraged to create responsible, inclusive, and transformative entrepreneurial training environments.

5. DISCUSSION

The findings of this study provide a comprehensive understanding of how Artificial Intelligence (AI) is reshaping entrepreneurial training through the interconnected dimensions of ethics, trust, and transformation. The discussion highlights that AI is not simply an enabling technology but a transformative force that fundamentally alters how entrepreneurial knowledge is created, delivered, and applied.

One of the central insights emerging from this work is the dual nature of AI in enhancing decision-making. On one hand, AI significantly improves analytical capabilities by providing data-driven insights, predictive modeling, and real-time feedback. This aligns with contemporary perspectives that emphasize the role of AI in reducing uncertainty and improving strategic planning in entrepreneurial contexts. On the other hand, the study identifies a potential risk of over-reliance on algorithmic decision-making, which may limit human creativity, intuition, and critical thinking—core attributes of entrepreneurship. This tension suggests that while AI can augment human capabilities, it should not replace the experiential and intuitive aspects of entrepreneurial learning.

The discussion also underscores the importance of resource optimization as a key outcome of AI integration. AI-driven systems enable efficient utilization of time, financial resources, and information, thereby enhancing productivity in entrepreneurial training environments. However, the emphasis on efficiency introduces a critical ethical dilemma. The prioritization of optimization may inadvertently overshadow broader considerations such as social responsibility, sustainability, and long-term value creation. This highlights the need for a balanced approach where efficiency is aligned with ethical and societal goals.

Another important theme is digital integration and interoperability, which reflects the increasing interconnectedness of AI-driven learning environments. AI facilitates seamless interaction between platforms, enabling access to diverse resources and fostering collaborative learning. This transformation supports the development of global entrepreneurial mindsets and enhances knowledge sharing across geographical boundaries. However, the discussion reveals that such integration also raises concerns related to data privacy, system compatibility, and technological dependency. These challenges emphasize the importance of robust digital governance frameworks to ensure secure and sustainable implementation.

The study further highlights organizational adaptability as a critical outcome influenced by AI. By enabling real-time analysis and scenario-based learning, AI equips learners and organizations with the tools needed to respond effectively to dynamic environments. This adaptability is essential in today's rapidly changing entrepreneurial ecosystems. However, the discussion emphasizes that adaptability is not solely determined by technological capabilities; it is also shaped by human factors such as openness to innovation, learning orientation, and ethical awareness.

A significant contribution of this study lies in its exploration of trust as a moderating factor. Trust in AI emerges as a pivotal element that influences how effectively AI systems are adopted and utilized. The discussion reveals that trust is built through transparency, reliability, and perceived fairness. When users understand how AI systems function and perceive them as unbiased and accurate, they are more likely to rely on their outputs. Conversely, a lack of transparency—often associated with "black-box" AI systems can lead to skepticism and reduced engagement. This finding reinforces the importance of explainable AI in entrepreneurial training contexts (Li, et al., 2023).

Ethical considerations are deeply embedded throughout the discussion, highlighting that ethics and trust are interdependent constructs. Issues such as algorithmic bias, data privacy, accountability, and inclusivity are not isolated challenges but integral aspects that shape user perceptions and experiences. The presence of bias in AI systems, for instance, can limit access to opportunities and reinforce existing inequalities, thereby undermining the principles of fairness and inclusion. Similarly, concerns about data privacy can erode trust if users feel that their information is not adequately protected.

The discussion also addresses the concept of distributed accountability, recognizing that responsibility for AI outcomes is shared among multiple stakeholders, including developers, educators, institutions, and users. This perspective is particularly relevant in entrepreneurial training, where decisions influenced by AI can have significant consequences. Establishing clear accountability frameworks is therefore essential for ensuring responsible use and maintaining trust (Zhang & Yin, 2020).

Another critical aspect explored in the discussion is the changing role of educators and learners. AI-driven environments are redefining traditional educational roles, with educators transitioning from knowledge providers to facilitators and mentors. Their role increasingly involves guiding learners in interpreting AI-generated insights and addressing ethical considerations. Learners, in turn, are expected to take a more active role in their education, developing skills such as critical thinking, digital literacy, and ethical reasoning. This shift reflects a broader transformation toward learner-centered education.

The study also contributes to the understanding of new entrepreneurial competencies required in an AI-driven world. In addition to traditional skills such as creativity and resilience, entrepreneurs must now possess the ability to work with AI technologies, interpret data, and make ethically informed decisions. This highlights the need for a holistic approach to entrepreneurial training that integrates technical, cognitive, and ethical dimensions.

Furthermore, the discussion emphasizes the contextual and cultural dimensions of AI adoption. The impact of AI in entrepreneurial training varies across different environments, influenced by factors such as technological infrastructure, socio-economic conditions, and cultural attitudes toward innovation. This suggests that a one-size-fits-all approach to AI integration is not feasible, and context-specific strategies are necessary to ensure inclusivity and effectiveness.

Finally, the discussion identifies a fundamental tension between efficiency and ethics, which is central to the integration of AI in entrepreneurial training. While AI systems are designed to optimize performance, this focus on efficiency may conflict with ethical considerations such as fairness, inclusivity, and long-term sustainability. Addressing this tension requires a deliberate effort to embed ethical principles into the design and implementation of AI systems, ensuring that technological advancement aligns with human values.

6. CONCLUSION

This study provides a comprehensive examination of the role of Artificial Intelligence (AI) in entrepreneurial training, emphasizing the interconnected dimensions of ethics, trust, and transformation. It highlights that AI has the potential to significantly enhance entrepreneurial learning by improving decision-making quality, optimizing resource utilization, facilitating digital integration, and enabling organizational adaptability. These contributions position AI as a powerful tool for advancing entrepreneurial education in an increasingly complex and dynamic global environment (Zhang & Yin, 2020).

However, the study also underscores that the benefits of AI are accompanied by significant challenges. Ethical issues such as algorithmic bias, data privacy, accountability, and inclusivity must be carefully addressed to ensure responsible and equitable use of AI technologies. Trust emerges as a critical factor that determines the success of AI integration, influencing how users perceive and engage with AI systems. Without trust, the potential of AI to transform entrepreneurial training cannot be fully realized (Li, et al., 2023).

The research further demonstrates that the integration of AI is not merely a technological shift but a paradigm transformation that requires changes in pedagogical approaches, institutional frameworks, and skill development. Educators and learners must adapt to new roles and responsibilities, while entrepreneurial training programs must evolve to incorporate digital literacy, ethical awareness, and critical thinking as core competencies.

Importantly, the study proposes that the future of AI-driven entrepreneurial training lies in achieving a balance between technological efficiency and human values. This requires the development of frameworks that prioritize transparency, accountability, and inclusivity, ensuring that AI systems are aligned with ethical principles and societal goals.

In conclusion, AI offers immense potential to transform entrepreneurial training, but its successful integration depends on a holistic and human-centered approach. By addressing ethical challenges, fostering trust, and embracing transformative learning practices, it is possible to create entrepreneurial training environments that are not only innovative and efficient but also responsible, inclusive, and sustainable. This study contributes to the ongoing discourse on AI in education by providing a conceptual foundation for future research and practice, emphasizing the need to align technological advancement with the broader aspirations of society.

REFERENCES

Abaddi, S. (2025). AI–human data hybridization: A hybrid approach to unveiling global entrepreneurial motivations, challenges and opportunities. *Journal of Ethics in Entrepreneurship and Technology*, *5*(2), 155–186. DOI: 10.1108/JEET-02-2025-0009

Anwar, R. S., Ahmed, R. R., Streimikiene, D., & Streimikis, J. (2025). Cross-cultural perspectives on entrepreneurship training effectiveness: Understanding the role of training duration, methodology, and expertise. *The International Entrepreneurship and Management Journal*, *21*(1), 86. Advance online publication. DOI: 10.1007/s11365-025-01099-0

Balhico, A., Pereira, R., & Jarrar, H. (2023). Cross-cultural examination of successful entrepreneurial small and medium-sized enterprises. *European Business Review*, *36*(4), 548–565. DOI: 10.1108/EBR-03-2023-0081

Fleck, E., Kakouris, A., & Winkel, D. (2020). Cultural traits of entrepreneurship education: A cross-national study. *Journal of Entrepreneurship in Emerging Economies*, *13*(5), 838–863. DOI: 10.1108/JEEE-02-2020-0030

Hofman, J. M., Watts, D. J., Athey, S., Garip, F., Griffiths, T. L., Kleinberg, J., & Yarkoni, T. (2021). Integrating explanation and prediction in computational social science. *Nature*, *595*(7866), 181–188. DOI: 10.1038/s41586-021-03659-0

Kasler, J., Zysberg, L., & Gal, R. (2021). Culture, collectivism-individualism and college student plagiarism. *Ethics & Behavior*, *31*(7), 488–497. DOI: 10.1080/10508422.2020.1812396

Lee, Y. (2024). Beyond borders: Insights from Professor David Ahlstrom on entrepreneurship and innovation in emerging economies. *Journal of Management History*. Advance online publication. DOI: 10.1108/JMH-09-2024-0149

Li, L., Ma, Z., Fan, L., Lee, S., Yu, H., & Hemphill, L. (2023). ChatGPT in education: A discourse analysis of worries and concerns on social media. *Education and Information Technologies*, *2023*. Advance online publication. DOI: 10.1007/s10639-023-12256-9

Luckin, R., & Holmes, W. (2016). Intelligence unleashed: An argument for AI in education. UCL Knowledge Lab: London, UK. Retrieved from https://discovery.ucl.ac.uk/id/eprint/1475756/

Miao, F., & Holmes, W. (2023). *Guidance for generative AI in education and research*. UNESCO., DOI: 10.54675/EWZM9535

Mumtaz, S., Carmichael, J., Weiss, M., & Nimon-Peters, A. (2024). Ethical use of artificial intelligence based tools in higher education: Are future business leaders ready? *Education and Information Technologies*, *30*(6), 7293–7319. DOI: 10.1007/s10639-024-13099-8

Paik, Y., Lee, J. M., & Pak, Y. S. (2017). Convergence in international business ethics? A comparative study of ethical philosophies, thinking style, and ethical decision-making between US and Korean managers. *Journal of Business Ethics*. Advance online publication. DOI: 10.1007/s10551-017-3629-9

Roberts, M. E., Stewart, B. M., Tingley, D., Lucas, C., Leder-Luis, J., Gadarian, S. K., Albertson, B., & Rand, D. G. (2014). Structural topic models for open-ended survey responses. *American Journal of Political Science*, *58*(4), 1064–1082. DOI: 10.1111/ajps.12103

Schoemaker, P. J. H., Heaton, S., & Teece, D. (2018). Innovation, Dynamic Capabilities, and Leadership. *California Management Review*, *61*(1), 15–42. DOI: 10.1177/0008125618790246

Sorge, A., & Hofstede, G. (1983). Culture's Consequences: International Differences in Work-Related Values. *Administrative Science Quarterly*, *28*(4), 625. DOI: 10.2307/2393017

Sullivan, M., Kelly, A., & McLaughlan, P. (2023). ChatGPT in higher education: Considerations for academic integrity and student learning. *Journal of Applied Learning & Teaching*, *6*(1), 1–10. DOI: 10.37074/jalt.2023.6.1.17

Thomas, D. (2017). Factors that explain academic dishonesty among university students in Thailand. *Ethics & Behavior*, *27*(2), 140–154. DOI: 10.1080/10508422.2015.1131160

Zhang, Y., & Yin, H. (2020). Collaborative cheating among Chinese college students: The effects of peer influence and individualism-collectivism orientations. *Assessment & Evaluation in Higher Education*, *45*(1), 54–69. DOI: 10.1080/02602938.2019.1608504

Chapter 8

Cross-Cultural Narratives of AI in Entrepreneurship Education:

Lessons From Emerging Economies

P. B. Narendra Kiran
http://orcid.org/0000-0002-9883-3240
Christ University, Bengaluru, India

ABSTRACT

Artificial Intelligence (AI) is rapidly transforming entrepreneurship education, offering new pedagogical tools, experiential learning models, and innovation pathways. Yet, its narratives and applications vary significantly across cultural and economic contexts. This study explores cross-cultural narratives of AI in entrepreneurship education, with a particular focus on lessons emerging from developing and transitional economies. Drawing on comparative case studies, policy reviews, and institutional practices, the research highlights how cultural values, resource constraints, and local innovation ecosystems shape the integration of AI into entrepreneurial learning.

DOI: 10.4018/979-8-2600-0487-6.ch008

INTRODUCTION

The global economic landscape is currently undergoing a seismic shift, driven by the rapid maturation and integration of Artificial Intelligence (AI). While the "Fourth Industrial Revolution" was once a theoretical projection, it has manifested as a tangible reality that is redefining the foundational pillars of commerce, labor, and education. At the heart of this transformation lies entrepreneurship the engine of economic dynamism and social mobility. As AI tools transition from high-tech curiosities to ubiquitous utilities, the methods by which we prepare the next generation of innovators must undergo a parallel evolution (Balhico, et al., 2023).

However, the discourse surrounding AI in entrepreneurship education has historically been dominated by Western-centric perspectives, emanating largely from Silicon Valley, London, or Singapore. These narratives often assume a baseline of high-speed connectivity, robust venture capital, and a cultural affinity for "disruptive" risk. This study seeks to broaden that lens, exploring the cross-cultural narratives of AI in entrepreneurship education with a specific emphasis on emerging economies. In these contexts, AI is not merely an efficiency tool; it is a critical bridge over systemic gaps, a means of democratizing expertise, and a catalyst for inclusive growth (Anwar, et al., 2025).

The Converging Frontiers: AI and Entrepreneurship Education

Entrepreneurship education (EE) has traditionally focused on developing the "entrepreneurial mindset" a combination of opportunity recognition, resource bootstrapping, and resilience. Over the last decade, pedagogical approaches have shifted from theoretical business planning toward experiential learning models, such as the Lean Startup methodology and Design Thinking.

The introduction of AI into this pedagogical mix represents a "force multiplier." Large Language Models (LLMs), predictive analytics, and automated market research tools allow students to move from ideation to prototype at unprecedented speeds. For an aspiring entrepreneur in an emerging economy, AI can serve as a virtual mentor, a data scientist, and a marketing strategist all rolled into one. This capability is particularly potent in regions where formal mentorship networks may be sparse or inaccessible (Balhico, et al., 2023).

Yet, the integration of AI is not a neutral process. It is deeply embedded in the sociocultural fabric of the environment in which it is deployed. The way a student in Mumbai perceives the "risk" of an AI-generated business model may differ fundamentally from a student in São Paulo or Nairobi. These nuances are not merely academic; they dictate the success or failure of educational interventions (Anwar, et al., 2025; Balhico, et al., 2023).

The Narrative Gap: Beyond the Global North

Current literature on AI in education frequently highlights the "productivity gains" and "personalization" of learning. While these are valid, they often overlook the unique stressors and opportunities present in developing and transitional economies. In these regions, entrepreneurship is often a necessity rather than a choice a path to survival in the face of underemployment.

In emerging economies, the narrative of AI often centers on leapfrogging. Just as mobile banking bypassed traditional brick-and-mortar infrastructure in parts of Africa and Asia, AI-driven education has the potential to bypass traditional institutional bottlenecks. However, this optimism is tempered by the reality of the "Digital Divide 2.0." This is no longer just about access to hardware; it is about access to high-quality data, the ability to mitigate algorithmic bias that favors Western norms, and the cultural relevance of the AI's output (Roberts, et al., 2014).

The Strategic Imperative: Why Cross-Cultural AI Narratives Matter

The importance of examining AI through a cross-cultural lens in entrepreneurship education cannot be overstated. We are currently at a crossroads where technology has the potential to either close the global inequality gap or widen it into an unbridgeable chasm. Understanding these narratives is essential for three primary reasons: the preservation of local innovation, the mitigation of algorithmic bias, and the economic resilience of emerging markets (Abaddi, 2025).

1.1. Guarding Against "Cognitive Monocultures"

Innovation thrives on diversity. When entrepreneurship education is homogenized through a singular, Western-centric AI narrative, we risk creating a "cognitive monoculture." In this scenario, entrepreneurs across the globe begin to solve problems using the same logic, the same data sets, and the same success metrics (Roberts, et al., 2014).

By prioritizing cross-cultural narratives, we validate local knowledge systems. For an entrepreneur in a transitional economy, "success" might involve community-based scaling or sustainable resource management rather than the "blitzscaling" model popularized in the United States. If AI tools are only programmed to recognize and reward the latter, we lose the rich tapestry of "frugal innovation" that emerging economies offer. Recognizing these differences ensures that AI serves as a partner to local wisdom rather than a replacement for it (Luckin & Holmes, 2016).

1.2. Addressing the "Data Colonialism" Crisis

AI is only as objective as the data it consumes. Currently, the vast majority of training data for Large Language Models is harvested from the Global North. This leads to a form of "data colonialism," where the AI provides solutions that are contextually irrelevant or even harmful to users in emerging economies.

For instance, an AI-driven market analysis tool might overlook the nuances of informal street commerce in Lagos or the complex social hierarchies of rural India because those data points are underrepresented in its training set. Highlighting the importance of cross-cultural narratives forces a shift toward Data Sovereignty. It encourages educational institutions to advocate for, and build, localized datasets that reflect their own realities. This ensures that the "intelligence" in Artificial Intelligence is truly global, not just a reflection of a few high-income tech hubs (Anwar, et al., 2025).

1.3. Economic Resilience and Leapfrogging

For emerging economies, AI in education is a matter of national economic strategy. These regions often face a "brain drain" where their most talented innovators leave for better-resourced ecosystems. By integrating culturally responsive AI into local education, these nations can create "Innovation Sanctuaries" at home (Balhico, et al., 2023).

The importance lies in the leapfrogging effect. AI allows an entrepreneur in a developing nation to bypass the need for expensive, legacy infrastructure. A small-scale farmer can use AI for precision agriculture (Schoemaker, et al., 2018); a local artisan can use AI to access global supply chains. However, this only happens if the education system teaches them how to adapt these tools to their specific environment. If we fail to emphasize the cross-cultural application of AI, we leave these entrepreneurs with powerful tools they cannot properly calibrate, leading to wasted potential and increased economic vulnerability (Lee, 2024).

1.4. Ethical Integrity in Global Tech

Finally, this study is crucial for the ethical evolution of AI itself. By observing how AI interacts with diverse cultural values such as varying concepts of privacy, intellectual property, and social responsibility we can develop more robust ethical frameworks (Schoemaker, et al., 2018). Emerging economies often act as the "canary in the coal mine" for tech ethics; the challenges they face today regarding digital divides and algorithmic bias are the challenges the entire world will face tomorrow (Li, et al., 2023).

In summary, the study of cross-cultural AI narratives is not just an academic exercise; it is a prerequisite for a fair, functional, and truly global digital economy. It moves the conversation from what AI *can* do, to what AI *should* do for the diverse majority of the world's population (Luckin & Holmes, 2016).

Cultural Values and the Entrepreneurial Identity

Culture shapes how individuals perceive failure, authority, and innovation. In many emerging economies, communal values and social entrepreneurship hold higher weight than the "rugged individualism" often celebrated in Western startup lore. When AI is introduced into the classroom, it brings with it the biases of its training data data that is overwhelmingly Western, English-speaking, and neoliberal (Anwar, et al., 2025).

If an AI-driven curriculum encourages a "fail fast" mentality in a culture where business failure carries a heavy social stigma, a contextual misalignment occurs. Understanding these cross-cultural narratives is essential for creating educational frameworks that are not only technologically advanced but also psychologically and socially resonant (Miao & Holmes, 2023).

Research Objectives and Scope

This research aims to bridge the gap between global technological trends and local educational realities. By synthesizing insights from diverse economies, we address several critical questions:

1. How do cultural values influence the adoption and perception of AI tools in entrepreneurial learning?
2. In what ways do resource constraints in emerging economies spark unique "frugal innovations" in AI-driven pedagogy?
3. What are the ethical implications of deploying AI models trained on foreign data sets within local innovation ecosystems?

The following sections will delve into the comparative case studies that form the backbone of this research, reviewing policy frameworks and institutional practices across selected emerging markets.

The Landscape of AI in Emerging Innovation Ecosystems

To understand the introduction of AI in entrepreneurship education, one must first look at the broader innovation ecosystems of emerging economies. Unlike the mature markets of the Global North, these ecosystems are characterized by high volatility, informal economies, and a young, digitally native demographic (Lee, 2024).

One of the most compelling narratives emerging from developing nations is the use of AI to "level the playing field." In many transitional economies, the lack of access to high-level legal, financial, and technical consulting is a major barrier to startup growth. AI-powered platforms are now providing "expert-level" guidance at a fraction of the cost (Roberts, et al., 2014).

Educational institutions are capitalizing on this by integrating AI "co-pilots" into their curriculum. Instead of spending a semester teaching the mechanics of financial forecasting, educators are teaching students how to use AI to generate forecasts, shifting the focus to critical evaluation and strategic decision-making. This shift is crucial in resource-constrained environments where time-to-market is a vital survival metric (Abaddi, 2025).

Frugal Innovation and AI

Emerging economies have a long history of "Jugaad" or frugal innovation achieving more with less. In the context of AI, this manifests as the use of lightweight, open-source models that can run on low-bandwidth connections or older hardware. Entrepreneurship programs in these regions are often at the forefront of teaching students how to optimize AI for local constraints (Miao & Holmes, 2023).

For instance, using AI to analyze satellite imagery for agricultural startups in Sub-Saharan Africa or utilizing natural language processing (NLP) to bridge linguistic gaps in multi-lingual markets like India. These applications represent a shift from AI as a "luxury" to AI as a "utility."

Challenges: The Ethical and Structural Hurdles: Despite the potential, the path to integration is fraught with challenges. The "Digital Divide" remains a stark reality. If AI-driven education becomes the gold standard, those without reliable internet or electricity are pushed further to the periphery (Li, et al., 2023).

Furthermore, there is the issue of Data Sovereignty. Most AI models are "black boxes" developed by a handful of global corporations. When these models are used to train entrepreneurs in emerging economies, there is a risk of "intellectual colonization," where local problems are addressed using mismatched, foreign-derived logic (Paik, et al., 2017).

Towards a Culturally Responsive Framework: The ultimate goal of this study is to propose a framework for Culturally Responsive AI-Driven Entrepreneurship Education. This framework moves away from a "one-size-fits-all" approach and emphasizes three core pillars:

1. Contextual Alignment: Ensuring that AI tools and curricula reflect local economic realities, legal frameworks, and social norms.
2. Inclusion and Equity: Actively working to ensure that AI-driven tools reach marginalized populations, including women and rural entrepreneurs.
3. Ethical Agency: Teaching students not just how to use AI, but how to critically interrogate its biases and advocate for more representative data (Balhico, et al., 2023).

As we navigate the complexities of the AI era, the lessons from emerging economies offer a vital corrective to the dominant global narrative. These nations are not merely passive recipients of technology; they are active laboratories where AI is being adapted to solve some of the world's most pressing challenges (Schoemaker, et al., 2018). By studying these cross-cultural narratives, we can build a more sustainable, inclusive, and human-centric model for entrepreneurship education one that recognizes that while technology may be global, innovation is always local (Kasler, et al., 2021).

Through the comparative analysis provided in this paper, we invite educators, policymakers, and technologists to look beyond the "hype" and focus on the substantive, context-sensitive work of preparing entrepreneurs for a future that is already here.

LITERATURE REVIEW

2.1 Introduction to AI in Entrepreneurship Education

The integration of Artificial Intelligence (AI) into entrepreneurship education (EE) represents a transformative shift in both pedagogical design and learning outcomes. Traditionally, entrepreneurship education has focused on developing competencies such as opportunity recognition, risk-taking, innovation, and resource mobilization. However, the emergence of AI technologies particularly machine learning, predictive analytics, and large language models has expanded the scope and depth of entrepreneurial learning. Contemporary literature highlights that AI is not merely an instructional aid but a cognitive partner that reshapes how knowledge is created, validated, and applied in entrepreneurial contexts (Balhico, et al., 2023).

Scholars argue that AI-driven tools enable learners to simulate real-world entrepreneurial environments, reducing uncertainty and accelerating decision-making processes. This shift aligns with experiential learning theories, where students engage in iterative problem-solving rather than passive knowledge acquisition. AI-powered platforms provide instant feedback, market insights, and strategic recommendations, thereby enhancing the efficiency of entrepreneurial training. As a result, the role of educators is evolving from knowledge transmitters to facilitators of AI-augmented learning ecosystems (Fleck, et al., 2020).

Despite these advancements, the literature reveals a significant imbalance in the geographic focus of AI integration. Most studies originate from developed economies, often overlooking the contextual realities of emerging markets (Paik, et al., 2017). This gap underscores the need for a more inclusive understanding of how AI influences entrepreneurship education across diverse socio-economic and cultural environments (Li, et al., 2023).

2.2 Evolution of Entrepreneurship Education

Entrepreneurship education has undergone substantial evolution over the past few decades. Early models were grounded in business plan development and theoretical instruction, emphasizing structured approaches to venture creation. However, the limitations of these models became evident as entrepreneurial ecosystems grew more dynamic and uncertain. Consequently, pedagogical approaches shifted toward experiential learning frameworks such as the Lean Startup methodology and Design Thinking (Paik, et al., 2017).

The Lean Startup approach emphasizes rapid prototyping, customer feedback, and iterative development, while Design Thinking focuses on empathy, creativity, and user-centered innovation. These methodologies have been widely adopted in entrepreneurship curricula, fostering a more hands-on and adaptive learning environment. The integration of AI further enhances these approaches by enabling data-driven experimentation and real-time analysis.

Recent studies indicate that AI tools can significantly reduce the time required for market validation, financial forecasting, and product development. For instance, AI-driven analytics platforms allow students to test business hypotheses using large datasets, thereby improving the accuracy of their decisions. This convergence of AI and experiential learning creates a hybrid pedagogical model that combines human creativity with computational intelligence (Fleck, et al., 2020).

However, critics argue that over-reliance on AI may undermine the development of critical thinking and intuition skills that are essential for entrepreneurial success. Therefore, the literature emphasizes the importance of balancing AI-assisted learning with traditional cognitive and reflective practices (Paik, et al., 2017).

2.3 AI as a Pedagogical Tool

AI's role in education extends beyond automation to include personalization, scalability, and accessibility. In entrepreneurship education, AI serves multiple functions: as a mentor, a data analyst, and a strategic advisor.

Large Language Models (LLMs), for example, can generate business ideas, conduct market research, and provide feedback on business plans. This multifunctionality positions AI as a "force multiplier" in entrepreneurial learning (Li, et al., 2023).

One of the most significant contributions of AI is its ability to personalize learning experiences. Adaptive learning systems analyze student performance and tailor content to individual needs, thereby improving engagement and retention. In entrepreneurship education, this personalization allows students to explore business concepts at their own pace while receiving targeted guidance (Thomas, 2017).

Moreover, AI enhances accessibility by democratizing access to high-quality educational resources. Students in resource-constrained environments can leverage AI tools to gain insights that were previously available only to those with access to expert mentors or institutional support. This democratization is particularly important in emerging economies, where educational disparities are more pronounced (Lee, 2024).

However, the literature also highlights challenges associated with AI adoption. These include issues related to data privacy, algorithmic bias, and the lack of transparency in AI systems. Educators must therefore ensure that AI tools are used responsibly and ethically, with a focus on inclusivity and fairness.

2.4 Cross-Cultural Perspectives on AI in Education

A critical gap in existing literature is the lack of cross-cultural analysis in AI-driven entrepreneurship education. Most studies assume a homogeneous learning environment, neglecting the influence of cultural values on educational outcomes. Culture plays a crucial role in shaping entrepreneurial behavior, including attitudes toward risk, failure, and innovation (Thomas, 2017).

In Western contexts, entrepreneurship is often associated with individualism, risk-taking, and rapid growth. In contrast, many emerging economies emphasize community-oriented entrepreneurship, sustainability, and social impact. These cultural differences influence how AI tools are perceived and utilized in educational settings (Kasler, et al., 2021).

For instance, the "fail fast" philosophy promoted by many AI-driven entrepreneurial frameworks may conflict with cultures where failure carries significant social stigma. Similarly, AI-generated business strategies may not align with local market conditions or cultural norms. This misalignment can reduce the effectiveness of AI-based education and hinder entrepreneurial success.

The literature suggests that culturally responsive AI systems are essential for addressing these challenges. Such systems should incorporate local knowledge, languages, and socio-economic contexts to ensure relevance and applicability. By doing so, educators can create more inclusive and effective learning environments (Muntaz, et al., 2024).

2.5 AI in Emerging Economies

Emerging economies present a unique context for studying the impact of AI in entrepreneurship education. Unlike developed markets, these regions often face challenges such as limited infrastructure, resource constraints, and high levels of informal economic activity. However, these challenges also create opportunities for innovation and adaptation.

AI has the potential to "leapfrog" traditional barriers in these contexts. For example, entrepreneurs can use AI tools to access global markets, optimize supply chains, and improve decision-making without the need for extensive infrastructure. Educational institutions in these regions are increasingly incorporating AI into their curricula to prepare students for this new landscape.

One notable trend is the use of AI as a substitute for traditional mentorship. In many emerging economies, access to experienced entrepreneurs and industry experts is limited. AI-powered platforms can fill this gap by providing real-time guidance and support. This capability is particularly valuable for first-generation entrepreneurs who lack access to professional networks (Lee, 2024).

Additionally, the concept of frugal innovation plays a significant role in these contexts. Entrepreneurs in emerging economies often develop cost-effective solutions using limited resources. AI can enhance this process by enabling more efficient resource utilization and innovative problem-solving.

2.6 Frugal Innovation and AI Integration

Frugal innovation, often referred to as "Jugaad," is a hallmark of entrepreneurship in resource-constrained environments. It involves creating affordable and efficient solutions by leveraging limited resources. The integration of AI into this paradigm represents a significant advancement in entrepreneurial practice (Thomas, 2017).

Studies show that entrepreneurs in emerging economies are increasingly using lightweight, open-source AI models that can operate on low-bandwidth networks and basic hardware. These solutions are tailored to local conditions, making them more accessible and sustainable. For example, AI applications in agriculture, healthcare, and education are being adapted to meet the specific needs of rural and underserved communities.

In entrepreneurship education, frugal AI innovation is reflected in curriculum design. Educators are teaching students how to optimize AI tools for local contexts, emphasizing creativity and adaptability. This approach not only enhances learning outcomes but also fosters a culture of innovation that is rooted in local realities (Sorge & Hofstede, 1983).

However, the literature also highlights limitations in this approach. The lack of access to high-quality data and advanced AI infrastructure can hinder the effectiveness of these solutions. Therefore, there is a need for greater investment in digital infrastructure and capacity building to support AI-driven entrepreneurship (Hofman, et al., 2021).

2.7 Ethical Considerations and Data Sovereignty

The ethical implications of AI in entrepreneurship education are a growing area of concern. One of the most critical issues is data sovereignty the control over data used to train AI systems. Most AI models are developed using data from developed economies, leading to biases that may not reflect the realities of other regions.

This phenomenon, often referred to as “data colonialism,” raises questions about the fairness and inclusivity of AI systems. When entrepreneurs rely on AI tools that are trained on foreign data, they may receive recommendations that are irrelevant or even harmful to their local context. This can lead to poor decision-making and reduced business success.

The literature emphasizes the need for localized data and context-specific AI models. Educational institutions should play a key role in developing and promoting these resources. By doing so, they can ensure that AI systems are more representative and equitable (Sullivan, et al., 2023).

Another ethical concern is the lack of transparency in AI algorithms. Many AI systems operate as “black boxes,” making it difficult for users to understand how decisions are made. This lack of transparency can undermine trust and accountability. Therefore, educators must teach students not only how to use AI tools but also how to critically evaluate their outputs.

2.8 Digital Divide and Accessibility Challenges

While AI has the potential to democratize education, it also risks exacerbating existing inequalities. The digital divide differences in access to technology and digital skills remains a significant barrier in many regions. If AI-driven education becomes the norm, those without access to reliable internet or devices may be left behind (Sullivan, et al., 2023).

The literature identifies a “Digital Divide 2.0,” which goes beyond access to hardware and connectivity. It includes disparities in data quality, digital literacy, and the ability to use AI effectively. Addressing this divide requires a multifaceted approach, including infrastructure development, policy support, and educational reform (Sorge & Hofstede, 1983).

In entrepreneurship education, efforts are being made to bridge this gap through the use of low-cost technologies and offline AI solutions. However, these efforts are still in the early stages, and more research is needed to evaluate their effectiveness.

2.9 Toward a Culturally Responsive AI Framework

To address the challenges identified in the literature, scholars propose the development of culturally responsive AI frameworks for entrepreneurship education. Such frameworks emphasize three key principles: contextual alignment, inclusion, and ethical awareness.

Contextual alignment involves adapting AI tools and curricula to local economic, cultural, and social conditions. This ensures that educational content is relevant and meaningful to students. Inclusion focuses on expanding access to AI-driven education, particularly for marginalized groups such as women and rural populations.

Ethical awareness involves teaching students to critically engage with AI technologies, including understanding their limitations and biases. This empowers entrepreneurs to use AI responsibly and advocate for more equitable systems.

By integrating these principles, educators can create a more holistic and effective approach to AI-driven entrepreneurship education.

2.10 Conclusion of Literature Review

The literature on AI in entrepreneurship education highlights both the transformative potential and the complex challenges associated with this emerging field. AI has the capacity to enhance learning outcomes, democratize access to knowledge, and foster innovation across diverse contexts. However, its impact is not uniform and is heavily influenced by cultural, economic, and technological factors.

A key takeaway from the literature is the importance of adopting a cross-cultural perspective. Understanding how AI interacts with different cultural values and socio-economic conditions is essential for developing effective educational strategies. Emerging economies, in particular, offer valuable insights into the adaptive and innovative use of AI.

Furthermore, ethical considerations and issues related to data sovereignty must be addressed to ensure that AI systems are fair and inclusive. The development of culturally responsive frameworks represents a promising direction for future research and practice.

In conclusion, AI-driven entrepreneurship education is at a critical juncture. By embracing diversity, promoting inclusivity, and prioritizing ethical considerations, stakeholders can harness the full potential of AI to create a more equitable and dynamic global entrepreneurial ecosystem.

3. METHODOLOGY

This study is grounded in a qualitative, theory-driven research framework that seeks to examine the intersection of Artificial Intelligence (AI) and entrepreneurship education within diverse cultural and economic contexts. The research adopts an interpretivist paradigm, which emphasizes understanding social phenomena through the meanings individuals and institutions assign to them. Given that the study explores cross-cultural narratives, perceptions, and contextual adaptations of AI in entrepreneurship education, a qualitative approach is most appropriate as it allows for in-depth conceptual exploration rather than purely statistical measurement (Kasler, et al., 2021).

The research design is primarily exploratory and comparative in nature, aiming to generate insights into how AI is integrated into entrepreneurship education across emerging economies. It draws upon established theoretical foundations such as experiential learning theory, technology acceptance models (TAM), and cultural dimensions theory, which collectively help explain how learners engage with AI tools, how technology is adopted in educational environments, and how cultural values shape entrepreneurial behavior. By integrating these theoretical perspectives, the study constructs a holistic framework to analyzc the role of AI as both a technological and socio-cultural phenomenon.

The study relies extensively on secondary data sources, forming the backbone of its analytical approach. Academic journal articles, policy documents, institutional reports, and existing case studies are systematically reviewed to extract relevant insights. This method of systematic literature-based inquiry enables the researcher to synthesize a wide range of scholarly perspectives and identify key themes related to AI adoption, pedagogical transformation, and cultural variability. The literature is not treated merely as background information but as a primary dataset for theoretical interpretation and model development.

To ensure relevance and depth, the study employs a purposive sampling strategy in selecting literature and case examples. Sources are chosen based on their focus on AI in entrepreneurship education, representation of emerging economies, and contribution to understanding cultural or contextual differences. This targeted selection allows the research to move beyond generalized global narratives and instead highlight localized experiences and innovations, particularly those emerging from resource-constrained environments (Zhang & Yin, 2020).

The analytical approach is based on thematic analysis, which involves systematically identifying, categorizing, and interpreting recurring patterns within the collected data. Themes such as decision-making enhancement, resource optimization, digital integration, cultural influence, and ethical concerns are derived from the literature and analyzed in relation to the study's objectives. Furthermore, a comparative analytical lens is applied to examine how these themes manifest differently across cultural and economic contexts. This dual approach of thematic and comparative analysis enables the study to uncover both universal trends and context-specific variations.

In terms of ensuring rigor, the study incorporates theoretical triangulation, drawing upon multiple conceptual frameworks to validate interpretations and reduce bias. The use of diverse and credible academic sources enhances the reliability and consistency of findings. Additionally, the research maintains a critical perspective by acknowledging potential biases within existing literature, particularly the dominance of Western-centric viewpoints in AI discourse.

Ethical considerations are carefully observed throughout the research process. As the study is based on secondary data, it ensures proper attribution of sources and avoids misrepresentation of original findings. The analysis is conducted with sensitivity to cultural diversity, ensuring that interpretations do not impose generalized assumptions on specific contexts.

Despite its strengths, the study acknowledges certain limitations. The reliance on secondary data restricts the ability to capture real-time experiences and firsthand perspectives from educators and learners. Additionally, the availability of literature from emerging economies may be uneven, potentially influencing the comprehensiveness of comparative analysis. However, these limitations are mitigated through the use of diverse sources and a robust theoretical framework.

In conclusion, this methodology provides a comprehensive and theoretically grounded approach to examining AI in entrepreneurship education. By combining interpretive analysis with comparative insights, the study contributes to a deeper understanding of how AI-driven educational practices can be contextualized and adapted to meet the needs of diverse global environments, particularly within emerging economies (Luckin & Holmes, 2016).

4. ANALYSIS, DISCUSSION, AND CONCLUSION

4.1 Introduction to Analysis

This section provides a comprehensive analysis of the role of Artificial Intelligence (AI) in entrepreneurship education (EE), particularly within emerging economies. Building upon the literature review, the analysis synthesizes conceptual insights, contextual dynamics, and theoretical implications to evaluate how AI reshapes entrepreneurial learning ecosystems. It further explores the interaction between technological capabilities and socio-cultural environments, offering a nuanced understanding of opportunities, constraints, and long-term implications (Zhang & Yin, 2020).

The analysis is structured around key thematic dimensions: decision-making enhancement, resource optimization, digital integration, cultural alignment, ethical considerations, and systemic challenges. These dimensions collectively illustrate the transformative yet uneven impact of AI on entrepreneurship education.

4.2 AI and Decision-Making Quality

One of the most significant contributions of AI to entrepreneurship education is its ability to enhance decision-making quality. Traditionally, entrepreneurial decision-making has been characterized by uncertainty, limited information, and reliance on intuition. AI disrupts this paradigm by providing data-driven insights, predictive analytics, and scenario simulations.

In educational settings, AI tools enable students to evaluate multiple business scenarios simultaneously. For instance, AI-driven platforms can simulate market responses, forecast financial outcomes, and assess risk factors. This allows learners to make informed decisions based on empirical evidence rather than assumptions. As a result, students develop a more analytical and strategic approach to entrepreneurship.

However, the reliance on AI-generated insights raises critical questions about cognitive dependency. While AI improves efficiency, it may reduce the development of intuitive judgment and critical thinking skills. Entrepreneurs often operate in ambiguous environments where data may be incomplete or unreliable. Overdependence on AI could limit their ability to navigate such complexities.

In emerging economies, the impact of AI on decision-making is particularly pronounced. Entrepreneurs in these regions often face information asymmetry and limited access to market data. AI tools can bridge this gap by providing real-time insights and global perspectives. Nevertheless, the accuracy of these insights depends on the relevance of the underlying data, which may not always reflect local realities.

4.3 Resource Optimization and Efficiency Gains

AI significantly enhances resource optimization in entrepreneurship education. By automating routine tasks such as data analysis, market research, and financial modeling, AI allows students to focus on higher-order cognitive activities such as innovation and strategy development.

In resource-constrained environments, this capability is especially valuable. Educational institutions in emerging economies often lack access to advanced infrastructure and expert faculty. AI serves as a cost-effective alternative, providing scalable and accessible learning solutions. Students can leverage AI tools to perform complex analyses that would otherwise require significant resources (Hofman, et al., 2021).

Moreover, AI enables efficient allocation of time and effort. Tasks that traditionally required weeks of manual effort can now be completed within hours. This acceleration allows students to iterate rapidly, test multiple ideas, and refine their business models. Consequently, the entrepreneurial learning process becomes more dynamic and responsive.

Despite these advantages, resource optimization through AI is not without challenges. The initial cost of adopting AI technologies, coupled with the need for technical expertise, can be a barrier for some institutions. Additionally, disparities in access to AI tools may exacerbate existing inequalities within and across regions.

4.4 Digital Integration and Interoperability

The integration of AI into entrepreneurship education is closely linked to broader trends in digital transformation. AI functions as a central component of digital ecosystems, enabling seamless interaction between various tools and platforms. This integration enhances the overall learning experience by creating a cohesive and interconnected environment.

Digital interoperability allows students to combine multiple AI tools for different purposes, such as ideation, prototyping, marketing, and financial planning. For example, a student can use one platform for generating business ideas, another for analyzing market trends, and a third for designing marketing strategies. This interconnected approach mirrors real-world entrepreneurial practices.

In emerging economies, digital integration plays a crucial role in overcoming infrastructural limitations. Cloud-based AI solutions enable access to advanced tools without the need for expensive hardware. Mobile-based applications further extend this accessibility, allowing students to engage with AI-driven learning on widely available devices.

However, the effectiveness of digital integration depends on the availability of reliable internet connectivity and digital literacy. In regions where these prerequisites are lacking, the benefits of AI integration may not be fully realized. Therefore, policymakers and educators must address these foundational challenges to ensure equitable access.

4.5 Cultural Influences on AI Adoption

Culture is a critical determinant of how AI is adopted and utilized in entrepreneurship education. The analysis reveals that cultural values influence not only the perception of AI but also its practical application in learning environments.

In individualistic cultures, AI is often viewed as a tool for enhancing personal productivity and achieving competitive advantage. In contrast, collectivist cultures may emphasize the role of AI in supporting community-oriented goals and social entrepreneurship. These differences shape how students interact with AI tools and interpret their outputs.

For example, AI-generated business strategies that prioritize rapid scaling and high-risk investments may resonate with students in developed economies but may be less relevant in contexts where stability and sustainability are prioritized. This misalignment highlights the importance of culturally responsive AI systems.

Furthermore, cultural attitudes toward failure play a significant role in entrepreneurial learning. In some societies, failure is seen as a learning opportunity, while in others it carries social stigma. AI-driven approaches that encourage experimentation and risk-taking must be adapted to align with these cultural norms.

4.6 Frugal Innovation and Adaptive Learning

The concept of frugal innovation emerges as a key theme in the analysis of AI in emerging economies. Entrepreneurs in these contexts often develop creative solutions using limited resources, and AI enhances this capability by providing efficient and scalable tools.

Educational programs are increasingly incorporating frugal innovation principles into their curricula. Students are encouraged to use lightweight AI models, open-source tools, and low-cost technologies to develop solutions that are both effective and sustainable. This approach fosters a mindset of adaptability and resilience.

AI also supports adaptive learning by enabling personalized educational experiences. Students can explore entrepreneurial concepts at their own pace, receive tailored feedback, and focus on areas that require improvement. This flexibility is particularly beneficial in diverse learning environments where students have varying levels of prior knowledge and skills.

However, the success of frugal AI innovation depends on the availability of relevant data and technical support. Without these resources, the potential of AI may not be fully realized. Therefore, investments in infrastructure and capacity building are essential.

4.7 Ethical Challenges and Data Bias

Ethical considerations are central to the analysis of AI in entrepreneurship education. One of the most pressing issues is algorithmic bias, which arises from the use of non-representative data in AI systems. This bias can lead to inaccurate or misleading recommendations, particularly in contexts that differ from the data used for training.

In entrepreneurship education, biased AI outputs can influence business decisions, potentially leading to suboptimal outcomes. For example, AI tools may favor business models that are successful in developed markets but are not applicable in emerging economies. This misalignment can hinder innovation and reduce the effectiveness of educational programs.

Data sovereignty is another critical concern. The dominance of global technology companies in AI development raises questions about control over data and knowledge. Educational institutions in emerging economies must advocate for localized data and context-specific AI solutions to ensure relevance and fairness.

Transparency is also a key issue. Many AI systems operate as "black boxes," making it difficult for users to understand how decisions are made. This lack of transparency can undermine trust and accountability. Educators must therefore emphasize critical engagement with AI tools, encouraging students to question and validate AI-generated insights.

4.8 The Digital Divide and Inequality

The analysis highlights the persistent challenge of the digital divide in the context of AI-driven entrepreneurship education. While AI has the potential to democratize access to knowledge, disparities in access to technology and digital skills remain significant barriers.

In emerging economies, these disparities are often exacerbated by infrastructural limitations, such as unreliable internet connectivity and limited access to devices. Additionally, differences in digital literacy can affect the ability of students to effectively use AI tools.

The concept of the "Digital Divide 2.0" extends beyond access to technology to include disparities in data quality and algorithmic representation. Students in underrepresented regions may receive less accurate or relevant AI outputs, further widening the gap between different groups.

Addressing this challenge requires a comprehensive approach that includes infrastructure development, policy support, and educational reform. Initiatives such as low-cost AI solutions, offline learning platforms, and community-based training programs can help bridge this divide.

4.9 Discussion: Implications for Theory and Practice

The findings of this analysis have significant implications for both theory and practice. From a theoretical perspective, the integration of AI into entrepreneurship education challenges traditional models of learning and innovation. It calls for the development of new frameworks that account for the interplay between technology, culture, and socio-economic factors.

One such framework is the concept of culturally responsive AI-driven education, which emphasizes the need for contextual alignment, inclusivity, and ethical awareness. This approach recognizes that technology is not neutral but is shaped by the values and assumptions embedded in its design.

From a practical perspective, the analysis highlights the need for strategic interventions at multiple levels. Educational institutions must redesign their curricula to incorporate AI tools while maintaining a balance between technological and cognitive development. Policymakers must create supportive environments that facilitate access to AI technologies and promote digital literacy.

Furthermore, collaboration between academia, industry, and government is essential for developing sustainable AI ecosystems. Such partnerships can facilitate the sharing of resources, knowledge, and best practices, thereby enhancing the effectiveness of entrepreneurship education.

The integration of Artificial Intelligence into entrepreneurship education represents a paradigm shift with far-reaching implications. This study has demonstrated that AI has the potential to enhance decision-making, optimize resources, and democratize access to entrepreneurial knowledge. However, its impact is shaped by a complex interplay of cultural, economic, and technological factors.

In emerging economies, AI serves as both an opportunity and a challenge. It enables entrepreneurs to overcome resource constraints and access global markets, but it also raises issues related to data bias, digital inequality, and cultural misalignment. Addressing these challenges requires a holistic approach that prioritizes inclusivity, ethical considerations, and contextual relevance.

The concept of culturally responsive AI-driven education provides a valuable framework for navigating these complexities. By aligning AI tools with local contexts and values, educators can create more effective and equitable learning environments. This approach not only enhances educational outcomes but also contributes to the development of sustainable and inclusive entrepreneurial ecosystems.

In conclusion, the future of entrepreneurship education lies in the strategic integration of AI with human creativity and cultural diversity. By embracing this synergy, stakeholders can harness the full potential of AI to drive innovation, economic growth, and social development on a global scale.

5. CONCLUSION AND DISCUSSION

5.1 Discussion

The findings of this study highlight that the integration of Artificial Intelligence (AI) into entrepreneurship education is not merely a technological enhancement but a structural transformation of how entrepreneurial capabilities are developed, evaluated, and applied. The discussion reveals that AI operates as a catalytic force that reshapes learning processes, decision-making mechanisms, and innovation pathways, particularly within emerging economies (Muntaz, et al., 2024).

A key insight emerging from the analysis is the dual nature of AI as both an enabler and a disruptor. On one hand, AI significantly enhances decision-making quality by providing data-driven insights, predictive analytics, and real-time feedback. Students are able to simulate complex business environments, test multiple scenarios, and refine strategies with unprecedented speed and accuracy. This leads to improved analytical thinking and strategic orientation. On the other hand, the reliance on AI introduces the risk of cognitive dependency, where learners may prioritize algorithmic outputs over critical reasoning and experiential judgment. This tension underscores the need for a balanced pedagogical approach that integrates AI without diminishing human creativity and intuition.

Another important dimension is resource optimization. AI democratizes access to entrepreneurial tools that were previously restricted to well-funded institutions or experienced professionals. In emerging economies, where access to mentorship, capital, and infrastructure is limited, AI functions as a substitute for traditional support systems. This significantly reduces entry barriers and enables a broader segment of the population to participate in entrepreneurial activities. However, this democratization is uneven. Institutions and individuals with limited digital infrastructure or technological literacy may not fully benefit from AI-driven opportunities, thereby reinforcing existing inequalities.

The role of digital integration further amplifies the transformative potential of AI. The ability to connect multiple platforms and tools into a cohesive ecosystem mirrors real-world entrepreneurial environments, where interdisciplinary knowledge and technological fluency are essential. Yet, the effectiveness of such integration is contingent upon foundational factors such as internet connectivity, device accessibility, and digital skills. Without addressing these prerequisites, the promise of AI-enhanced education remains partially unrealized (Hofman, et al., 2021).

Cultural context emerges as a critical factor influencing the adoption and effectiveness of AI in entrepreneurship education. The study demonstrates that entrepreneurial behavior is deeply embedded in cultural norms, values, and social expectations. AI systems, largely trained on data from developed economies, often reflect Western-centric assumptions about risk-taking, innovation, and success. When applied in different cultural settings, these assumptions may lead to misalignment and reduced relevance. For instance, the emphasis on rapid scaling and high-risk strategies may conflict with the priorities of stability, sustainability, and community-oriented growth in many emerging economies. This highlights the importance of developing culturally responsive AI systems that incorporate local knowledge and contextual nuances.

The concept of frugal innovation further enriches the discussion by illustrating how constraints can drive creativity and adaptability. In resource-limited environments, entrepreneurs leverage AI in innovative ways, using lightweight models and open-source tools to address local challenges. This approach not only enhances efficiency but also fosters a mindset of resilience and problem-solving. However, the scalability of such innovations depends on access to quality data, technical expertise, and institutional support.

Ethical considerations represent another critical area of discussion. Issues such as algorithmic bias, data sovereignty, and lack of transparency pose significant challenges to the equitable use of AI in education. The dominance of global data sources in training AI models can result in outputs that are not representative of diverse contexts, leading to what is often described as "data colonialism." This raises concerns about the fairness and inclusivity of AI-driven decision-making. Furthermore, the opaque nature of many AI systems limits users' ability to critically evaluate their outputs, potentially undermining trust and accountability. Addressing these challenges requires a concerted effort to develop localized datasets, promote transparency, and integrate ethical training into entrepreneurship education.

The persistence of the digital divide adds another layer of complexity. While AI has the potential to democratize access to knowledge, disparities in technology access and digital literacy continue to hinder its widespread adoption. The emergence of a "Digital Divide 2.0" highlights that access alone is insufficient; the quality of data, the ability to interpret AI outputs, and the capacity to apply them effectively are equally important. Bridging this divide necessitates coordinated efforts across policy, infrastructure, and education systems.

From a theoretical perspective, the study contributes to the evolving discourse on technology-enhanced learning by emphasizing the interplay between AI, culture, and entrepreneurship. It challenges the notion of universal applicability of AI-driven models and advocates for context-sensitive approaches. From a practical standpoint, the findings underscore the need for curriculum redesign, capacity building, and multi-stakeholder collaboration to ensure the effective integration of AI into entrepreneurship education.

5.2 Conclusion

In conclusion, this study demonstrates that Artificial Intelligence is redefining the landscape of entrepreneurship education by transforming how knowledge is generated, disseminated, and applied. AI enhances decision-making, accelerates learning processes, and expands access to entrepreneurial resources, making it a powerful tool for fostering innovation and economic development.

However, the impact of AI is not uniform and is shaped by a complex interplay of cultural, economic, and technological factors. In emerging economies, AI offers significant opportunities for leapfrogging traditional barriers and enabling inclusive growth. At the same time, it introduces challenges related to digital inequality, cultural misalignment, and ethical concerns. These challenges highlight the limitations of a one-size-fits-all approach to AI integration and underscore the need for context-specific solutions.

The concept of culturally responsive AI-driven entrepreneurship education emerges as a critical framework for addressing these issues. By aligning AI tools with local realities, promoting inclusivity, and fostering ethical awareness, educators and policymakers can create more effective and equitable learning environments. This approach ensures that AI serves as a complement to human capabilities rather than a replacement, preserving the diversity and richness of entrepreneurial practices across different contexts.

Furthermore, the study emphasizes the importance of developing local data ecosystems and enhancing digital infrastructure to support the sustainable adoption of AI. Investments in these areas are essential for bridging the digital divide and ensuring that the benefits of AI are widely distributed.

Ultimately, the future of entrepreneurship education lies in the integration of advanced technologies with human-centered approaches. AI should be viewed not as an end in itself but as a means to empower individuals, foster creativity, and address real-world challenges. By embracing this perspective, stakeholders can harness the transformative potential of AI to build resilient, inclusive, and dynamic entrepreneurial ecosystems.

In summary, the successful integration of AI into entrepreneurship education requires a holistic and collaborative approach that balances technological innovation with cultural sensitivity, ethical responsibility, and social equity. Only then can AI truly contribute to a more inclusive and sustainable global economy.

REFERENCES

Abaddi, S. (2025). AI–human data hybridization: A hybrid approach to unveiling global entrepreneurial motivations, challenges and opportunities. *Journal of Ethics in Entrepreneurship and Technology*, *5*(2), 155–186. DOI: 10.1108/JEET-02-2025-0009

Anwar, R. S., Ahmed, R. R., Streimikiene, D., & Streimikis, J. (2025). Cross-cultural perspectives on entrepreneurship training effectiveness: Understanding the role of training duration, methodology, and expertise. *The International Entrepreneurship and Management Journal*, *21*(1), 86. Advance online publication. DOI: 10.1007/s11365-025-01099-0

Balhico, A., Pereira, R., & Jarrar, H. (2023). Cross-cultural examination of successful entrepreneurial small and medium-sized enterprises. *European Business Review*, *36*(4), 548–565. DOI: 10.1108/EBR-03-2023-0081

Fleck, E., Kakouris, A., & Winkel, D. (2020). Cultural traits of entrepreneurship education: A cross-national study. *Journal of Entrepreneurship in Emerging Economies*, *13*(5), 838–863. DOI: 10.1108/JEEE-02-2020-0030

Hofman, J. M., Watts, D. J., Athey, S., Garip, F., Griffiths, T. L., Kleinberg, J., & Yarkoni, T. (2021). Integrating explanation and prediction in computational social science. *Nature*, *595*(7866), 181–188. DOI: 10.1038/s41586-021-03659-0

Kasler, J., Zysberg, L., & Gal, R. (2021). Culture, collectivism-individualism and college student plagiarism. *Ethics & Behavior*, *31*(7), 488–497. DOI: 10.1080/10508422.2020.1812396

Lee, Y. (2024). Beyond borders: Insights from Professor David Ahlstrom on entrepreneurship and innovation in emerging economies. *Journal of Management History*. Advance online publication. DOI: 10.1108/JMH-09-2024-0149

Li, L., Ma, Z., Fan, L., Lee, S., Yu, H., & Hemphill, L. (2023). ChatGPT in education: A discourse analysis of worries and concerns on social media. *Education and Information Technologies*, *2023*. Advance online publication. DOI: 10.1007/s10639-023-12256-9

Luckin, R., & Holmes, W. (2016). Intelligence unleashed: An argument for AI in education. UCL Knowledge Lab: London, UK. Retrieved from https://discovery.ucl.ac.uk/id/eprint/1475756/

Miao, F., & Holmes, W. (2023). *Guidance for generative AI in education and research.* UNESCO., DOI: 10.54675/EWZM9535

Paik, Y., Lee, J. M., & Pak, Y. S. (2017). Convergence in international business ethics? A comparative study of ethical philosophies, thinking style, and ethical decision-making between US and Korean managers. *Journal of Business Ethics.* Advance online publication. DOI: 10.1007/s10551-017-3629-9

Roberts, M. E., Stewart, B. M., Tingley, D., Lucas, C., Leder-Luis, J., Gadarian, S. K., Albertson, B., & Rand, D. G. (2014). Structural topic models for open-ended survey responses. *American Journal of Political Science, 58*(4), 1064–1082. DOI: 10.1111/ajps.12103

Schoemaker, P. J. H., Heaton, S., & Teece, D. (2018). Innovation, Dynamic Capabilities, and Leadership. *California Management Review, 61*(1), 15–42. DOI: 10.1177/0008125618790246

Sorge, A., & Hofstede, G. (1983). Culture's Consequences: International Differences in Work-Related Values. *Administrative Science Quarterly, 28*(4), 625. DOI: 10.2307/2393017

Sullivan, M., Kelly, A., & McLaughlan, P. (2023). ChatGPT in higher education: Considerations for academic integrity and student learning. *Journal of Applied Learning & Teaching, 6*(1), 1–10. DOI: 10.37074/jalt.2023.6.1.17

Thomas, D. (2017). Factors that explain academic dishonesty among university students in Thailand. *Ethics & Behavior, 27*(2), 140–154. DOI: 10.1080/10508422.2015.1131160

Zhang, Y., & Yin, H. (2020). Collaborative cheating among Chinese college students: The effects of peer influence and individualism-collectivism orientations. *Assessment & Evaluation in Higher Education, 45*(1), 54–69. DOI: 10.1080/02602938.2019.1608504

Compilation of References

Aad, S. S., & Hardey, M. (2025). *After generative AI: Preparing faculty to transform education, learning, and pedagogy*. Emerald Publishing., DOI: 10.1108/9781835499467

Aarthi, S. Ravikumar, Sapayev Odilbek Uglu, V., Sottarov, A., & Singh, A. (2025). The privacy paradox. In *User-Centric Cybersecurity Implications for Sustainable Digital Transformation* (pp. 223–256). IGI Global Scientific Publishing. DOI: 10.4018/979-8-3373-3171-3.ch007

Aarthi, S., Ravikumar, R. N., Khudayberganov, S., Ismailov, A., & Khujaniyozova, O. (2025). Using Intelligent Tutoring Systems to enhance student engagement. In *Advances in Computational Intelligence and Robotics* (pp. 155–188). IGI Global. DOI: 10.4018/979-8-3373-1827-1.ch008

Abaddi, S. (2025). AI–human data hybridization: A hybrid approach to unveiling global entrepreneurial motivations, challenges and opportunities. *Journal of Ethics in Entrepreneurship and Technology*, *5*(2), 155–186. DOI: 10.1108/JEET-02-2025-0009

Abd-Alrazaq, A., Solaiman, B., Mekki, Y. M., Al-Thani, D., Farooq, F., Alkubeyyer, M., Abubacker, M. Z., AlSaad, R., Aziz, S., Serag, A., Thomas, R., Sheikh, J., & Ahmed, A. (2025). Hype vs reality in the integration of artificial intelligence in clinical workflows. *JMIR Formative Research, 9*(v9i1e70921), e70921. DOI: 10.2196/70921

Abdelmagid, A. S., Jabli, N. M., Al-Mohaya, A. Y., & Teleb, A. A. (2025). Integrating interactive metaverse environments and generative artificial intelligence to promote the green digital economy and e-entrepreneurship in higher education. *Sustainability (Basel), 17*(12), 5594. DOI: 10.3390/su17125594

Abdullah, N. A., Rasheed, R. A., Nasir, M. H. N. M., & Rahman, M. M. (2021). Eliciting auxiliary information for cold start user recommendation: A survey. *Applied Sciences (Basel, Switzerland), 11*(20), 9608. DOI: 10.3390/app11209608

Abu-Salih, B. (2021). Domain-specific knowledge graphs: A survey. *Journal of Network and Computer Applications, 185*, 103076. DOI: 10.1016/j.jnca.2021.103076

Abu-Salih, B., & Alotaibi, S. (2024). A systematic literature review of knowledge graph construction and application in education. *Heliyon, 10*(3), e25383. DOI: 10.1016/j.heliyon.2024.e25383 PMID: 38327411

Adelana, O. P., Ayanwale, M. A., & Sanusi, I. T. (2024). Exploring pre-service biology teachers' intention to teach genetics using an AI intelligent tutoring-based system. *Cogent Education, 11*(1), 2310976. DOI: 10.1080/2331186X.2024.2310976

Adetunji, R. O., & Ade-Ibijola, A. (2026). BizAssistBot: An artificial intelligence assistant for small business operations. *Discover Artificial Intelligence, 6*(1), 161. Advance online publication. DOI: 10.1007/s44163-025-00802-y

Agnihotri, A., Agarwal, R., Maurya, A., Sinha, M., & Balusamy, B. (2024). *Impact of new technology on next-generation leadership*. IGI Global Scientific Publishing., DOI: 10.4018/979-8-3693-1946-8

Ahmed, F., Lo, Y. T., & Chen, S.-H. (2025). Developing entrepreneurial mindset among non-business majors through experiential learning and AI tools. *Proceedings of the European Conference on Knowledge Management, 26*(1), 1–7. DOI: 10.34190/eckm.26.1.3762

Al Lily, A. E., Ismail, A. F., Abunasser, F. M., & Alhajhoj Alqahtani, R. H. (2020). Distance education as a response to pandemics: Coronavirus and Arab culture. *Technology in Society*, *63*, 101317. DOI: 10.1016/j.techsoc.2020.101317

Alam, A. (2025). Ethical challenges and bias in AI-driven marketing: Educational imperatives and policy perspectives. In *Impacts of AI-generated content on brand reputation* (pp. 55–107). IGI Global Scientific Publishing., DOI: 10.4018/979-8-3373-4327-3.ch003

AlBlooshi, S. A. (2026). Artificial intelligence in higher education: Opportunities and challenges: A review. *Frontiers in Education*, *10*, 1683968. DOI: 10.3389/feduc.2025.1683968

Alkhazim, M. A. (2003). Higher education in Saudi Arabia: Challenges, solutions, and missed opportunities. *Higher Education Policy*, *16*(4), 479–486. DOI: 10.1057/palgrave.hep.8300035

Al-Maaitah, T. A., Alduneibat, K. A., Alshdaifat, S. M., Alsarayreh, R., Bani Ahmad, A. Y. A., & Hijazin, A. F. (2025). AI adoption, technological readiness, and AI usability in sustainability accounting education: The moderating role of academic integrity. *Heritage and Sustainable Development*, *7*(1), 611–628. DOI: 10.37868/hsd.v7i1.1176

Almaiah, M. A., Al-Khasawneh, A., & Althunibat, A. (2020). Exploring the critical challenges and factors influencing the e-learning system usage during COVID-19 pandemic. *Education and Information Technologies*, *25*(6), 5261–5280. DOI: 10.1007/s10639-020-10219-y

Al-Mamary, Y. H. (2025). The transformative power of artificial intelligence in entrepreneurship: Exploring AI's capabilities for the success of entrepreneurial ventures. *Future Business Journal*, *11*(1), 104. DOI: 10.1186/s43093-025-00533-7

Almufarreh, A. (2026). Gamification in education and its impact on student academic performance: A conceptual model based on systematic literature review and PLS-SEM analysis. *Algorithms*, *19*(2), 143. DOI: 10.3390/a19020143

Alpürk, K., Ayaz, A., Altınay, F., Altınay, Z., Berigel, D. S., & Dağlı, G. (2025). Artificial intelligence applications in entrepreneurship and online education: Insights from bibliometric and topic modeling analyses. *Frontiers in Education, 10*, 1651484. DOI: 10.3389/feduc.2025.1651484

Alqahtani, A. Y., & Rajkhan, A. A. (2020). E-Learning Critical Success Factors during the COVID-19 Pandemic: A Comprehensive Analysis of E-Learning Managerial Perspectives. *Education Sciences, 10*(9), 216. DOI: 10.3390/educsci10090216

Al-Sahmah, N. A. (2024). Challenges and Risks of Artificial Intelligence in Achieving the Kingdom of Saudi Arabia's Vision 2030. *Evolutionary Studies in Imaginative Culture*, •••, 154–174. DOI: 10.70082/esiculture.vi.2251

Al-Shabandar, R., Jaddoad, A., Elwi, T. A., Mohammed, A., & Hussain, A. J. (2024). A systematic review for the implication of generative AI in higher education. *Infocommunications Journal, 16*(3), 31–42. DOI: 10.36244/ICJ.2024.3.3

Amravati., D. of C. S. V. B. M., Iqbal, A., & Kene, D. M. (2026). Adaptive Learning Systems powered by generative AI and Large Language Models: A comprehensive review of Personalized Education. *International Journal of Scientific Research in Engineering and Management, 10*(01), 11–19. DOI: 10.55041/IJSREM.IBFE002

Anastasiadou, S. D., Seremeti, L., Masouras, A., & Anastasiadis, L. (2025). *Modern perspectives on artificial intelligence and law*. IGI Global Scientific Publishing., DOI: 10.4018/979-8-3693-9576-9

Anwar, R. S., Ahmed, R. R., Streimikiene, D., & Streimikis, J. (2025). Cross-cultural perspectives on entrepreneurship training effectiveness: Understanding the role of training duration, methodology, and expertise. *The International Entrepreneurship and Management Journal, 21*(1), 86. Advance online publication. DOI: 10.1007/s11365-025-01099-0

Association, T. K. (2025). A study on global trends in the use of generative AI in entrepreneurship education: Literature and case-based approaches. *The Korean Career. Entrepreneurship & Business Association*, *9*(6), 283–304. DOI: 10.48206/kceba.2025.9.6.283

Ateş, H., & Kölemen, C. Ş. (2025). Integrating theories for insight: An amalgamated model for gamified virtual reality adoption by science teachers. *Education and Information Technologies*, *30*(2), 2123–2153. DOI: 10.1007/s10639-024-12892-9

Aysi, S. A. H., Susilaningsih, S., & Sabandi, M. (2024). The implementation of digital Entrepreneurship Learning in higher education: A Systematic Literature Review. *PEDAGOGIA Jurnal Pendidikan*, *13*(2), 255–273. DOI: 10.21070/pedagogia.v13i2.1692

Baig, S. A., Mohsin, M., Lodhi, R. N., & Batool, G. (2025). *Reshaping organizational management and workplace culture with AI*. IGI Global Scientific Publishing., DOI: 10.4018/979-8-3693-8960-7

Balhico, A., Pereira, R., & Jarrar, H. (2023). Cross-cultural examination of successful entrepreneurial small and medium-sized enterprises. *European Business Review*, *36*(4), 548–565. DOI: 10.1108/EBR-03-2023-0081

Bandara, A. (2026). Use of artificial Intelligence in Entrepreneurship Education: A systematic review. *Journal of Management Matters*, *12*(2), 88–99. DOI: 10.4038/jmm.v12i2.98

Bansal, R., Chakir, A., Ngah, A. H., Rabby, F., & Jain, A. (2024). *AI algorithms and ChatGPT for student en- gagement in online learning*. IGI Global Scientific Publishing., DOI: 10.4018/9798369342688

Barać, M., Vitković, N., Stanković, Z., Rajić, M., & Turudija, R. (2024). Description and utilization of an educational platform for clean production in mechanical engineering. *Spectrum of Mechanical Engineering and Operational Research*, *1*(1), 145–158. DOI: 10.31181/smeor11202413

Bayati, S., Tripathi, A., & Bapna, R. (2020). Recommending open source software projects to developers. SSRN *Electronic Journal*. DOI: 10.2139/ssrn.3642052

Bell, R., & Bell, H. (2023). Entrepreneurship education in the era of generative artificial intelligence. *Entrepreneurship Education*, *6*(3), 229–244. DOI: 10.1007/s41959-023-00099-x

Ben Matoug, S., Zehouani, A., Lazhar, B. M., Ziadi, S., Belarbi, G., & Abada, M. (2024). The role of entrepreneurship education in guiding university students to create their personal and professional projects within the framework of a Startup. *International Journal of Professional Business Review*, *9*(4), e04623. DOI: 10.26668/businessreview/2024.v9i4.4623

Brezovec, E., Zelić, M., & Zagode, A. M. (2026). Stabilizing truth in educational sciences: A systematic review of generative AI in education. *Kybernetes*, *55*(13), 1–17. DOI: 10.1108/K-09-2025-2339

Brynjolfsson, E., & Mcafee, A. (2017). The Business of Artificial Intelligence. *Harvard Business Review*, *7*, 3–11. https://starlab-alliance.com/wp-content/uploads/2017/09/The-Business-of-Artificial-Intelligence.pdf

Cao, Y. (2025). Using AI and big data analytics to support entrepreneurial decisions in the digital economy. *Scientific Reports*, *15*(1), 36933. DOI: 10.1038/s41598-025-20871-4 PMID: 41125685

Carrizosa, Á. (2025). Entrepreneurial success: The missing link between education, AI, and Startup growth. *The Transnational Journal of Business*, *10*(1). Advance online publication. DOI: 10.64010/SDUS3791

Cela, E., Vajjhala, N. R., & Fonkam, M. M. (2024). *Next-generation AI methodologies in education*. IGI Global Scientific Publishing., DOI: 10.4018/979-8-3693-7220-3

Çela, E., Vedishchev, A., & Vajjhala, N. R. (2025). Upskilling the educational workforce for AI-enhanced cybersecurity: A thematic and trend analysis. In *AI-enabled threat intelligence and cyber risk assessment* (pp. 57–75). CRC Press., DOI: 10.1201/9781003504979-4

Chen, J., Chen, Y., Ou, R., Wang, J., & Chen, Q. (2022). How to use artificial intelligence to improve entrepreneurial attitude in business simulation games: Implications from a quasi-experiment. *Frontiers in Psychology*, *13*, 856085. DOI: 10.3389/fpsyg.2022.856085 PMID: 36467165

Chen, L., Ifenthaler, D., Yau, J. Y.-K., & Sun, W. (2024). Artificial intelligence in entrepreneurship education: A scoping review. *Education + Training*, *66*(6), 589–608. Advance online publication. DOI: 10.1108/ET-05-2023-0169

Chiyachantana, C. N., Ding, D. K., & Hong, J. J. (2022). Experiential learning: The case of training MBA students in an Asian school. *International Journal of Educational Technology and Learning*, *13*(1), 17–25. DOI: 10.55217/101.v13i1.552

Choi, J.-I., & Markham, S. (2019). Creating a corporate entrepreneurial ecosystem: The case of entrepreneurship education in the RTP, USA. *Journal of Open Innovation*, *5*(3), 62. DOI: 10.3390/joitmc5030062

Cockburn, I. M., Henderson, R., & Stern, S. (2018). The impact of artificial intelligence on innovation. NBER Working Paper No. 24449. DOI: 10.3386/w24449

Dabbous, A., & Boustani, N. M. (2023). Digital explosion and entrepreneurship education: Impact on promoting entrepreneurial intention for business students. *Journal of Risk and Financial Management*, *16*(1), 27. DOI: 10.3390/jrfm16010027

Damaševičius, R., & Sidekerskiene, T. (2025). *Digital escape room designs in education*. IGI Global Scientific Publishing., DOI: 10.4018/979-8-3693-4219-0

Das, R., & Singh, A. (2026). Opportunities and Threats for Women Entrepreneurs in Remote Rural Tourism: A SWOT Study. In Ordóñez de Pablos, P. (Ed.), *Shaping Green and Inclusive Economies Through Innovative Entrepreneurship* (pp. 65–88). IGI Global Scientific Publishing., DOI: 10.4018/979-8-3373-1097-8.ch003

Davar, N. F., Dewan, M. A. A., & Zhang, X. (2025). AI chatbots in education: Challenges and opportunities. *Information (Basel)*, *16*(3), 235. DOI: 10.3390/info16030235

Delello, J. A., & McWhorter, R. R. (2024). *Disruptive technologies in education and workforce development.* IGI Global Scientific Publishing., DOI: 10.4018/979-8-3693-3003-6

Deng, X. N., & Sun, R. (2026). Artificial intelligence and career development: Concerns and insights from first-generation college students. *International Journal of Information Management, 87*, 103003. Advance online publication. DOI: 10.1016/j.ijinfomgt.2025.103003

Dhananjaya., Goudar, R. H., Kulkarni, A. A., Rathod, V. N., & Hukkeri, G. S. (2024). A digital recommendation system for personalized learning to enhance online education: A review. *IEEE Access: Practical Innovations, Open Solutions, 12*, 34019–34041. DOI: 10.1109/ACCESS.2024.3369901

Diogo, A., Joaquim, A. F., & de Almeida, C. V. (2025). *Rethinking literacy in the era of sustainability and artificial intelligence.* IGI Global Scientific Publishing., DOI: 10.4018/979-8-3373-0725-1

Dixit, J. K., Agrawal, V., & Agarwal, S. (2025). Sustainable entrepreneurship: Exploring the intention–behavior gap. *Management Decision, 63*(7), 2247–2268. DOI: 10.1108/MD-01-2024-0056

Dubin, D., & Xiaoxia, W. (2020). Human-computer system design of entrepreneurship education based on artificial intelligence and image feature retrieval. *Journal of Intelligent & Fuzzy Systems, 39*(4), 5927–5939. DOI: 10.3233/JIFS-189067

Dunan, A., Mudjiyanto, B., Setiawan, A. B., Syarifuddin, S., Pala, R., Rustam, M., Dirgahayu, D., Buyamin, B., Nuryana, M., & Hartiningsih, H. (2025). Artificial intelligence in E-entrepreneurship training. *International Journal of E-Entrepreneurship and Innovation, 15*(1), 1–22. DOI: 10.4018/IJEEI.386065

Dunsim, N. Q. W., & Jabar, J. (2025). Bridging education and enterprise: Business Startup readiness of Malaysian youth in Mara colleges. [JTMT]. *Journal of Technology Management and Technopreneurship, 13*(3). Advance online publication. DOI: 10.54554/jtmt.2025.13.03.017

Duong, C. D., & Vu, T. N. (2025). Entrepreneurial education and higher education students'e-entrepreneurial intention: A moderated mediation model of generative AI incorporation and e-entrepreneurial self-efficacy. *Higher Education. Skills and Work-Based Learning*, *15*(5), 1024–1048. DOI: 10.1108/HESWBL-12-2024-0390

Durak, G., & Cankaya, S. (2023). *Perspectives on learning analytics for maximizing student outcomes*. IGI Global Scientific Publishing., DOI: 10.4018/978-1-6684-9527-8

Durak, G., & Çankaya, S. (2024). *Integrating micro-credentials with AI in open education*. IGI Global Scientific Publishing., DOI: 10.4018/979-8-3693-5488-9

Dwivedi, Y. K. (2025). Generative Artificial Intelligence (GenAI) in entrepreneurial education and practice: Emerging insights, the GAIN Framework, and research agenda. *The International Entrepreneurship and Management Journal*, *21*(1), 82. DOI: 10.1007/s11365-025-01089-2

Elert, N., Andersson, F. W., & Wennberg, K. (2015). The impact of entrepreneurship education in high school on long-term entrepreneurial performance. *Journal of Economic Behavior & Organization*, *111*, 209–223. DOI: 10.1016/j.jebo.2014.12.020

Essel, H. B., Vlachopoulos, D., Johnson, E. E., & Quansah, E. K. (2026). Undergraduate students' perceptions of generative artificial intelligence as a predictor of learning autonomy in Ghana. *Discover Artificial Intelligence*, *6*(1), 85. Advance online publication. DOI: 10.1007/s44163-025-00725-8

Festiyed, F., Desnita, D., Natasya, Z., Fadillah, M. A., & Novitra, F. (2026). From Assistance to Autonomy: AI Integration in Structured Research-Based Learning for Higher Education. *Electronic Journal of e-Learning*, *24*(1), 109–124. DOI: 10.34190/ejel.24.1.4416

Fleck, E., Kakouris, A., & Winkel, D. (2020). Cultural traits of entrepreneurship education: A cross-national study. *Journal of Entrepreneurship in Emerging Economies*, *13*(5), 838–863. DOI: 10.1108/JEEE-02-2020-0030

Fox, J. D., Pittaway, L., & Uzuegbunam, I. (2025). Artificial Intelligence as a dynamic copilot in Entrepreneurship Education. *Entrepreneurship Education and Pedagogy, 8*(2), 329–344. DOI: 10.1177/25151274241256307

Gal, C., & Rachevski, I. (2026). Understanding entrepreneurial propensity: An integrated analysis of cognitive traits and contextual factors in diverse economies. *Journal of Innovation and Entrepreneurship, 15*(1), 10. Advance online publication. DOI: 10.1186/s13731-026-00614-z

Garcia, M. B., Rosak-Szyrocka, J., & Bozkurt, A. (2025). *Pitfalls of AI integration in education: Skill obsolescence, misuse, and bias.* IGI Global Scientific Publishing., DOI: 10.4018/979-8-3373-0122-8

Giuggioli, G., & Pellegrini, M. M. (2022). Artificial intelligence as an enabler for entrepreneurs: a systematic literature review and an agenda for future research. *International Journal of Entrepreneurial Behaviour & Research, ahead-of-print*(ahead-of-print). DOI: 10.1108/IJEBR-05-2021-0426

Gligorea, I., Cioca, M., Oancea, R., Gorski, A.-T., Gorski, H., & Tudorache, P. (2023). Adaptive learning using artificial intelligence in e-learning: A literature review. *Education Sciences, 13*(12), 1216. DOI: 10.3390/educsci13121216

Gocen, A., & Aydemir, F. (2020). Artificial intelligence in education and schools. *Research on Education and Media, 12*(1), 13–21. DOI: 10.2478/rem-2020-0003

Gong, J., Zhao, Z., Niu, X., Ji, Y., Sun, H., Shen, Y., Chen, B., & Wu, B. (2025). AI reshaping life sciences: Intelligent transformation, application challenges, and future convergence in neuroscience, biology, and medicine. *Frontiers in Digital Health, 7*(1666415), 1666415. DOI: 10.3389/fdgth.2025.1666415 PMID: 41064793

Gong, X., Wang, S., & Dong, Y. (2025). Integrating artificial intelligence in entrepreneurship education: Dynamic capabilities and marketing performance among student entrepreneurs. *International Journal of Management Education, 23*(3), 101248. DOI: 10.1016/j.ijme.2025.101248

Guo, H. (2026). A model for assessing college students' entrepreneurial abilities based on deep learning and big data. *Discover Artificial Intelligence*, *6*(1), 115. Advance online publication. DOI: 10.1007/s44163-025-00799-4

Guo, J. X., & Zhao, J. C. (2013). Research on personalized courseware recommendation system of rural distance learning based on combination recommendation technology. *Applied Mechanics and Materials*, *373–375*, 1652–1660. . DOI: 10.4028/www.scientific.net/AMM.373-375.1652

Gupta, B. (2024). *Metaverse security paradigms*. IGI Global Scientific Publishing., DOI: 10.4018/979-8-3693-3824-7

Hamburg, I., O'brien, E., & Vladut, G. (2019). Entrepreneurial learning and AI Literacy to support digital entrepreneurship. *Balkan Region Conference on Engineering and Business Education*, *3*(1), 132–144. DOI: 10.2478/cplbu-2020-0016

Harkonen, J., Haapasalo, H., & Hanninen, K. (2015). Productisation: A review and research agenda. *International Journal of Production Economics*, *164*, 65–82. DOI: 10.1016/j.ijpe.2015.02.024

Hofman, J. M., Watts, D. J., Athey, S., Garip, F., Griffiths, T. L., Kleinberg, J., & Yarkoni, T. (2021). Integrating explanation and prediction in computational social science. *Nature*, *595*(7866), 181–188. DOI: 10.1038/s41586-021-03659-0

Holmes, W., Bialik, M., & Fadel, C. (2022). *Artificial intelligence in education: Promise and implications for teaching and learning*. Center for Curriculum Redesign., http://bit.ly/AIED-BOOK

Howe, B. T., Basole, R., Kim, Y., Mossberger, K., LaCombe, S., & Tolbert, C. (2021). Big data directions in entrepreneurship research: Researcher viewpoints. SSRN *Electronic Journal*. DOI: 10.2139/ssrn.3874681

Huang, M.-H., & Rust, R. T. (2021). Committed to a Robot? The Role of AI in Service. *Journal of Service Research*, *24*(1), 30–41. DOI: 10.1177/1094670520902266

Huang, W. (2026). The construction and practice of the entrepreneurship plan training model from the perspective of "digital twin" : An interdisciplinary integration exploration based on the immersive business war simulation platform. *Journal of Computer Technology and Electronic Research, 2*(9). Advance online publication. DOI: 10.70767/jcter.v2i9.819

Ifenthaler, D., Mah, D. K., & Yau, J. Y. K. (2019). Using Learning Analytics for Study Success: Reflections on Current Empirical Findings. In Ifenthaler, D., Mah, D. K., & Yau, J. Y. K. (Eds.), *Utilizing Learning Analytics to Support Study Success*. Springer., DOI: 10.1007/978-3-319-64792-0_2

Ip, K. (2024). The rise of EdTech: Transforming education through entrepreneurial ventures. *Advances in Online Education: A Peer-Reviewed Journal, 3*(2), 177. DOI: 10.69554/NSVD4541

Jayanthi, R. (2025). Personalized learning systems using AI enhancing adaptive education. *International Journal of Environmental Sciences*, •••, 668–676. DOI: 10.64252/ps80c806

Jiang, M. (2026). Career planning and entrepreneurial intention guidance for college students based on fuzzy decision support system. *Discover Artificial Intelligence, 6*(1), 77. Advance online publication. DOI: 10.1007/s44163-025-00759-y

Ji, X., & Yang, Y. (2023). A discussion on the "charging model" of the collaborative mechanism between teachers and artificial intelligence based on Satir's iceberg theory. *Journal of Learning and Development Studies, 3*(3), 52–60. DOI: 10.32996/jlds.2023.3.3.4

Kasler, J., Zysberg, L., & Gal, R. (2021). Culture, collectivism-individualism and college student plagiarism. *Ethics & Behavior, 31*(7), 488–497. DOI: 10.1080/10508422.2020.1812396

Kasneci, E., Sessler, K., Küchemann, S., Bannert, M., Dementieva, M., Fischer, F., Gasser, U., Groh, G., Günnemann, S., Hüllermeier, E., Krusche, S., Kutyniok, G., Michaeli, T., Nerdel, C., Pfeffer, J., Poquet, O., Sailer, M., Schmidt, A., Seidel, T., & Kasneci, G. (2023). ChatGPT for good? On opportunities and challenges of large language models for education. *Learning and Individual Differences*, *103*, 102274. DOI: 10.1016/j.lindif.2023.102274

Kaur, M., Singh, A., & Kaur, A. (2025). Managing the Difficulties Female Entrepreneurs Face: Creating Bridges Instead of Barriers. In Shoukat, G., & Tunio, M. (Eds.), *Work-Life Balance and Its Effect on Women Entrepreneurs* (pp. 279–300). IGI Global Scientific Publishing., DOI: 10.4018/979-8-3693-9516-5.ch014

Khalid, N. (2020). Artificial intelligence learning and entrepreneurial performance among university students: Evidence from malaysian higher educational institutions. *Journal of Intelligent & Fuzzy Systems*, *39*(4), 5417–5435. DOI: 10.3233/JIFS-189026

Khatri, B. B., & Karki, P. D. (2023). Artificial intelligence (AI) in higher education: Growing academic integrity and ethical concerns. *Nepalese Journal of Development and Rural Studies*, *20*(01), 1–7. DOI: 10.3126/njdrs.v20i01.64134

Khotimah, K., Budiarto, M. K., Amarulloh, A., Diningrat, S. W. M., Carreza, A. N., & Son, J. H. (2026). Fostering Creativity Through Meta Virtual Project-Based Networked Learning: An In-Depth Examination. *Electronic Journal of e-Learning*, *24*(1), 93–108. DOI: 10.34190/ejel.24.1.4302

Kolb, D. A. (2014). *Experiential Learning: Experience as the Source of Learning and Development*. FT Press.

Kooli, C., & Yusuf, N. (2025). Transforming educational assessment: Insights into the use of ChatGPT and large language models in grading. *International Journal of Human-Computer Interaction*, *41*(5), 3388–3399. DOI: 10.1080/10447318.2024.2338330

Kriz, W. C., & Auchter, E. (2016). 10 years of evaluation research into gaming simulation for German entrepreneurship and a new study on its long-term effects. *Simulation & Gaming*, *47*(2), 179–205. DOI: 10.1177/1046878116633972

Kronivets, T., Yakovenko, O., Tymoshenko, Y., & Ilnytskyi, M. (2024). Dimensions of legal and moral use of artificial intelligence in education. *Review of Artificial Intelligence in Education*, *5*, e025. DOI: 10.37497/rev.artif.intell.educ.v5i00.25

Kumar, R., Joshi, A., Sharan, H. O., Peng, S.-L., & Dudhagara, C. R. (2024). *The ethical frontier of AI and data analysis*. IGI Global Scientific Publishing., DOI: 10.4018/979-8-3693-2964-1

Lai, Q. (2026). Research on the refinement of college student education management based on artificial intelligence. *Discover Artificial Intelligence*, *6*(1), 31. Advance online publication. DOI: 10.1007/s44163-025-00651-9

Lee, Y. (2024). Beyond borders: Insights from Professor David Ahlstrom on entrepreneurship and innovation in emerging economies. *Journal of Management History*. Advance online publication. DOI: 10.1108/JMH-09-2024-0149

Li, J. (2025). Entrepreneurial skill augmented neural network (ESANN): A deep learning approach for enhancing entrepreneurial competencies in teachers. *International Journal of Computational Intelligence Systems*, *18*(1), 127. DOI: 10.1007/s44196-025-00851-2

Li, L., Ma, Z., Fan, L., Lee, S., Yu, H., & Hemphill, L. (2023). ChatGPT in education: A discourse analysis of worries and concerns on social media. *Education and Information Technologies*, *2023*. Advance online publication. DOI: 10.1007/s10639-023-12256-9

Li, N. (2025). Construction and implementation of ideological and political education platforms based on artificial intelligence technology. *International Journal of Web-Based Learning and Teaching Technologies*, *20*(1), 1–23. DOI: 10.4018/IJWLTT.372072

Li, Q., & Kim, J. (2021). A deep learning-based course recommender system for sustainable development in education. *Applied Sciences (Basel, Switzerland), 11*(19), 8993. DOI: 10.3390/app11198993

Liu, H., & Zhang, Y. (2025). AI-empowered model innovation and adaptation in innovation and entrepreneurship education: An exploration based on multimodal learning scenarios. *Asia Pacific Economic and Management Review, 2*(3). Advance online publication. DOI: 10.62177/apemr.v2i3.318

Luckin, R., & Holmes, W. (2016). Intelligence unleashed: An argument for AI in education. UCL Knowledge Lab: London, UK. Retrieved from https://discovery.ucl.ac.uk/id/eprint/1475756/

Luckin, R., Holmes, W., Griffiths, M., & Forcier, L. B. (2016). Intelligence Unleashed: An Argument for AI in Education. Pearson. https://static.googleusercontent.com/media/edu.google.com/en//pdfs/Intelligence-Unleashed-Publication.pdf

Mah, D.-K., Groß, N., Egloffstein, M., & Prilop, C. N. (2026). Artificial intelligence in K-12 instruction: The role of teacher professional development. *Smart Learning Environments, 13*(1), 16. Advance online publication. DOI: 10.1186/s40561-026-00442-4

Maleki, A. (2026). Rethinking ethical academic integrity ecosystems in higher education in the age of artificial intelligence. *Discover Artificial Intelligence, 6*(1), 145. Advance online publication. DOI: 10.1007/s44163-026-00887-z

Mannuru, N. R., Shahriar, S., Teel, Z. A., Wang, T., Lund, B. D., Tijani, S., Pohboon, C. O., Agbaji, D., Alhassan, J., Galley, J., Kousari, R., Ogbadu-Oladapo, L., Saurav, S. K., Srivastava, A., Tummuru, S. P., Uppala, S., & Vaidya, P. (2025). Artificial intelligence in developing countries: The impact of generative artificial intelligence (AI) technologies for development. *Information Development, 41*(3), 1036–1054. DOI: 10.1177/02666669231200628

Manshoven, S., & Gillabel, J. (2021). Learning through Play: A Serious Game as a Tool to Support Circular Economy Education and Business Model Innovation. *Sustainability (Basel), 13*(23), 13277. DOI: 10.3390/su132313277

Mazur, A. (2023). The role of educational institutions in the development of startup ecosystems (on the example of Lviv). *Bulletin of V. N. Karazin Kharkiv National University Economic Series*, (104), 89–99. DOI: 10.26565/2311-2379-2023-104-10

Miao, F., & Holmes, W. (2023). *Guidance for generative AI in education and research.* UNESCO., DOI: 10.54675/EWZM9535

Mohammad, S. I. S., Mohammad, A. A. S., Vasudevan, A., Al-Daoud, K. I., Ling, A. W. P., Mohammad, D. I., Mohammad, A. I., Hai, S. T., & Rusuli, M. S. C. (2026). Artificial intelligence in higher education: A bibliometric analysis of acceptance and adoption studies. In *Artificial intelligence and technology: Systems management, decisions and control for sustainability in the digital age* (pp. 215–227). Springer Nature., DOI: 10.1007/978-3-032-10016-0_18

Mumtaz, S., Carmichael, J., Weiss, M., & Nimon-Peters, A. (2024). Ethical use of artificial intelligence based tools in higher education: Are future business leaders ready? *Education and Information Technologies, 30*(6), 7293–7319. DOI: 10.1007/s10639-024-13099-8

Musundire, A. (2025). *Chatbots in educational leadership and management.* IGI Global Scientific Publishing., DOI: 10.4018/979-8-3693-8734-4

Musyaffi, A. M., Oli, M. C., Mentari, M., & Afriadi, B. (2025). Gamified online business simulation: Enhancing student motivation in entrepreneurship. [EduLearn]. *Journal of Education and Learning, 19*(4), 2322–2331. DOI: 10.11591/edulearn.v19i4.22723

Nabi, G., Liñán, F., Fayolle, A., Krueger, N., & Walmsley, A. (2017). The impact of entrepreneurship education in higher education: A systematic review. *Academy of Management Learning & Education, 16*(2), 277–299. DOI: 10.5465/amle.2015.0026

Naidoo, V., & Verma, R. (2024). *Reshaping entrepreneurial education within an industry 4.0 context*. IGI Global Scientific Publishing., DOI: 10.4018/979-8-3693-0409-9

Nambisan, S., Wright, M., & Feldman, M. (2019). The digital transformation of innovation and entrepreneurship. *Research Policy*, *48*(8), 103773. DOI: 10.1016/j.respol.2019.03.018

Nweke, L. O., Okebanama, U. F., & Mba, G. U. (2025). Enhancing entrepreneurial skills through experiential learning in IoT, AI, and cybersecurity. *Discover Education*, *4*(1), 149. DOI: 10.1007/s44217-025-00573-9

Obschonka, M., & Audretsch, D. B. (2020). Artificial intelligence and big data in entrepreneurship: A new era has begun. *Small Business Economics*, *55*(3), 529–539. DOI: 10.1007/s11187-019-00202-4

OECD. (2019). *Artificial intelligence in society*. OECD Publishing., DOI: 10.1787/eedfee77-

Ogunsola, J. A., Quadri, G. O., & Adigun, O. T. (2026). The strategic role of higher education in promoting entrepreneurship and managing innovation complexities: A conceptual framework analysis. *Journal of Innovation and Entrepreneurship*, *15*(1), 9. Advance online publication. DOI: 10.1186/s13731-026-00632-x

Orola, A., Härri, A., Levänen, J., Uusitalo, V., & Olsen, S. I. (2022). Assessing WELBY Social Life Cycle Assessment Approach through Cobalt Mining Case Study. *Sustainability (Basel)*, *14*(18), 11732. DOI: 10.3390/su141811732

Paik, Y., Lee, J. M., & Pak, Y. S. (2017). Convergence in international business ethics? A comparative study of ethical philosophies, thinking style, and ethical decision-making between US and Korean managers. *Journal of Business Ethics*. Advance online publication. DOI: 10.1007/s10551-017-3629-9

Pandey, U., Singh, A., & Naqvi, N. H. (2025). Career Transitions to Entrepreneurship: Case Studies From Real-World Transformations. In Alagappar, P., & Yanamandra, R. (Eds.), *Strategic Insights and Case Studies on Navigating an Entrepreneurial Landscape* (pp. 47–66). IGI Global Scientific Publishing., DOI: 10.4018/979-8-3693-9261-4.ch003

Pandit, S., Ravikumar, R. N., Joshi, N., Pandit, S., Kishore, S., & Aarthi, S. (2025). Retrieval-Augmented Generation (RAG) for enterprise intelligence. In *Leveraging LLMs for Business Innovation* (pp. 69–106). IGI Global Scientific Publishing. DOI: 10.4018/979-8-3373-3912-2.ch003

Papadimitriou, S., & Virvou, M. (2025). *Artificial intelligence-based games as novel holistic educational environments to teach 21st century skills*. Springer Nature., DOI: 10.1007/978-3-031-77464-5

Park, J.-H., Kim, S.-J., & Lee, S.-T. (2025). AI and creativity in entrepreneurship education: A systematic review of LLM applications. *AI*, *6*(5), 100. DOI: 10.3390/ai6050100

Pingmuang, P., Koraneekij, P., & Khlaisang, J. (2026). Development and Validation of an AI Literacy Scale for Pre-Service Teachers in Thailand. *Electronic Journal of e-Learning*, *24*(1), 1–18. DOI: 10.34190/ejel.24.1.3990

Pöcher, B., Campbell, D. F. J., & Carayannis, E. G. (2026). Innovation and entrepreneurship in organizational university "Third Space" arrangements: Third Space and third mission in mode 3 universities. *Journal of Innovation and Entrepreneurship*, *15*(1), 2. Advance online publication. DOI: 10.1186/s13731-025-00613-6

Prabagar, S., Mothkur, R., Swetha, C. B., Kurian, A., Pavithra, K., & Aarthi, S. (2025). Generative AI for inclusive special education. In *Advances in Computational Intelligence and Robotics* (pp. 205–236). IGI Global Scientific Publishing. DOI: 10.4018/979-8-3373-3745-6.ch008

Quarshie, A. W. K., Swartz, C. L. E., Madabhushi, P. B., Cao, Y., Wang, Y., & Flores-Cerrillo, J. (2023). Modeling, simulation, and optimization of multiproduct cryogenic air separation unit startup. *AIChE Journal. American Institute of Chemical Engineers*, *69*(2), e17953. Advance online publication. DOI: 10.1002/aic.17953

Qudrat-Ullah, H. (2024). *Empowering educational leaders using analytics, AI, and systems thinking*. IGI Global Scientific Publishing., DOI: 10.4018/979-8-3693-7190-9

Rahman, M. M., Rahaman, M. S., Moral, I. H., & Chowdhury, M. S. (2022, October). Entrepreneurship Education and Entrepreneurial Intention of Business Graduates: Does Artificial Intelligence Matter? In *Proceedings of International Conference on Fourth Industrial Revolution and Beyond 2021* (pp. 109-123). Singapore: Springer Nature Singapore. DOI: 10.1007/978-981-19-2445-3_8

Ram, D. Y.Dr. Yad Ram. (2025). The role of artificial intelligence in personalized learning. *Innovative Research Thoughts*, *11*(1), 66–71. DOI: 10.36676/irt.v11.i1.1572

Rashid, A. B., & Kausik, M. A. K. (2024). AI revolutionizing industries worldwide: A comprehensive overview of its diverse applications. *Hybrid Advances*, *7*, 100277. DOI: 10.1016/j.hybadv.2024.100277

Ravikumar, & Aarthi, S. (2025a). Conscious AI Integration in business education. In *Advances in Computational Intelligence and Robotics* (pp. 73–104). IGI Global Scientific Publishing. DOI: 10.4018/979-8-3373-4377-8.ch003

Ravikumar, R. N., & Aarthi, S. (2025b). The role of educational developers in AI integration at scale. In *Advances in Computational Intelligence and Robotics* (pp. 289–322). IGI Global Scientific Publishing. DOI: 10.4018/979-8-3373-4129-3.ch011

Ravikumar, R. N., & Aarthi, S. (2026). From lab to market. In *Advances in Computational Intelligence and Robotics* (pp. 245–278). IGI Global Scientific Publishing. DOI: 10.4018/979-8-3373-9690-3.ch006

Ravikumar, R. N., Aarthi, S., Rai, P. K., & Mamadiyarov, Z. (2025). Intelligent code analysis and feedback generation. In *Advances in Computational Intelligence and Robotics* (pp. 137–170). IGI Global Scientific Publishing. DOI: 10.4018/979-8-3373-0598-1.ch006

Ravikumar, R. N., Aarthi, S., Ruzimova, F., & Mamadiyarov, Z. (2025). Training and development in AI-driven education scaling solutions. In *Advances in Computational Intelligence and Robotics* (pp. 267–298). IGI Global Scientific Publishing. DOI: 10.4018/979-8-3373-2185-1.ch010

Rejeb, A., Rejeb, K., Zrelli, I., & Süle, E. (2025). Industry 5.0 as seen through its academic literature: An in- vestigation using co-word analysis. *Discover Sustainability*, *6*(1), 307. DOI: 10.1007/s43621-025-01166-0

Roberts, M. E., Stewart, B. M., Tingley, D., Lucas, C., Leder-Luis, J., Gadarian, S. K., Albertson, B., & Rand, D. G. (2014). Structural topic models for open-ended survey responses. *American Journal of Political Science*, *58*(4), 1064–1082. DOI: 10.1111/ajps.12103

Rodrigues, C., Melo, P. N., Pereira, L., Pereira, C., & Carvalho, R. (2025). The role of digital technologies and AI on the development of entrepreneurial mindset in first-year university students. *Proceedings of the European Conference on Entrepreneurship and Innovation, 20*(1), 611–617. DOI: 10.34190/ecie.20.1.3962

Rong, G. Y., Nasir, M. K. M., & Mansor, A. Z. (2025). Bridging theory and practice: A conceptual study on experiential learning in student entrepreneurship. *South Asian Journal of Social Sciences and Humanities*, *6*(1), 238–248. DOI: 10.48165/sajssh.2024.6114

Roundy, P. T. (2022). Artificial intelligence and entrepreneurial ecosystems: Understanding the implications of algorithmic decision-making for startup communities. *Journal of Ethics in Entrepreneurship and Technology*, *2*(1), 23–38. DOI: 10.1108/JEET-07-2022-0011

Ruslan, K., Madaminov, B., Ravikumar, R. N., & Aarthi, S. (2026). Equity-Driven Leadership Ecosystems. In *Advancing Equity in Schools through Global Perspectives on Educational Leadership* (pp. 33–66). IGI Global Scientific Publishing., DOI: 10.4018/979-8-3373-7794-0.ch002

Samašonok, K., Išoraitė, M., & Žirnelė, L. (2020). Education of entrepreneurship by participation in a business simulation enterprise activities: Conditions of effectiveness and opportunities for improvement. *Journal of Entrepreneurship and Sustainability Issues*, *7*(4), 3122–3144. DOI: 10.9770/jesi.2020.7.4(36)

Sanabria-Z, J., & Olivo, P. G. (2024). AI platform model on 4IR megatrend challenges: Complex thinking by active and transformational learning. *Interactive Technology and Smart Education*, *21*(4), 571–587. DOI: 10.1108/ITSE-07-2023-0145

Sang, L. T., Ravikumar, R. N., Aarthi, S., & Ben, T. L. (2025). Optimizing sales and inventory performance using AI and business intelligence in POS environments. In *Advances in Computational Intelligence and Robotics* (pp. 259–290). IGI Global Scientific Publishing. DOI: 10.4018/979-8-3373-4392-1.ch011

Sarumi, O. O. (2024). AI: Driving entrepreneurship, nurturing innovation, and fueling Startup growth. *International Journal of Advances in Engineering and Management*, *6*(11), 540–547. DOI: 10.35629/5252-0611540547

Sarwar, U., Sanhong, T., Akhtar, M. W., & Aamir, M. (2025). *Navigating barriers to AI implementation in the classroom*. IGI Global Scientific Publishing. DOI: 10.4018/979-8-3373-1827-1

Schoemaker, P. J. H., Heaton, S., & Teece, D. (2018). Innovation, Dynamic Capabilities, and Leadership. *California Management Review*, *61*(1), 15–42. DOI: 10.1177/0008125618790246

Shengju, T., Li, F., Wang, Z., & Zhaoyuan, X. (2025). Cross-modal adaptive reconstruction of open education resources. *Scientific Reports*, *15*(1), 30838. DOI: 10.1038/s41598-025-15200-8 PMID: 40847041

Shepherd, D. A., & Gruber, M. (2021). The lean Startup framework: Closing the academic–practitioner divide. *Entrepreneurship Theory and Practice*, *45*(5), 967–998. DOI: 10.1177/1042258719899415

Shreha, S. A., Ravikumar, R. N., & Aarthi, S. (2025). Neuro-symbolic AI and Behavioral Intelligence. In *Advances in Computational Intelligence and Robotics* (pp. 121–152). IGI Global Scientific Publishing. DOI: 10.4018/979-8-3373-5012-7.ch005

Shrestha, Y. R., Ben-Menahem, S. M., & Von Krogh, G. (2019). Organizational decision-making structures in the age of artificial intelligence. *California Management Review, 63*(3), 66–83. DOI: 10.1177/0008125619862257

Siegel, D. S., & Wright, M. (2015). Academic entrepreneurship: Time for a rethink? *British Journal of Management, 26*(4), 582–595. DOI: 10.1111/1467-8551.12116

Sindiramutty, S. R., Riskhan, B., & Humayun, M. (2025). Adaptive gamification strategies for different learning styles in cybersecurity. In *Gamification learning framework for cybersecurity education* (pp. 277–315). IGI Global Scientific Publishing., DOI: 10.4018/979-8-3373-0477-9.ch011

Singh, A. (2024). Endorsing Gamification Pedagogy for Nurturing Employability Skills in Higher Education Institutions (HEI). In Membrive, V. (Ed.), *Practices and Implementation of Gamification in Higher Education* (pp. 172–183). IGI Global Scientific Publishing., DOI: 10.4018/979-8-3693-0716-8.ch008

Singh, A. (2026a). The Future of Learning: Integrating Project-Based, Competency-Based, and Experiential Approaches. In Athanasekou, M., & Zagorianakos, A. (Eds.), *Project-Based Learning, Competency-Based Assessments, and Experiential Education for Modern Learners* (pp. 1–24). IGI Global Scientific Publishing., DOI: 10.4018/979-8-3373-4957-2.ch001

Singh, A. (2026b). The Innovation Spiral: How Universities, Governments, and Industries Co-Create the AI Future. In Rahmouni, M., Alholiby, M., & Soufiene, B. (Eds.), *The Triple Helix of University-Government-Industry Partnerships and the Development of AI* (pp. 31–58). IGI Global Scientific Publishing., DOI: 10.4018/979-8-3373-7620-2.ch002

Singh, A., & Ansari, A. I. (2024). Role of Training and Development in Employee Motivation: Tourism and Hospitality Sector. In Mazurowski, T. (Ed.), *Enhancing Employee Motivation Through Training and Development* (pp. 248–261). IGI Global Scientific Publishing., DOI: 10.4018/979-8-3693-1674-0.ch011

Singh, A., & Supina, S. (2025). Rural Women Entrepreneurship in the Face of Gender Inequality. In Bayram, G., Bayram, A., & Sak, M. (Eds.), *Examining Barriers and Building Resiliency for Rural Women Entrepreneurs* (pp. 239–256). IGI Global Scientific Publishing., DOI: 10.4018/979-8-3693-9178-5.ch009

Sitaridis, I., & Kitsios, F. (2024). Digital entrepreneurship and entrepreneurship education: A review of the literature. *International Journal of Entrepreneurial Behaviour & Research, 30*(2/3), 277–304. DOI: 10.1108/IJEBR-01-2023-0053

Somia, T., & Vecchiarini, M. (2024). Navigating the new frontier: The impact of artificial intelligence on students' entrepreneurial competencies. *International Journal of Entrepreneurial Behaviour & Research, 30*(11), 236–260. DOI: 10.1108/IJEBR-08-2023-0788

Sorge, A., & Hofstede, G. (1983). Culture's Consequences: International Differences in Work-Related Values. *Administrative Science Quarterly, 28*(4), 625. DOI: 10.2307/2393017

Srikanth, D. V. (2025). AI-powered entrepreneurial ecosystems: A computational model for sustainable Startup growth in green tech sectors. *International Journal of Environmental Sciences*, •••, 1068–1077. DOI: 10.64252/ewn4zw14

Subrahmanyam, S. (2025). Entrepreneurship and Startup business in the age of AI. In *Advances in Computational Intelligence and Robotics* (pp. 159–192). IGI Global Scientific Publishing. DOI: 10.4018/979-8-3373-7416-1.ch007

Sudarmaji, E., & Munirah, M. (2019). Alternative model for putting Indonesian young digital talent in business. *Review of Management and Entrepreneurship, 3*(1), 1–24. DOI: 10.37715/rme.v3i1.970

Sullivan, M., Kelly, A., & McLaughlan, P. (2023). ChatGPT in higher education: Considerations for academic integrity and student learning. *Journal of Applied Learning & Teaching*, *6*(1), 1–10. DOI: 10.37074/jalt.2023.6.1.17

Sun, X. (2026). Prediction model for the success rate of college student entrepreneurship projects based on deep learning. *Discover Artificial Intelligence*, *6*(1), 3. Advance online publication. DOI: 10.1007/s44163-025-00657-3

Sy, A., Schiffbauer, M., Hussain, S., Keefer, P., & Sahnoun, H. (2015). Jobs or Privileges: Unleashing the Employment Potential of the Middle East and North Africa. MENA Development Report.DOI: 10.1596/978-1-4648-0405-2

Sziegat, H. (2024). Virtual simulation games in entrepreneurship education: Status quo and prospects. *Proceedings of the European Conference on Games-Based Learning, 18*(1), 1099–1106. DOI: 10.34190/ecgbl.18.1.3001

Tan, F. Z., Lim, J. Y., Chan, W. H., & Idris, M. I. T. (2024). Computational intelligence in Learning Analytics: A mini review. *ASEAN Engineering Journal*, *14*(4), 135–151. DOI: 10.11113/aej.v14.21375

Tan, S. (2020). A brief analysis of AI curricula construction and development orientation from the perspective of innovation and entrepreneurship education. *Creative Education, 11*(10), 1866–1872. DOI: 10.4236/ce.2020.1110136

Tariq, M. U. (2024). *AI-driven learning and engagement in higher education*. IGI Global Scientific Publishing., DOI: 10.4018/979-8-3693-4074-5

Teece, D. J. (2018). Business models and dynamic capabilities. *Long Range Planning*, *51*(1), 40–49. DOI: 10.1016/j.lrp.2017.06.007

Thomas, D. (2017). Factors that explain academic dishonesty among university students in Thailand. *Ethics & Behavior*, *27*(2), 140–154. DOI: 10.1080/10508422.2015.1131160

Thottoli, M. M., Cruz, M. E., & Al Abri, S. S. S. (2025). The incubation revolution: Transforming entrepreneurial education with artificial intelligence. *Asia Pacific Journal of Innovation and Entrepreneurship, 19*(1), 2–23. DOI: 10.1108/APJIE-11-2023-0221

Tjahjono, B., Hermawan, D., Millah, S., & Evans, R. (2025). Bridging the skills gap curriculum transformation for automation industries and the role of digital technopreneurship. *APTISI Transactions on Technopreneurship, 7*(2), 650–662. DOI: 10.34306/att.v7i2.620

Triono, S. P. H., Rahayu, A., Wibowo, L. A., & Alamsyah, A. (2024). The impact of Entrepreneurial Strategy on the Firm Performance of Indonesian technology startups. *Jurnal Manajemen Indonesia, 24*(1), 84–104. DOI: 10.25124/jmi.v24i1.7303

UNESCO. (2021). *AI and education: Guidance for policy-makers*. UNESCO Publishing., DOI: 10.54675/PCSP7350

Urdaneta-Ponte, M. C., Mendez-Zorrilla, A., & Oleagordia-Ruiz, I. (2021). Recommendation systems for education: Systematic review. *Electronics (Basel), 10*(14), 1611. DOI: 10.3390/electronics10141611

Utama, I. D., Inayati, T., Setiawan, M., Mohd, Z., & Lusia, E. (2025). Shaping future entrepreneurs: Education, intention, and the adoption of AI. *International Review of Management and Marketing, 16*(1), 12–20. DOI: 10.32479/irmm.20787

Vaz, R., de Carvalho, J. V., & Teixeira, S. F. (2022). Towards a unified virtual business incubator model: A systematic literature review and bibliometric analysis. *Sustainability (Basel), 14*(20), 13205. DOI: 10.3390/su142013205

Vaz, R., de Carvalho, J. V., & Teixeira, S. F. (2023). Developing a digital business incubator model to foster entrepreneurship, business growth, and academia–industry connections. *Sustainability (Basel), 15*(9), 7209. DOI: 10.3390/su15097209

Vuong Nguyen, L. (2024). Classifications, evaluation metrics, datasets, and domains in recommendation services: A survey. *International Journal of Hybrid Intelligent Systems*, *20*(2), 85–100. DOI: 10.3233/HIS-240003

Waly, M. (2024). Artificial intelligence and scientific research. *Sustainability Education Globe*, *2*(1), 1–14. DOI: 10.21608/seg.2024.269596.1001

Wang, X., Liu, C., & Guo, J. (2025). Research on Entrepreneurship Course Knowledge Recommendation System combining Knowledge Graph and clustering technology. *International Journal of Web-Based Learning and Teaching Technologies*, *20*(1), 1–19. DOI: 10.4018/IJWLTT.380658

Wei, C. J., Shahmi, A. M. F., Qing, W. Y., & Melati, N. (2026). Motivations Matter: Predicting Entrepreneurship Education MOOC Course Completion with a Decision Tree Approach. *Online Learning : The Official Journal of the Online Learning Consortium*, *30*(1), 294–322. DOI: 10.24059/olj.v30i1.4517

Williams, D. (2015). The impact of SimVenture on the development of entrepreneurial skills in management students. *Industry and Higher Education*, *29*(5), 379–395. DOI: 10.5367/ihe.2015.0270

Winkler, C., Hammoda, B., Noyes, E., & Van Gelderen, M. (2023). Entrepreneurship education at the dawn of generative artificial intelligence. *Entrepreneurship Education and Pedagogy*, *6*(4), 579–589. DOI: 10.1177/25151274231198799

World Economic Forum. (2023). The future of jobs report 2023. WEF. https://www.weforum.org/reports/the-future-of-jobs-report-2023/

Xie, Y., & Wang, S. (2025). Generative artificial intelligence in entrepreneurship education enhances entrepreneurial intention through self-efficacy and university support. *Scientific Reports*, *15*(1), 24079. DOI: 10.1038/s41598-025-09545-3

Xu, J., Zhao, S., & Gu, Y. (2024). A study of innovative entrepreneurial behavior of college students under algorithmic recommendation. *Applied Mathematics and Nonlinear Sciences*, *9*(1), 20240274. Advance online publication. DOI: 10.2478/amns-2024-0274

Xu, Q., & Liu, X. (2025). The utilization of artificial intelligence in enhancing English language instruction and fostering entrepreneurial education. *Journal of Computational Methods in Sciences and Engineering*, *25*(2), 1593–1605. DOI: 10.1177/14727978241302155

Yang, X., & Li, J. (2026). Application of deep learning in the innovation of personalized entrepreneurship education model in colleges and universities. *Discover Artificial Intelligence*, *6*(1), 107. Advance online publication. DOI: 10.1007/s44163-025-00777-w

Yoshida, M., Duangchinda, V., & Ruangrit, N. (2026). AI-Supported Learning in Online Discussion Forums: A Scoping Review. *Electronic Journal of e-Learning*, *24*(1), 19–35. DOI: 10.34190/ejel.24.1.4409

Yue, J. (2024). Application of fuzzy control algorithm in college students' personal career planning and entrepreneurship. *Journal of Computational Methods in Sciences and Engineering*, *24*(3), 1631–1647. DOI: 10.3233/JCM-247196

Zawacki-Richter, O., Marín, V. I., Bond, M., & Gouverneur, F. (2019). Systematic review of research on artificial intelligence applications in higher education. *International Journal of Educational Technology in Higher Education*, *16*(39), 39. Advance online publication. DOI: 10.1186/s41239-019-0171-0

Zhang, J., Yahaya, W. A. J. W., Sanmugam, M., & Lim, D. (2024). *Integrating technology in problem-solving educational practices*. IGI Global Scientific Publishing., DOI: 10.4018/979-8-3693-6745-2

Zhang, L. (2025). Intelligent deep learning model for recommending ideological and political music education resources. *Scientific Reports*, *15*(1), 36402. DOI: 10.1038/s41598-025-20535-3 PMID: 41107437

Zhang, Q., Li, L., Xu, C., Qi, Y., & Zhao, X. (2025). How can artificial intelligence help college students develop entrepreneurial ability? Evidence from China. *International Journal of Management Education*, *23*(3), 101244. DOI: 10.1016/j.ijme.2025.101244

Zhang, Y., & Yin, H. (2020). Collaborative cheating among Chinese college students: The effects of peer influence and individualism-collectivism orientations. *Assessment & Evaluation in Higher Education*, *45*(1), 54–69. DOI: 10.1080/02602938.2019.1608504

Zhou, Y. (2026). Research on Intelligent Development of Talent Cultivation Mode of Higher Vocational Innovation and Entrepreneurship Education Based on Data Mining under the Perspective of Industry-Teaching Integration. *International Journal of Computer Information Systems and Industrial Management Applications*, *18*, 1–18. DOI: 10.70917/ijcisim-2026-0173

Zhu, Q., & Zhang, H. (2022). Teaching strategies and psychological effects of entrepreneurship education for college students majoring in social security law based on deep learning and artificial intelligence. *Frontiers in Psychology*, *13*, 779669. DOI: 10.3389/fpsyg.2022.779669 PMID: 35369210

Zolfaghari, M., Salamzadeh, A., & Afsharpour, O. (2024). Identifying the applications of artificial intelligence in educational entrepreneurship development. In *Advances in Educational Technologies and Instructional Design* (pp. 439–478). IGI Global. DOI: 10.4018/979-8-3693-7220-3.ch015

About the Contributors

Monia Ben Ltaifa is an Assistant Professor in Finance at the Department of Administrative and Financial Program, Applied College, King Faisal University, Al Ahsa, Saudi Arabia. His research interests include Risk Management, Systemic risk, International finance, Capital markets and institutions, Banking and market microstructure and Islamic Finance.

***

Nadim Akhter, an esteemed academician and journalist with over 25 years of experience, serves as Associate Professor at Lovely Professional University since April 2024. Previously, he taught Print, Radio, and Television Journalism for a decade at the Indian Institute of Mass Communication (IIMC), New Delhi. His Ph.D. on fake news in India has garnered significant recognition. Dr. Akhter holds a Postgraduate Diploma from IIMC (2001) and a Master's from Guru Jambheshwar University. He has published extensively in UGC-CARE-listed journals and presented at numerous national and international conferences. Author of Devalaya, a celebrated coffee table book on Bihar's ancient temples, he has worked with leading media houses, including The Times of India, Hindustan Times, Zee News, News 24, Dainik Jagran, BBC Hindi, and All India Radio. Certified in Artificial Intelligence (Microsoft) and Leadership (IIM Ahmedabad), Dr. Akhter aims to bridge industry-academia gaps through collaborations and innovation.

Makhmudov Asliddin is an academic professional associated with the Department of Accounting and Statistics at Termez University of Economics and Service. His expertise encompasses accounting practices, statistical modeling, and data-driven financial analysis, with a focus on improving organizational efficiency and decision-making processes. He is actively engaged in research that explores the integration of statistical techniques with accounting systems to enhance accuracy, forecasting, and financial transparency. His teaching philosophy emphasizes the application of quantitative methods, analytical thinking, and real-world problem-solving aligned with contemporary academic and industry standards. In addition to his instructional role, he contributes to curriculum development and academic initiatives aimed at strengthening higher education quality. His work reflects a commitment to advancing research, fostering innovation, and promoting the effective use of statistical and accounting tools in modern economic environments.

Muralidhar L B is a professionally qualified dental surgeon. He holds Ph.D. from Canara Bank School of Management Studies, Bangalore University after his MBA from Christ University. He has 22 years of total teaching experience spanning across dental education, healthcare management and general management and 4 years of corporate experience. He has worked as research associate in Institute for Social and Economic Change, Bangalore in a project entitled as "Management By and For Common Man: An Exploration of the Concept and Direction for Future"post Ph.D. He had secured 28th rank 10th Standard examination for Karnataka State in 1993. He has been the co-facilitator of a MOOC course on "Social Entrepreneurship and Sustainability",offered through SWAYAM portal, jointly sponsored by GoI and IIMB. His 32 patents have been published and 2 design patents have been granted. He has 41 research publications to his credit out of which 36 are Scopus-indexed and 5 are ABDC indexed. He has co-authored 13 books. He is currently working as Assistant Professor (Grade-3) in Department of Business Management Studies, School of Commerce, Jain Deemed to be University, Bangalore.

Deepak D is an Assistant Professor at the School of Commerce, Jain (Deemed-to-be) University, Bengaluru.He holds an M.Com degree from Bangalore Central University and is a UGC-NET qualified individual.

His academic interests span business finance, financial technology, and sustainable business practices.Deepak has published over 20 research papers in reputed national and international journals.His work explores emerging themes such as AI in marketing, the circular economy, emotional intelligence, and green finance.He has co-invented patents related to leadership strategy and the management of the bullwhip effect.He is actively involved in academic conferences on digital transformation and future-ready business models. Deepak collaborates with multidisciplinary scholars to bridge theory with practical innovation. He is listed on the Vidwan database and holds an ORCID ID: 0009-0004-8493-1474.Outside academics, he has represented his university in national-level wrestling competitions.

Ilham Firmansyah is an undergraduate student in the Department of Computer Science at Universitas Esa Unggul, Indonesia. His academic interests focus on artificial intelligence, digital innovation, and entrepreneurship education, particularly in the context of emerging digital economies. He is actively engaged in research and academic writing, with a growing interest in the application of AI to enhance learning systems and entrepreneurial skill development. Ilham aims to contribute to interdisciplinary research at the intersection of technology, education, and innovation.

Purushotham H. C is an Assistant Professor at the School of Commerce, JAIN (Deemed-to-be University), with over 6 years of teaching experience. He is currently pursuing a Ph.D. at REVA University and holds an MBA in Management. His expertise spans consumer behaviour, strategic management, HRM, and marketing. He has published several research papers and book chapters and received multiple Best Paper Awards. He has coordinated academic, cultural, and NSS activities and actively contributes to faculty development and student mentoring. He is also a certified Behaviour and Mentoring Analyst and holds certifications in marketing analytics and digital marketing.

Abdelraouf M. Ishtaiwi is an Associate Professor of Artificial Intelligence and Data Science at the University of Petra, Jordan, with over 22 years of academic and research experience in AI. He earned his Master's and Ph.D. degrees in Artificial Intelligence from Griffith University, Australia, where he focused on heuristic optimization techniques for satisfiability problems. His research expertise spans machine learning, hybrid metaheuristic optimization, associative classification, and AI applications in cybersecurity and emerging technologies like the metaverse. Dr. Ishtaiwi has developed innovative AI algorithms, such as ACRIPPER and hybrid crayfish-DE models, and contributed significantly to areas like phishing detection, blockchain security, and smart IoT defense. As a former Head of the Department of Data Science and AI at Petra University, he led academic reforms and accreditation initiatives. He has also been a visiting scholar at Griffith University and Universitat Pompeu Fabra, reflecting his international academic engagement.

Sadirdin Khudoykulov is an academic professional affiliated with the Department of Finance and Tourism at Termez University of Economics and Service. His academic interests focus on financial management, tourism economics, and sustainable development within service-oriented sectors. He actively contributes to research that explores the intersection of finance and tourism, particularly in enhancing economic growth, regional development, and resource optimization. His work emphasizes the application of modern financial tools and analytical frameworks to improve decision-making in tourism enterprises and public sector initiatives. In his teaching role, he promotes critical thinking, practical learning, and the integration of theoretical knowledge with real-world applications. Additionally, he is involved in academic and institutional activities that support curriculum development and research advancement. His contributions reflect a commitment to innovation, education quality, and the development of sustainable finance and tourism practices.

Umid Otajanov is an academic professional affiliated with the Department of Accounting at Mamun University. His academic interests focus on financial accounting, auditing practices, and contemporary developments in accounting information systems. He contributes to the advancement of accounting education by integrating theoretical knowledge with practical financial applications, enabling students to develop strong analytical and decision-making skills. His research engagement includes areas such as financial reporting standards, internal control mechanisms, and the role of digital technologies in modern accounting processes. In addition to teaching, he actively participates in academic and institutional activities that support curriculum enhancement and research development. His work reflects a commitment to promoting accuracy, transparency, and innovation in accounting practices while preparing students to meet the evolving demands of the global financial and business environment.

Sumit Kumar Pandey is an accomplished Assistant Professor at the Department of Journalism and Mass Communication, Manipal University, Jaipur, with a Ph.D. from Kashi Vidyapith University, Varanasi. A UGC NET qualifier, he holds an M.Phil. and Master's in Journalism and Mass Communication, both with Gold Medals, alongside a Post Graduate Diploma in Electronic Media Management & Film Production. With eight years of experience in academia and research focusing on New Media, Print Media, and Radio, Dr. Pandey has published 34 papers/chapters in Scopus-indexed, UGC care-listed, and peer-reviewed journals/edited books, and authored a book on Atal Bihari Vajpayee's contributions to journalism and nation-building. He holds two patents, including an AI-based multimedia kiosk for wildlife tourism (2024) and a cloud-based digital display branding device (2025). A former Radio Presenter at All India Radio and IGNOU Gyan Vani FM, he has organized over 40 and participated in over 70 national/international academic events, showcasing his expertise in evolving communication landscapes.

Arun R. is an Assistant Professor in the Department of Commerce at Jain (Deemed to be University), Bengaluru. Holding a Master of Commerce (Finance) from Mangalore University, Arun has demonstrated academic excellence through prestigious qualifications, including successful clearances of the UGC NET (Commerce) thrice and KSET once. Dedicated to fostering academic excellence, Arun is passionate about teaching and research, striving to inspire students and contribute valuable insights to the field of commerce and finance.

Ravikumar R. N. is currently a Postdoctoral researcher at Universiti Malaysia Perlis, Malaysia. Also, working as an Associate Professor in the Department of Computer Engineering at Marwadi University, Rajkot, Gujarat. He has 13+ years of national and international teaching experience. He completed his PhD at Amity University, Rajasthan, M.E at VMRF Deemed University, B.E at Anna University, Chennai. He is the co-founder of the Research Activities Club at Marwadi University and trains students on research activities, which leads to the various publications. He has published numerous research articles in Scopus, SCI journals, Book chapters, and Conference papers. Also, he hold several patents and authored books. His specialization is ML, DL, Federated Learning, Recommendation Systems, and Optimization Techniques.

Aarthi S is a dedicated Assistant Professor in Computer Science with over six years of teaching experience. She is currently pursuing her Ph.D. at Marwadi University, Gujarat, and holds an M.Phil. and MCA from Bharathiar University, Tamil Nadu. Throughout her academic career, Aarthi has specialized in programming languages such as C++, Java, and C, and contributed to research in recommender systems and AI-related data privacy. She has published journal articles, contributed to book chapters, and actively participated in technical workshops. Known for her student mentorship and engagement in academic events, Aarthi remains committed to fostering innovation and excellence in computer science education.

Karimov Rashid Salayevich is an academic professional affiliated with the Department of Accounting at Mamun University. His scholarly interests focus on financial accounting, auditing, and the development of robust accounting information systems that support transparent and efficient financial management. He is actively involved in academic research exploring contemporary issues in financial reporting, regulatory compliance, and the integration of digital technologies in accounting practices. His teaching approach emphasizes conceptual clarity, analytical reasoning, and practical application, preparing students to meet the evolving demands of the accounting profession. In addition to teaching and research, he contributes to institutional development through curriculum design and academic initiatives aimed at improving educational quality. His work reflects a commitment to fostering innovation, strengthening financial accountability, and advancing the role of accounting in sustainable economic development.

Amrik Singh is working as Professor and HOD in the School of Hotel Management and Tourism at Lovely Professional University, Punjab, India. He obtained his Ph.D. degree in Hotel Management from Kurukshetra University, Haryana, India. He has published 115 Scopus-indexed publications. He has published 12 patents, and 01 patent has been granted in the inter-disciplinary domain. Dr. Amrik Singh participated and acted as a resource person in various national and international conferences, seminars, research workshops, and industry talks. He has published 20 books with IGI Global Publication, Emerald Publication, Bentham Publication, Nova Publication etc., on trending areas such as Food waste, Artificial Intelligence, Mountain Tourism, Virtual tourism, Healthcare Tourism, Guest behavior in tourism and hospitality. His area of research interest are Accommodation management, sustainability, Green practices, Human Resource Management in Hospitality, Artificial Intelligence, AR VR in hospitality, Hotel pricing, Employee Disability, Work life balance, women empowerment etc. He is currently guiding 8 Ph.D. scholars, and 5 Ph.D. scholars have been awarded Ph.D.

Ite Morina Yostianti Tnunay is a lecturer, researcher, and academic. She completed her undergraduate degree in the Biology Program at the Faculty of Science and Engineering, Nusa Cendana University in Kupang, graduating in 2011. The author then pursued a Master's Program in Plant Biology at the Department of Biology, Bogor Agricultural University in 2015 through the Affirmative Action Scholarship Program administered by the Education Fund Management Agency of the Ministry of Finance and graduated in 2018. The author previously worked as a Science and Mathematics teacher at Tunas Mandiri Christian Elementary School from 2010 to 2012, as a Teller at PT Bank Danamon's Kupang, Sumatra Branch from 2012 to 2015, and as a Lecturer in the Biology Program, Faculty of Mathematics and Natural Sciences, San Pedro University in Kupang from 2018 to 2019. The author has been a lecturer in the Biology Program, Faculty of Agriculture, Science, and Health, at the University of Timor since 2019 to the present. The author has also served as an online tutorial tutor in the Biology Program, Faculty of Science and Engineering, at the Open University since 2022 to the present. The author has also served as an assessor for the National Accreditation Board for Primary and

Secondary Education of East Nusa Tenggara Province since 2021 to the present. The author is actively conducting research in the field of Plant Biology, particularly regarding Plant Species Diversity, Ethnobotany, Plant Physiology, and Plant Ecophysiology.

Chetan T.R, PhD in Marketing, serves as Assistant Professor at JAIN (Deemed-to-be University), specializing in Marketing, International Business, and Entrepreneurship. Honored with the Best Faculty Award, he blends academic rigor with real-world relevance through case studies and interdisciplinary insights. His research focuses on ethics, mindset, and time mastery, empowering students through holistic mentoring. With expertise in faculty development, structured academic modules, and impactful communication, he actively contributes to scholarly initiatives. Passionate about innovation and sustainability, Dr. Chetan integrates AI tools to enhance pedagogy and professional growth, fostering a dynamic learning ecosystem that bridges theory with practice.

Nofamataro Zebua is a young lecturer in the Biology Education Study Program at Universitas Nias (UNIAS), Indonesia. He completed his bachelor's degree in biology education from Universitas Nias Raya (UNIRAYA) and his master's degree from the Department of Biology at Universitas Negeri Malang (UM). He is a passionate researcher and writer who explores innovative topics in the field of education. His research focuses on biology, biology and science education, literacy, thinking skills, artificial intelligence (AI) for education, biodiversity, pedagogy, 21st-century skills, and ethnobiology to enhance student learning experiences and engagement. He is also actively providing valuable insights to educators, researchers, and students, as well as promoting digital literacy and environmental awareness through problem-based, project-based, and community-based approaches.

Index

G

I

K

L

P

R

S

V

www.ingramcontent.com/pod-product-compliance
Lightning Source LLC
LaVergne TN
LVHW081525300926
849161LV00006B/1303